D1154488

Orion Blinded

Orion Blinded

Essays on Claude Simon

Edited by
Randi Birn *and* Karen Gould

Lewisburg:
Bucknell University Press

London and Toronto: Associated University Presses

Associated University Presses, Inc.
4 Cornwall Drive
East Brunswick, N.J. 08816

Associated University Presses Ltd.
69 Fleet Street
London EC4Y 1EU, England

Associated University Presses
Toronto, Ontario, Canada M5E 1A7

Library of Congress Cataloging in Publication Data

Main entry under title:

Orion blinded.

   Bibliography: p.
   1. Simon, Claude--Criticism and interpretation
--Addresses, essays, lectures. I. Birn, Randi.
II. Gould, Karen.
PQ2637.I547Z83   843'.9'14   79-17687
ISBN 0-8387-2420-5

Printed in the United States of America

For Jay, in fond memory

Contents

Note

In referring to Simon's novels the translations into English by Richard Howard and Helen R. Lane will be used throughout.

Translated by Richard Howard:
The Wind. New York: George Braziller, 1959 (abbreviation: *Wind*).
The Grass. New York: George Braziller, 1960 (abbreviation: *Grass*).
The Flar ders Road. New York: George Braziller, 1961 (abbreviation: *Flanders*).
The Palace. New York: George Braziller, 1963 (abbreviation: *Palace*).
Histoire. New York: George Braziller, 1967.
The Battle of Pharsalus. New York: George Braziller, 1971 (abbreviation: *Pharsalus*).

Translated by Helen R. Lane:
Conducting Bodies. New York: Viking, 1974 (abbreviation: *Bodies*).
Triptych. New York: Viking, 1976.

The following works have never been translated into English:
Le Tricheur (abbreviation: *Tricheur*).
La Corde raide (abbreviation: *Corde*).
Gulliver.
Le Sacre du printemps (abbreviation: *Sacre*).
Femmes.
Orion aveugle (abbreviation: *Orion*).
Leçon de choses (abbreviation: *Leçon*).

In referring to these works the original French titles will be used, and, unless otherwise stated, translations are the responsibility of the authors of the respective articles.

Preface: Why Claude Simon?

Serge Doubrovsky

Following the special issue of *Entretiens* and the *Colloque Claude Simon* at Cerisy (I will not even concern myself with the ever-growing list of books and individual articles), here is a new volume of essays. This collective probing glance, cast from America this time, extends in many directions and bears witness to the global dimension of the work.

If we consider that the writer has been working for over thirty years, why all this belated interest—especially when one compares the destiny of Simon to that of Robbe-Grillet, seized upon still palpitating by the critics? Perhaps it is because Robbe-Grillet, maker of enigmatic tales, inspires—if only to thwart—an instant desire to interpret. Simon's work, slower, heavier, growing like *The Grass*, with an often imperceptible growth, is opaque in a different way; and this particular notion of time, motionless and destructive, where everything moves and makes no headway, this major theme of *The Wind* and *The Flanders Road* is also, and probably above all, the time of the reading. This work could be called, after Mallarmé, one of patience (*Atlas, herbier ou rituel*), a stranger to all haste, and especially to that of the present moment.

What then is this richness that international criticism is so gradually, and increasingly, discovering? To this proliferation of commentary, issuing from every ideological shore, that every great writer's work elicits and rejects, what density, what depth of text serves as both springboard and obstacle? To reply in detail would require a lengthy study, an additional article to swell this already substantial collection. The writer of the preface is generally granted the privilege (by virtue of seniority, in criticism as in the army) of being more succinct or cavalier. So I will simply say that for me this Simonian density remains the famous *pâte romanesque*: but it has turned into *clay*. "Sentences, words, this sort of gummy and difficult material from which he undoubtedly could not disentangle himself" (*Wind*). There is a double entanglement—not only in the verbal matter, but also in a narrative design in search of itself. "There was no link in his story between the different episodes or rather tableaux that he described, as in those dreams where you move suddenly from one place to another, from one situation to another without transition, the only continuity at last this obscure and overpowering obsession with something he absolutely had to do despite obstacles and hindrances, without being able to imagine what" (ibid.). What is here said in the context of the fiction about the "character" of Montès is a clinically precise analog for the very movement of scription.

There has been talk—in order to simplify things and because the French love textbook classifications— of a New Novel "school" and of a structuralist "movement." Just as we realize today that the projects of Lévi-Strauss, Lacan, or Foucault have nothing in common, unless it be to oppose a previous ideology, it is obvious that the only thing uniting Sarraute, Robbe-Grillet, and Simon is an identical rejection of worn-out conventions. Character, plot, verisimilitude, pseudo-mimesis of a "real" world: during the 1950s writers began to discard all this, at least the best or least sheep-like among them. Some have spoken of this period as a "reducing diet" for the novel. The *dépeupleur* is not only the title of one of Beckett's latest texts, it might be said to be the guiding principle behind the functioning of the modern text in general, diametrically opposed to the works of a Balzac or a Zola, which were described as "swarming" or "teeming" with life. In their extreme undertakings, Borges, Robbe-Grillet, and

Beckett have undoubtedly attained this uttermost point of fictional bareness where nothing is exposed to view but the mechanisms of the fiction itself, this is writing "degree zero" where nothing is written but the simple possibilities (or even impossibilities) of language.

Such is not the case with Simon's work. And this is what gives it its unique status. Certainly we must not fail to recognize its evolution and its diversity: we have come a long way from *Le Tricheur* to *Conducting Bodies* or *Triptych*. No critical formula can be indiscriminately applied to a whole of such richness and profusion with phases and cycles that critics (in this very collection) are only now beginning to catalogue. From the writing of the "collage" that is *Orion aveugle* to the still humanist, occasionally Camus-like tones of *The Wind*—to read through Simon backwards is like retracing the history of the ideologies of our time. Without then in any way belittling the value of the discovery that any experiment in writing constitutes when it is sustained, cogent, inventive, and arduous, as is the work of Claude Simon, I personally am struck by certain constants which place the writer outside of any school and which, if I may say so, make him dear to me: he is an *impure* writer. Ludovic Janvier has well described the principal characteristic of the Simonian sentence as "cumulative": "One sentence joining another, engendering a paragraph, a page, the entire book, this is the genesis of an irresistible and vertiginous movement" (*Une parole exigeante*). Jean Ricardou has in turn accurately stated that "the sentence is no longer closed upon itself like an organism. It is formless . . . .Here language, disjointed, frees words from their subservience to a higher order of significance. From this point on, words become *foci of semantic irradiation*" ("Un ordre dans la débâcle"). Lumpy, rocky, swollen, grating, carrying its *signifiant* like a glacial moraine that imprisons linguistic debris belonging to the most diverse levels, Simon's sentence has a transgressive power that has become, since Proust, very rare in works of such scope: this writing, in fact, deals a blow, and a deep one, to the language it is supposed to promote and, as DuBellay would say, "illustrate." Simon's audacity is

remarkable among his New Novel confreres: while all of them
attack the sclerosis of the narrative code, in general they
scrupulously respect the classical rules for good writing; and
although Beckett may give the rules a few swift kicks in passing, although Roussel and Brisset may be decorated
posthumously for their temerity, even the most innovative
French writer remains, in his writing, much closer to Madame
de La Fayette than to Joyce. Certainly the narrative no longer
follows the aristotelian esthetic model with a beginning, a
middle, and an end, but sentences still dutifully have a subject, a verb, and a complement. Simon is the only one—with a
few exceptions, and in any case the only one so persistently
and at such length—to attack the heritage of "the French
language," which he desecrates with perverse subtlety.
Distended or distorted syntax, parentheses at the wrong time,
punctuation in the wrong place, "he" and "she" with multiple
antecedents, "which" where it is impossible to determine
which what, and I could go on: everything sacrosanct in
language is subverted. But what is more serious, the
vocabulary itself is affected, by permanent semantic glides,
approximations that jolt the period by way of verbal sallies,
stumbling blocks in the form of puns filling in as rhetorical
relays. One might say, to parody Rimbaud, that Simon's
writing is words "catching hold of other words and pulling."
In this impure French, not even Frenchness itself is left uncontested, as it constantly rubs elbows with foreign words
whose litanies interlard the text (Latin, Italian, Spanish, what
not, depending on the circumstances). Deconstructor of the
language, dismantler of the *signifiant*, he is also a
demonstrator: as the one who brings into play all the
possibilities of language, he also brings them pleasure—and us
as well. This polymorphous monstration, this display of the
treasure of the French language unrivaled in today's
literature, erogenizes all zones of language. Cumulative, certainly, but the Simonian sentence is also an astonishing, explosive brew. Whereas the contemporary novel often espouses
a verbal economy that borders on poverty, reworking the
same highly refined, effete vocabulary that delights the
classroom where basic French is taught (oh, pedagogical end

of avant-garde literature, from *The Stranger* to *Jealousy!*),
Simon manhandles the lexicon, mauls about the slang of bar-
racks and stables—at ease with the terminology of the country
or urban agglomerations, as at home in art criticism as bicycle
racing, tireless technician of the verb, lover of words, which
he laces from one level to another with consummate mastery,
or to which he abandons himself to the point of babbling
glossolalic ecstasy. A sort of Balzac of the New Novel, vigor
and poor taste included.

This is no accident. At the moment when he appears to be
swept along by the linguistic material, immersed in it, Simon,
like Balzac, but differently of course, is obsessed by the world
that is tangible, sensual, human, mineral, historical, where an
incessant and searching look transforms sign into saga. This
work may be read as a metaphorical epic of the *eye*, owing to
the constant narrative currency of the photograph, the painting, postcard, or engraving which perpetually gives new impetus to the fiction, articulates its functioning from book to
book. Seeing, for Simon, is the driving force behind saying;
vision is the awareness of the absolute distance (from words)
to things, but inversely, it is the fascination of the language-
master with reality. We are dealing here with nothing less
than the old mimetic code of the traditional pseudo mirror /
novel; in any case, *his* mirror is in pieces: "a little as if one
were trying to stick together the scattered remnants—incomplete—of a mirror" (*Wind*). We are dealing rather with a
doubly contradictory postulation of writing, which is felt in an
extreme tension. When Jakobson reminds us that the poetic
function, "which reveals the tangible side of signs, deepens at
the same time the fundamental dichotomy between signs and
objects," he nevertheless specifies a bit later: "The supremacy
of the poetic function over the referential function does not
obliterate the reference (denotation) but renders it
ambiguous." ("Linguistique et poétique"). Unlike the other
practitioners of the New Novel, Simon never attempts to
obliterate the references—historical, geographical, cultural,
or personal—which on the contrary abound in his work. This
is what creates its extraordinary richness, denotative and connotative, inducing the frenzied flow of words, their vibratile

proliferation, in a prodigious competition, no longer between the writer and "the bureau of vital statistics" but with *Weltlichkeit* itself, the being of the world as world. But just as the reference is being endlessly multiplied, the text confuses it, defies it, unties it, relaces it, replaces it in the code and logic proper to its texture, rendering the system of representation impossible or inadequate, finding only apparent support in it, progressing through it only in order to transgress it incessantly. Corresponding to the equivocal status of description is the joyous, triumphant impurity of scription. Fiction knows henceforth that it is no more than narration, but no less either, and this is why Simon has put it to use, put it to *work* with all the sources and resources of speech, projected beyond speaker and spoken toward the mute *Other* which is the horizon of all language.

Translated by Jane Carson.

Acknowledgments

The editors would like to express their appreciation to Bucknell University, Lewisburg, Pennsylvania, for a summer grant awarded to undertake work on this volume. In addition, we want to give special thanks to Professor Mills F. Edgerton for his helpful suggestions on some difficult translation problems. And lastly, thanks go to Ms. Sheri Daniel who worked so quickly to give us the necessary technical drawings.

Introduction

> Now, signs, all signs, are open to a new
> reading—necessarily fragmentary—but liberated
> from the shackles of an arbitary and sterilizing
> "taste."
>
> **Jacques Ehrmann**

Until a decade ago, most critics interested in what has come
to be known as the French *nouveau roman* did little more than
quietly acknowledge the creative talent of Claude Simon. By
no means a newcomer to the current French literary scene,
Simon has been publishing novels since the end of World War
II. But, for the most part, his early works (1945-1957) were
given only a passing glance from respected critics. It was not
until the late 1950s, with the publications of *The Wind, The
Grass*, and *The Flanders Road*, that Simon's artistic
endeavors began to attract some critical notice. Yet even then
he was all too often dismissed as a highly skilled technician
and imitator of Proust and Faulkner (whose influence on
Simon has been, admittedly, substantial). Since the early
1960s, Simon's name, along with those of Alain Robbe-
Grillet, Michel Butor, Nathalie Sarraute, and Samuel Beckett
(all of whom have published at the audacious but now
fashionable Editions de Minuit), has been at the forefront of
critical discussions on radical directions in contemporary
French fiction. But unlike the texts of other "Midnight
novelists," Simon's fictional works, now numbering fifteen in
all, failed to receive serious consideration until recently.[1]

Some scholars have suggested that the prolonged absence of
rigorous studies on Simon during the first twenty years of his

19

literary career was primarily due to the artist's own avoidance
of formal polemics on the novel. This position appears to have
some validity if one considers how successfully Robbe-Grillet
and Sarraute were able to launch themselves into the very
heart of the literary arena with their dramatic and controver-
sial theories on the novel set forth in *Pour un nouveau roman*
(For a New Novel) and *L'Ere du soupçon (The Age of Suspicion)*.[2] Still other critics, however, dispute this point, arguing
rather convincingly that criticism abounds on numerous con-
teporary writers who, like Beckett, have refused to engage in
lengthy theoretical discourse. Some readers also believe that
the difficulty of Simon's prose precludes a wider critical audience. But whatever the reason for Simon's slow rise in the
critics' estimation, it now seems clear that he has at last moved
into the literary limelight during the past decade, although
few American readers are familiar with his novels. Since
Simon's recent critical recognition, he has also begun to express an increasing interest in theoretical discussions on the
future of the novel as well as in the critical reception and
analysis of his works.

Although undeniably arbitrary in some respects, 1969 appears to be a kind of threshold year for Simon studies, due
most notably to the publication of John Sturrock's seminal
work *The French New Novel*,[3] in which he stressed the need
for a more extensive critical appraisal of Simon's fiction. The
year 1969 also marks the appearance of Simon's *La Bataille de
Pharsale (The Battle of Pharsalus)*, which, most critics agree,
displays a major turning point in Simon's evolution as a
novelist. *Pharsalus* establishes, more emphatically than any
previous work, the importance placed by Simon on the
development of the literary text from within itself through
what he has recently termed "la fiction mot à mot." Since
Pharsalus Simon's novels have focused increasingly on the
raw materials and their generative power in the text, out of
which *meanings* are *produced*. The text is thus primarily conceived as *process* rather than as *intentional design*. The
publication of *Pharsalus* prompted a measurably heightened
interest in Simon emerging from several critical circles, particularly from those whom we now refer to as "structuralists,"

but whose backgrounds and concerns are as varied as the fields that have molded them.

Certainly, Jean Ricardou is the most influential of these new "structural" critics to analyze the *nouveau roman* in recent years. His dazzling, though sometimes opaque, commentary on the Simonian text, especially after the appearance of *Pharsalus*, is at least partially responsible for having provoked a new and significantly more vital phase in Simon studies. But Ricardou has also been criticized, and sometimes sharply, for having led Simon criticism down the relatively narrow path of structural review in an almost dictatorial fashion. Fortunately, the pursuit of complementary as well as opposing critical perspectives has recently given rise to the publication of book-length studies on Simon in the U.S. and abroad by critics such as J.A.E. Loubère, S. Jiménez-Fajardo, Gérard Roubichou, and John Fletcher, as well as two special journal numbers on Simon in *Sub-stance* (1974) and *Études littéraires* (1976). After more than three decades of artistic exploration, Simon's works finally appear to be capturing the attention and the imagination of European and American publics alike.

A number of critics, including the late Roland Barthes, deny that there is now, or has ever been, such a thing as a "Robbe-Grillet school" or *nouveau roman*. Their dismay with those who choose to talk in one breath about writers as diverse as Beckett, Robbe-Grillet, Butor, Pinget, and Simon is, doubtless, justifiable and, in the final analysis, indicates a sensitivity to the unique quality of the literary text that must be applauded. Yet the fact that Simon was first brought to the public's attention as one of a number of New Novelists, whose literary creations presumably shared similar philosophical, psychological, and aesthetic concerns, should not be dismissed too quickly. For it is certain that many of the New Novels to emerge in the last two decades exhibit common structural elements and narrative techniques that sometimes parallel Simon's own experimentations in fiction.

Critics have noted, for instance, that one of the most striking realizations made when first reading Simon or Robbe-Grillet is the way in which the very process of storytelling is subverted, as the more traditional lines of development such

as characterization, plot, and subplot undergo a series of
unrelenting assaults and intentional detours from within the
text itself. No longer satisfied with describing to us *what* happens in a given tableau, the novelist insists, instead, on showing us how what takes place is *perceived* and *reflected upon* by
a particular consciousness. In fact, the words "perception"
and "reflection" have become virtually synonymous with
the notion of the New Novel, whose central literary focus
is shaped almost entirely by brief descriptive images, fragmentary thoughts, memories, dreams, and hallucinations, all of
which compose the complex substance of human consciousness. Whether we read Robbe-Grillet's *In the Labyrinth*
or Simon's *Histoire*, the "new" narrator, whose wandering
thoughts and fantasies we follow at every turn, casts little
more than a vague physical outline. It is his mind and senses
that we inhabit, and it is through them that we order human
experience and attach meaning to it whenever possible.

Because the fictional emphasis in a novel such as Butor's *A
Change of Heart*, Beckett's The *Unnamable*, or Simon's *The
Flanders Road* has indeed turned inward—even as it looks at
the world "outside"—the rational depictions of time and
space, which once provided the more traditional novel with a
sense of order, have also disappeared, leaving in their wake a
sense of temporal and spatial fluidity and, at times, uncertainty. Following in the footsteps of Proust's masterpiece, transitions in the narrative movement of these contemporary texts
are no longer based on the chronological development of a set
of given events but, more often than not, on organic associations, the juxtaposition of mental images, and parallelisms
between memory or fantasy and present-tense phenomena.

In short, while the traditional novel, however complex,
took great pains to situate its readers, giving them all the
salient physical, psychological, sociological, and even political
features necessary to uncover and determine the *essence* of its
characters and milieu, a *nouveau roman* as basic as Robbe-
Grillet's *Jealousy* or as intentionally disorienting as one of his
more recent works such as *Project for a Revolution in New
York* or Simon's *Conducting Bodies* demands that its readers
enter into a realm of fleeting perceptions, of fragmentary im-

ages that come forth from whatever preoccupies or disturbs the reflective consciousness at a given moment in the narration. All of this means, to be sure, that the individual reader's response to this new novelistic form must be to acknowledge, accept and, to some degree, struggle with the challenge to play a more active role in following and interpreting the text as it develops. At its best, Simon's fiction, like that of Sarraute, Robbe-Grillet, and Beckett, becomes a daring exploration into the nature of perception, sensation, and the *production* of *meanings*, an exploration that gains multiple *meanings* only as we, the readers, create them out of the perplexing network of fragmentary, shifting, and, at times, disjunctive narrative techniques.

The real thrust of this volume, however, is not aimed at restating the more or less obvious narrative and structural parallels that do, in fact, exist between many of Simon's works and those of the so-called *nouveau roman* school. Instead, we intend to establish new and perhaps more fruitful grounds for studying Simon's uniquely creative contribution to recent French fiction. Among the persistent preoccupations that expressly distinguish Simon from other contemporary writers, his densely metaphorical prose, the richness and complexity of his imagery, the dynamic role of description, and the highly personal treatment of universal themes and historic settings from his own past constitute some of the essential fictional elements that bring Simon's individual imagination to light. One significant trademark that has frequently furnished a prominent backdrop to Simon's thematic concerns is the recurrent use in his writing of what are both historical and autobiographical events such as the Spanish Civil War, the defeat of the French Army in 1940, his own German prison camp experiences and eventual escape, his early training as a painter, and his family ties and residence in the southern French countryside. Thematically speaking, what evolves out of these and other historical and geographical settings is a loosely woven web of interconnecting themes reflecting the crucial expectations, discoveries, and disappointments of human life as they are encountered in nature, love, war, imprisonment, betrayal, death, and extinction. Whether ex-

plicitly stated in dialogue and point of view or implicitly
presented in the vivid and minutely recorded descriptions of
the pictorial phenomena of consciousness, Simon's themes
meander throughout the text, as large and as intensely drawn
as life itself.

Early on, a number of critics made note of the potentially
cynical and pessimistic world view which seemed to emanate
from Simon's early and middle novelistic periods. The haunting role of chance in a work such as *Le Sacre du printemps* or
The Flanders Road, coupled with the questionable nature of
human progress as depicted in *La Corde raide*, *The Palace*, or
Histoire, might well lend credence to arguments maintained
by those who believe that the discoveries made by Simon's
protagonists culminate with the realization that, as John Sturrock has put it, "time operates independently of human
aspirations, so that progress, when it comes about, does so in a
wholly fortuitous manner which is a further bitterly ironic
comment on the optimism of reformers."[4] Although we find
evident signs of this cynicism in most of Simon's fiction, it is
also true that much of what his protagonists come to realize
throughout their fictional journeys allows them to identify certain truths about themselves and their relations with the world
outside. "Any work that implies thought," Simon once said,
"is both an affirmation and an interrogation, within a vast
horizon of answers concerning the meaning, the wherefore of
history, of the universe, of being."[5] Affirmative and interrogative elements surely go hand in hand in the Simonian text,
offering us, at most, tentative conclusions about the human
condition, but always urging us to reconsider attentively the
world in which we live.

Almost everyone who has written about Simon comes
around to talking about the originality of his style at one point
or another. Some critics even complain—especially with the
recent critical interest in structural analysis—that too much
attention has been directed in this area. Nevertheless, there is
little doubt that an investigation of Simon's intricate and continually evolving style clearly belongs at the very core of any
earnest study of his writings.

Perhaps more so than with most writers, it is difficult as
well as misleading to generalize about Simon's stylistic traits in

an all-inclusive manner since his formal techniques differ so greatly during his early (1945-54), middle (1957-67), and later (1969 to present) creative periods. However, what the best critics tell us about the author's early period is that his style was inconsistent, artificial, and somewhat confused until the publication of *The Wind* and *The Grass*, where he finally began to exert a comfortable technical mastery over his material. And yet, the generating principles at work in a text such as *La Corde raide* (1947) could surely tell us a great deal about the kinds of materials that were appropriate or inappropriate to the gradual development of a quite different style such as we find in Simon's most recent works. Only in the last few years have critics begun to discuss some of the relevant connections between these earlier novels and Simon's more mature fiction.

Much more critical attention has been focused on the novels written from *The Wind* up to and including *The Battle of Pharsalus*, all of which reveal an intensely metaphorical vision, filled with complex symbols, literary allusions, and mythological motifs. "The metaphor," wrote Ortega y Gasset, "is perhaps one of man's most fruitful potentialities. Its efficacy verges on magic."[6] For many critics, Simon's use of the metaphor seems to possess just such an enchanting quality, oftentimes expanding into a long and complicated pattern that reemerges in a refined form at some later point in the narrative. Likewise, the reflective movements of Simon's narrative consciousness move in and out of past, present, or imagined phenomena in lengthy spirals that may be repeated at numerous other instances in the text. The importance Simon places on the present participle as a key verb tense in works such as *The Flanders Road* and *Histoire* tends to bring about the blurring of past and present, which, in turn, reinforces the notion that we are never free of the past: the individual makes his or her joyful discoveries and saddening mistakes in an apparently repetitive, mechanical, or, some might even say, archetypal fashion.

One of Simon's most noted stylistic features from this middle novelistic period takes the form of descriptions, which are often sidetracked by the use of brackets within brackets in order to build upon the original image or permit the inclusion of contrasting images. Like the complex and, at times, disorienting treatment of time and space, visual description and mental contemplation do not progress linearly in Simon's works, particularly since *The Wind*, but instead proliferate outward in many varying and, at times, contradictory directions. This technical device underscores the complexity and confusion stemming from the disorderly nature of perception itself and coincides with the author's thematic concerns and general misgivings about ultimate, enduring answers that order our world.

The proliferating style that marks Simon's middle period has given way, in the last few years, to a more constricted, less undulating rhythm. His previously long and expansive sentences are now noticeably shorter and considerably more contained. For while Simon continues to construct an elaborate metaphorical network of signs and symbols, he admits that he is, of late, increasingly taken with the textual exploration of the generating power of language. Hence word associations and juxtapositions are more thoroughly developed in *Triptych* than they were, for example, in *The Palace*. Like the painters he admires most—Miró, Dubuffet, Rauschenberg—Simon wants to "return to the source, to the basic, to the concrete" which, he believes, is often most appropriately expressed in the form of collages and constructions: "The work of art which exists only to show its constituent parts."[7] And in his later novels, it is precisely as if the texts are emerging from themselves, from a handful of generating images or pictorial phenomena so that the possibilities of language become the focus of the evolving fiction. In this regard, Stephen Heath has aptly observed that "it is language that is the space of consciousness"[8] in the recent Simonian novel.

Among Simon's theoretical utterances and writings about artistic endeavor, which have become more frequent in the last several years, some of the most significant statements are found in the preface to *Orion aveugle*, a rather unusual volume that allows us to see, in pictorial form, the visual stimulators for the fiction alongside the text. It is here, in *Orion aveugle*, that Simon likens his creative pursuits to those of Orion, the Greek mythological hero depicted in Nicolas Poussin's painting, who was blinded by a jealous rival but later was told that he would regain his sight by traveling eastward to the point where the sun first rises from the ocean. The painting by Poussin, on the cover of *Orion aveugle*, shows the blinded Orion guided in the direction of the sun by a tiny apprentice whom the giant carries on his shoulders. For Simon, the metaphorical journey of the artist closely resembles that of the blinded hero since both must advance slowly, step by step or "word by word," unable to evaluate their progress clearly and blinded to their final destinations until they have been reached. Emphasizing how the novel does, in effect, develop by self-consciously reflecting on its own problems and expansion, Simon thus identifies his artistic struggle with the "singular adventure of the narrator who doesn't stop searching, discovering the world gropingly in and through writing."[9] In a recent interview in *Diacritics* Simon comments further on the image of the artist as a blinded Orion: "The complete title of this painting (*Orion aveugle*) is, 'Blind Orion Searching for the Rising Sun.' That seems to symbolize my own work: the writer advancing blindly in his language, groping in the midst of a forest of signs toward something he will never attain. . . . And this allegory is all the more complete given that Orion is, as you know, a constellation and that as the sun, toward which it advances, rises, the constellation disappears. The writer (the scriptor) is, in a similar manner, erased by the text which he has written and which was not the one he had projected. Isn't that extraordinary?"[10] For Simon, both the artist and the Greek hero, Orion, are consciously engaged in the slow, yet profound struggle of a journey forward into vastly new and previously unknown territory.

Critical attention to the formal properties of Simon's recent fiction is indeed necessary as well as understandable at a time when studies on the psychological, sociological, and linguistic nature of language are on the rise. Yet although, for critics of the *nouveau roman* in general, the temptation is sometimes great to illuminate the detailed systems of cross-references and associative structures, it is important to bear in mind that

Simon's fiction is far too rich in its scope and complicated in its design to be reduced to a series of sophisticated word games or highly intricate, intellectual puzzles. If the essence of contemporary literary productivity is no longer rooted in *mimesis*, in an earlier belief in representational art, but instead, in what might be termed "an opacity, a resistance to recuperation which exercizes sensibility and intelligence," as Jonathan Culler has suggested,[11] then our critical evaluation of Simon's texts must take this "opacity" into serious account. As critics, we must therefore be content to cast new light on a particular system of textual signs, knowing full well that other systems exist concomitantly, which neither time, energy, nor perhaps even insight allow us to decipher.

This volume offers, it is hoped, a representative sampler of contemporary critical essays on varying aspects of Simon's writings, the purpose of which is to widen our critical appraisal and perspective of his work and to place Simon in an important literary tradition that begins with modern masters such as Proust and Joyce and encompasses the increasingly radical artistic visions of contemporary writers such as Butor and Robbe-Grillet. But above all, the essays contained in this collection have been gathered together in order to provide a framework within which to analyze the unique and influential stature of Claude Simon in contemporary fiction.

The volume has been divided into three sections, which emphasize three distinctly different points of reference that have been used in the explication of Simon's novels. His work is first examined in an evolutionary context, then in light of recent innovative trends in critical methodology, and finally, within a larger context of literary tradition and world views.

The first and largest section is concerned with commentary on the patterns and evolution of Simon's literary style and thought from his early writings up to and including his most recent work. All of the articles in this section essentially view Simon's fiction from the perspective of his own artistic development. Thus, although individual novels are often discussed in detail, the thematic and formalistic concerns are acknowledged within a larger, developmental process. The opening essays by Elizabeth Weed and Philip Solomon deal with Simon's first novels, *Le Tricheur* and *Le Sacre du printemps* respectively, works that have usually been slighted, if not ignored altogether, by the critics but which have much to tell us about the roots of the author's artistic vision. Both critics succeed in pointing out the origins of a series of persistent thematic patterns and technical devices that recur throughout Simon's subsequent fiction. Weed's essay also demonstrates how the failures of the more conventional narrator in *Le Tricheur* foreshadow the eventual failures and outright abolition of the narrator in Simon's later fiction. Solomon's critical viewpoint grows out of an interest in the archetypal approach to literature, which seeks to establish an intimate relationship between literary creativity and mankind's mythic heritage. My own essay on *The Grass* analyzes the various roles of language in the mind of the central protagonist and examines the implications of these roles in view of the work's thematic content.

Randi Birn's analysis of eighteenth-century literary motifs in *The Flanders Road*, which, she affirms, is a novel about its own genesis, and the essay by Tobin Jones on the problems of authorial control and narrative vision in *Histoire*, link certain thematic considerations of this middle novelistic period to emerging aesthetic concerns about the possibilities of fictional organization and development. The tension that Jones notes between reading the text as a chronological progression of events or reading it as a pattern of changing analogical relationships is one that continues to dominate Simon's later novels. In her essay on the proliferation of interconnecting signs and images in Simon's recent fiction, particularly *The Battle of Pharsalus*, *Triptych*, and *Leçon de choses*, J.A.E. Loubère shows how Simon's texts have moved even more completely in the direction of the exploitation of analogical contructions as structural ordering principles. But she also argues, persuasively, that the proliferation of images does, in fact, form substantive geometric patterns or groupings which continue to inform us about Simon's thematic preoccupations. The final essay in this section is Karin Holter's thought-provoking investigation of intertextual relationships in a number of Simon's novels, particularly in *Leçon de choses*.

Her examples of self-quotation provide a basis for discussing
the recurring themes, images, and situations that permeate
much of Simon's fiction.

The second section brings together a series of essays that offer new critical approaches to different phases of Simon's
work. C. G. Bjurström's essay takes a new look at the
language used by Simon in his first few novels and
demonstrates how many of the author's later syntactic and
structuring principles are already at work in *Le Tricheur*,
Gulliver, and *Le Sacre du printemps*. Echoing Ricardou's insistence on "the adventure of the text," Gérard Roubichou's
essay on *Histoire* examines several serial combinations of
phenomena from the past and present as well as imaginary
images that are all formed by either psychological or scriptorial associations. Because the thematic tension of order and
disorder—long acknowledged by many critics as one of
Simon's primary thematic pairs—has been underscored by a
scriptorial tension involving the ordering and disordering of
linguistic signs, Roubichou maintains that *Histoire* invites us
to reconsider the process of writing/reading (Sollers' *écriture/
lecture*) and that, in so doing, this novel announces a new and
continuing phase in the architectural development of Simon's
texts.

The next two articles, by J. A. E. Loubère and Claud
DuVerlie, complement one another since both studies consider the function of particular kinds of generators in Simon's
work. Loubère takes a close look at a rather unique Simonian
phenomenon, occurring in much of his fiction, which is
Simon's use of translated phrases and parts of larger texts in
his own novels. She contends that these translated fragments
have particular generative properties, serving as linguistic and
thematic stimulators to the narration while causing the reader
to pause and reflect on the process of writing in a new way.
DuVerlie attends to another unusual form of generator, but
one that plays a major role in both *Orion aveugle* and *Conducting Bodies*, the pictorial referent. Emphasizing the tenuous
link between the initial picture and its linguistic transformation, DuVerlie has found that, ultimately, pictures chosen by
Simon as textual referents become the structural or architectural models for the narrative.

The concluding essay in this section, which delineates an altogether different critical vantage point from any of the preceding essays, is Christiane Makward's feminist perspective on the sexual forces and identities at work in Simon's novels from *The Wind* to *Leçon de choses*. Makward analyzes three trends in his texts that she considers essential for an understanding of the psychosexual drama of the narration: homosexuality, psychological transsexualism, and the significant attention paid to the erotic qualities of the body.

The third and final section of this volume contains essays by John Fletcher, S. Jiménez-Fajardo, and Morton Levitt, all of whom attempt to evaluate Simon's work as it relates to literary traditions, both in France and abroad, and to the artist's own perspectives on the individual's place in the modern world. The section concludes with a series of written comments by Simon in response to questions posed to him by Randi Birn and myself.

It has been a common practice among Simon critics over the past fifteen years to make frequent references to the stylistic similarities in Faulkner and Simon, but discussions about the thematic parallels in their works have been rare. Using Faulkner's *Sanctuary* (1931) and Simon's *Gulliver* (1952) as bases of comparison, John Fletcher points out the affinities and differences found in the two artists' literary treatment of evil and examines their respective psychological and moral conclusions.

In his article on Simon and the Latin American context, S. Jiménez-Fajardo indicates the range of social and ideological concerns as well as the experimentations with fictional form that link Simon to current Latin American writers, Borges and Alejo Carpentier in particular. Foreshadowing Morton Levitt's critical perspective, Jiménez-Fajardo argues that, although Simon's latest fiction, which resembles that of Julio Cortázar, demonstrates an increasing interest in self-generating compositions, where language itself becomes the narration's "instrument of discovery," Simon has not in any way abandoned earlier humanistic concerns. Even more emphatic than Fajardo in this respect, Levitt insists that a humanistic perspective is at the very center of Simon's work, even in novels as recent as *Triptych*. Levitt also places Simon in a rich literary tradition and establishes a number of thoughtful parallels as well as contrasts between Simon's literary outlook and that of Proust, Joyce, Butor, and especially Robbe-Grillet, which helps us to more fully appreciate Simon's place in and contribution to such a literary tradition. Finally, Simon's own remarks address themselves to issues that reveal, for example, his attitude toward the creative process, the role he envisions for the artist in modern society, his interest in his reading public, and the direction of his current literary activity.

If the critic's task to present his or her arguments as honestly, thoroughly, and competently as possible oftentimes appears foredoomed, the obligation of an editor to search out and accurately reflect a large body of critical views on a given author seems utterly futile. For this reason, it is not expected that the varied approaches presented in this volume will even begin to exhaust all of the possible critical paths open to Simon studies or to mirror properly the entire scope of critical investigation to date. We trust, however, that out of these diverse perspectives a general literary form will take shape that can incorporate the complementary, occasionally disparate, and at times even contradictory views assembled here on Claude Simon.

Karen Gould

Notes

1. Ludovic Janvier's *Une Parole exigeante* (Paris: Minuit, 1964) is a notable exception to the more common critical disregard of Simon's fiction throughout most of the sixties.

2. See Alain Robbe-Grillet, *Pour un nouveau roman* (Paris: Minuit, 1963), and Nathalie Sarraute, *L'Ere du soupçon* (Paris: Gallimard, 1956).

3. John Sturrock, *The French New Novel* (London: Oxford University Press, 1969).

4. Ibid., p. 50.

5. Claude Simon, "Littérature: Tradition et révolution," *La Quinzaine litteraire* (May 1-15, 1967), pp. 12-13, translated by J. A. E. Loubère.

6. José Ortega y Gasset, The Dehumanization of Art (Princeton: Princeton University Press, 1968), p. 33

7. Claude Simon, "Interview: The Crossing of the Image," *Diacritics* (Winter, 1972), p. 48

Introduction

8.   Stephen Heath, *The Nouveau Roman: A Study in the Practic* (Philadelphia: Temple University Press, 1972), p. 160.

9.   Claude Simon, *Orion aveugle* (Geneva: Skira, Collection "Les Sentie, tion," 1970), preface. My translation.

10.   Claude Simon, "Interview: The Crossing of the Image," *Diacriti* 1977), p. 52.

11.   Jonathan Culler, "Towards a Theory of Non-Genre Literature," in *Fiction Now and Tomorrow*, ed. Raymond Federman (Chicago: Swall 1975), p. 258.

Orion Blinded

I Simon's Evolving Creative Process

1
A Rereading of Claude Simon's *Le Tricheur*

Elizabeth Weed

When Claude Simon's first book, *Le Tricheur*, appeared in 1945, one reviewer, Maurice Nadeau, praised it as the newest novel of the Absurd, noting at the same time that its impact would have been greater had it appeared immediately after its completion in 1941, the year of the publication of *The Stranger*.[1] With Simon's next book, *La Corde raide*, a semifictitious "livre de souvenirs," it became clear that Simon wished to defy attempts to classify him as a writer of the Absurd. For more than a decade after *Le Tricheur* it was difficult to determine just what role Simon was to play in the French literary world. Neither his second novel, *Gulliver*, nor his third, *Le Sacre du printemps*, seemed to realize the literary promise that Nadeau had found in *Le Tricheur*. It was not until 1957, with the publication of *The Wind*, that Simon received enthusiastic critical acclaim. For Jean-Luc Seylaz, as for many readers, "this novel marks the true beginning of Claude Simon's work;" for him "a reading of *Le Tricheur*, or *Gulliver*, is rather disappointing; one doesn't experience, as one does when reading *The Wind*, the feeling of being in the presence of a remarkably gifted novelist."[2]

Although one can hardly contest Seylaz's judgment, the early books are more than literary curiosities; they are sources of enlightening perspectives on later developments in Simon's work. Maurice Merleau-Ponty, one of the first to note the meaningful continuity between the early books and subsequent ones, found in *La Corde raide* the germ of all of the later works.[3] It is possible to say the same thing of *Le Tricheur*. In it one finds in embryonic form many of the anecdotal elements which appear in the later works, most of the thematic elements, and some of the technical devices. By examining the early books, one can better understand the transformation of Simon's work and its relationship to contextual literary activities. Most important, one can participate more fully in the rich enterprise that is his writing, an enterprise which Stephen Heath describes as "a ceaseless process of textualization from novel to novel, of continuation, repetition, modification—'une permanente remise en question.' "[4]

During the early period of the New Novel, Simon often spoke of his inability to invent characters and situations. Indeed, to a greater extent than many writers, he has reworked and developed a relatively limited body of fictional (and quasi-autobiographical) material. The sketchy details of the life of Louis, the young protagonist of *Le Tricheur*, contain a number of elements shared by later Simon characters: a father who was an army officer, who spent some time in a French colony (Madagascar perhaps), and who was killed in World War I when the protagonist was a small child; a mother who died after a long illness when the boy was still young; unhappy years as ward of an uncle, a period of time at a boarding school, and several years of naval service. While there are aspects of the character of Louis which appear in almost all of Simon's major characters, the most direct line of parentage may be traced from Louis through Bernard of *Le Sacre du printemps*, to the narrator of *The Palace*, a fusion of Louis and Bernard.

Fundamental to the first novel is a view of life as a perpetual and futile contest between human volition and everything that challenges it. Louis, a boy in his early twenties, is unable to reconcile himself to the contingency of the human situation, and stubbornly and vainly attempts to impose his will on the many internal and external forces that mold his life. Whether those forces are governed by necessity or chance, for Louis, as for the narrator in *The Wind*, they amount to the same thing, for they invariably elude whatever rational order man tries to impose on them: "either everything is only chance. . . . or else reality is endowed with a life of its own, disdainful and independent of our perceptions and consequently of our knowledge and especially of our thirst for logic" (*The Wind*, p. 10).[5] From Louis's perspective, all is chance, and his great desire is to correct that chance.

A relatively simple episodic framework supports the essentially psychological ordeal of the protagonist. When the book opens he has just returned from five years at sea and has run off with his girlfriend, Belle. In the course of the narrative they go to a provincial city where he assists a friend in one brief, comic escapade of petty larceny, and then kills a priest whom he barely knows. It is this murder, in particular, which led critics such as Nadeau to compare *Le Tricheur* with *The Stranger*. Yet, in spite of some incidental similarities between the two books, Louis bears little significant resemblance to Camus's "absurd man." Nor does he resemble Gide's Lafcadio. Simon's character is more conventional than either, and his act, though seemingly gratuitous, is both psychologically motivated and premeditated.

Louis kills the priest because the man unwittingly plays a highly charged symbolic role in the psychological-sexual-religious drama that is his life, a drama continually reenacted in the form of obsessive memories.[6] At the source of Louis's problems is the traumatic loss of his mother, followed by miserable years at schools, where he hated both the priests with their dogma and discipline, and the happy, secure students who obeyed them. More than anyone, perhaps, Louis resembles Stephen Dedalus, for his anguish at the death of his mother is compounded by his guilt for his filial transgressions—particularly his refusal to become a priest as his mother had wished—and by his Oedipal hostilities. These hostilities are directed toward a group of rivals beginning with his father and ending with God the Father, to whom Louis's mother transferred her unquestioning devotion after the death of her husband. Like the narrator of *Histoire*, Louis is tormented by the loss of his mother to his combined rivals of God and father: "God. . .

And probably she attributed to him the form, the beard and moustache and look of the man, and when she thought of going to meet God, it was he, he as she had loved him, in his dazzling uniform and his polished boots and his riding whip and his absolute power over the natives" (pp. 228-29).

Besieged by emotional problems and faced with an uncertain future, Louis conceives of the murder as a defiant act of volition in a hostile universe. A Hamlet figure, he must banish the "familiar and sickly ghosts of acts never accomplished" (p. 219). The murder is the act that will save him, a symbolic gesture entirely dependent on his will and thus an adequate proof of that will. And yet, when the moment arrives, the ideal act is aborted. Louis loses control and is driven as if by an external force. In place of the revolver he had planned to use, he grabs a brick, attacks the man from behind, and bludgeons him to death. This clumsy caricature of his great gesture accomplishes nothing. He returns to the hotel, his unused revolver the mocking reminder of his failure: "the heavy solid shape of my will, forgotten, useless, and derisive, in my pocket" (p. 250).

The defeat is all the more derisory because Louis is a *tricheur*, a cheater. As Simon indicates *en exergue* in the novel, the *Littré* definition of *tricher*, "to cheat," is precisely "to correct chance." Destined to fail by the very nature of his endeavors, Louis invents tests of strength for himself, only to discover that he will not, or cannot, stay within the boundaries of the rules of the games he has created. In the case of the murder he merely puts into play the forces of chance and necessity. It is by chance that Louis ever meets the priest, by chance that the man is the brother of an unfaithful boyhood friend, and by chance that Louis finds him on the street and not at home on the night of the murder. And it is because of psychological necessity, because of the relentless nature of his own obsessions, that Louis murders. At the end he is driven to acknowledge his impotence in the face of the tangled web of forces that is his reality. It is this movement from defiance to defeat, this desire to translate will into action and the complete failure to do so, that forms the thematic focal point of the work.

Although Louis's ordeal appears idiosyncratic within the contrived episodic framework of the novel, it is the prototype not only for the ordeal of the narrator of *Histoire*, but for the particular dilemma at the core of much of Simon's work. In the early novels, an individualized protagonist tries to impose his will on events. In later books, the effort of the protagonist, or narrator, or consciousness, becomes one of extricating some significance from an experienced reality. From *The Wind* through *Histoire* this experienced reality coincides ever more completely with the text itself, with the result that the fictional narrator or consciousness becomes lost, a sign among signs, in the text of his own construction.[7] Like Louis, he suffers defeat, and such a radical defeat, finally, that after *Histoire*, or more precisely within *The Battle of Pharsalus*, the fictional narrator himself is abolished. With *The Battle of Pharsalus* it becomes evident that the anguish and epistemological failure of the fictional narrators have been a metaphorical enactment of Simon's gradual abandonment of the narrator as fictional generator of the text; henceforth, the functioning consciousness becomes merely one of a number of elements operating within it. What begins in *Le Tricheur* as a rather conventional failure of a protagonist to exercise control over his life thus culminates some two and a half decades later in the expulsion of the fictional consciousness from its privileged position in the text.

In all of the books from *Le Tricheur* through *Histoire*, the fictional reality confronted by the characters and narrators is one of permanent flux, of the onslaught of time experienced through the processes of history and nature. The most explicit indication in the first novel of a human failure to order the experience of time occurs in the opening pages where Louis angrily throws away his watch because it fails to work. Throughout the rest of the chapter his thoughts return to the lost watch, which he imagines is now ticking in the grass, and to all the passing moments he cannot record.

Although the forces of history do not play the major role in *Le Tricheur* that they play in later books, they are present. For example, Belle's father, Gauthier, remembers his own vigil and his wife's vigil on the eve of his departure for war, and the scene is one that appears often in Simon's novels, with the same failure of sexual contact to bring consolation, the same isolation and silence, and the same rectangular window opening on the night serving as a correlative for man's perspective on time and history: "side by side, silent, their eyes open in the darkness, the rectangle of the window filled with the dense blue of the night, and that tragic presence of time which no longer belonged to them, and the inescapable force of the whole hostile universe which bore down on them. Both of them crushed at the bottom of the illusory refuge of that room and that bed" (p. 95).

As in later books, the characters in *Le Tricheur* must also struggle against the forces of nature. Louis is besieged by an obsessive heat which threatens to paralyze his will on the day of the murder. Gauthier, long disillusioned with all action, is obsessed by the processes of nature that lead to death and oblivion. Having once been near death, he feels he understands its secret: "since he had seen what there was behind things—and that there was nothing" (p. 81). Beyond the flux, the process, there is nothing, an abyss. It is this void, this absence of all human significance, that is at the heart of the human dilemma in Simon's works. Like Robbe-Grillet a decade later, Simon rejects the myth of depth, as well as the myth of the Absurd: "I think that non-meaning is another invention of the poets and philosophers. A sort of compensatory value. . . . To say that the world is absurd amounts to the same thing as admitting that one still believes in a meaning" (p. 64). Unlike Robbe-Grillet, however, Simon is concerned, through *Histoire*, with the human anguish of the experience of the void, "that huge disparity between our actions and the immensity at the heart of which they are immersed" (*The Grass*, p. 89).

Increasingly, Simon's books are dominated by incessant cycles of decomposition-recomposition-decomposition, and by cycles of physical and historical exchange. Throughout the books this meaningless exchange, this eternal motion without progression, is rendered as a paradoxical motionless movement, whether through the present participles which replace inflected verbs in many of the novels, or in the image of the cavalry as "a petrified procession of mannequins swaying jerkily on their pedestals" (*The Flanders Road*, p. 285), or in the "Achilles running motionless" of *The Battle of Pharsalus*.

In each of the novels where the characters or the narrators struggle to order their experience of an elusive reality, there are various interplays of movement and immobility, flux and stasis. In *Le Tricheur* this interplay is less complex than in later works, but it is based on the same paradox of motionless or meaningless movement. Louis wanders through much of the novel in quest of his own acts of volition, but his wanderings take the form of derisive circular patterns. Like the wind against which Montès struggles in *The Wind*, Louis is swept along by what Ludovic Janvier calls "the horizontal flow of fate,"[8] a horizontal continuum as devoid of meaning as the circular patterns he traces. At times Louis is tempted to surrender passively to his condition or, as in the following passage, to its correlative: "carried along by the swift gliding of the bus, one can reach the point of being nothing more than this horizontal movement, gentle and restful" (pp. 216-17).

In resisting such surrender and in attempting to realize his will, he fights not against the maelstrom of *The Wind*, but against its antithesis, a petrified, immobile universe. In the summer heat the landscape of *Le Tricheur* is as static and two-dimensional as a theatrical set, "a smooth surface where space no longer exists, at least not in depth" (p. 215). For Louis an act of will represents an escape from the static stage set into a more human dimension of significance: "just an act. Trying to get outside the stage set, to find the limits of the coagulated landscape" (p. 238). The effort is futile. In spite of a moment of deceptive relief at the end of the novel, an "illusory and calming flow" (p. 250), nothing changes with the murder. Louis's world remains static, like the world of Montès near the end of *The Wind*, or like the memory world of Georges at the end of *The Flanders Road*.

Caught in the paradox of static flux, Simon's characters are torn between contrary impulses of volition and passive release. Janvier has observed that Louis makes a severe distinction between two possible attitudes toward existence—wakefulness and somnolence—and that his ordeal is a movement from one pole to the other: "Beginning with a deep desire to be aware, to give all his attention to 'his life,' which raises him for a time above himself, he ends up by giving up and by letting himself be carried away by events, by chance."[9] Janvier has also pointed out that in his movement from defiance to defeat, Louis, like later Simon characters, passes through three types of tests or temptations: games of chance, women, and "nature."[10] More than simple temptations, these categories describe three basic areas in which the dilemma of Simon's characters is enacted, areas in which the characters are both repelled by the fate awaiting them and drawn irresistibly to it.

The importance of games of chance in Simon's work is apparent from the title of the first novel. In *Le Tricheur*, the game of chance is a metaphor for a view of life that Louis consciously rejects, a "conception of existence based on a mutual bet" (p. 46). Unlike the other characters in the novel, all of whom yield readily to external forces, Louis refuses even to gamble on the horses as Belle urges him to do. Characters such as Louis, and Max, in *Gulliver*, try to resist such temptation. By *The Flanders Road*, where horse racing, war, and daily events all converge, the prisoners of war form a microcosmic society dominated by the exchange of commodities, which is, as John Sturrock says, "controlled quite directly by the operations of chance, and not by decisions of the individual reason or will."[11]

The characters' attempts to order reality, and their fears of powerlessness, are closely related to the role of the woman in the novels, which is, in turn, inseparable from the role of nature. Like Bernard in *Le Sacre du printemps*, who is haunted by the myth of the giant goddess spilling out Titan's sperm ("the impetuous dew, the impetuous principle of all life, of all thought," p. 58), the male characters dread the archetypal threat of female nature to the male (human) will to order. They are obsessed by the thought that "at any moment the orderly and reassuring world can suddenly capsize, turn over and lie on its back like an old whore tucking up her skirts and, reverting to the original chaos, disclose the hidden surface" (*Histoire*, p.52). For Louis, the female stands outside the realm of acts and it is against the animal-like docility he finds in her that he measures his own energy and determination. At the beginning of the book he abandons Belle sleeping in the grass, passive and bovine; shortly before he murders the priest, he strengthens his resolve by walking away from a girl who has offered herself to him, "lying on the floor, her skirt lifted up to her belly" (p. 230). Yet, in spite of Louis's masculine will, he fails, and the failures are invariably linked to a woman.

Louis's experience is common to most of Simon's male characters. Hence the fears of cuckoldry and castration that run through the books. Gauthier's tormented doubts about his wife's fidelity and the parentage of his child are related to the hypothetical cuckoldry of Reixach and his ancestor, which is at the fictional source of death itself in *The Flanders Road*. The old woman in *Le Tricheur* who cuts out a chicken's tongue with a scissor; the association of eroticism and violence in Belle's attitude toward Louis: "he is completely mine, how I love him! I could kill him without his . . ." (p. 147); the red, open mouth and teeth of a woman waiting for "men without faces, a decapitated crowd" (p. 229); the face of Louis's mother like a "knife-blade" (p. 247), are all related to the knives, the blades, the drops of blood, the mutilated limbs, and the harpies of *Histoire*. Hence, also, the mocking reminders in Simon's book of the failure of the human (male) will to order. The unused gun that weighs down Louis's pocket is related to the ironically upraised swords and brandished guns of the later novels, and its dark "disquieting mouth" (p. 221) to the recurring eye of the penis, that blind Cyclops which forces men to follow it into darkness and chaos.

In the novels from *The Wind* through *Histoire*, where the narrator's effort to order his reality becomes a generalized fictional, narrative, and linguistic struggle, his failure becomes increasingly catastrophic. Tragically for him, there is no meaning, no final order to be discovered. The void evoked thematically in *Le Tricheur* becomes to the fictional consciousness in later novels the absence at the center, or better, the absent center of the work. It is the unattainable point of immanence, the "always future hollowness," which remains hypothetical, unknowable, unnamable. It is in this void, this absence, that the narrator finally loses himself, to be replaced by the textual "O" of *The Battle of Pharsalus*. As the narrator's ordeal is reenacted from novel to novel, his failure to achieve a stable point of reference and, hence, a stable coherence, undermines ever more radically his existence. At the end of *The Flanders Road* Georges drifts into sleep as his entire construct becomes static and hollow and gradually falls apart, the fragments abandoned to the work of time. In *The Palace* the narrator becomes lost in a vertiginous oscillation between his present and the past until all that is left is abortion and death (that of the narrator himself, perhaps) in an underground urinal. In *Histoire*, where the figure who says "I" is identifiable only by reference to dead or absent relatives, the end of the book is a return to darkness as he transforms himself into a hideous fetus made up of various elements of the text, thus effacing his life as he confronts himself (perhaps) in the womb.

Although Louis is far from the textual annihilation awaiting later Simon characters, the seeds of the annihilation are already present in the fiction of *Le Tricheur*. Throughout the book Louis struggles against his desire to abandon himself to the dark holes and cavities waiting everywhere. At the very end, after the bungled murder, he contemplates the drop from his balcony into the black abyss, a drop he imagines to be like the fall one sometimes experiences in dreams: "an endless fall, a vertigo where everything slipped away and where one only had to let oneself go" (p. 250). The private drama that began with the death of his mother, "death of the mother, annihilation of one's origins, a perfect circle of destruction,"[12] ends with his passive abandonment of will as he stands on his balcony at the end: "my body upright, filling with silence and shadows, as if it were never going to end" (p. 250).

A major difference between *Le Tricheur* and later works is that Louis is trapped not by textual reflections of his own production, but by the convergence of episodic and thematic elements created through rather conventional narrative means. As Jacques Guicharnaud has pointed out, the early works are composed of familiar modernist devices, of "prefabricated techniques: the stream of consciousness and pointillism, as developed by the American novel, resulting in the mixture of Faulkner, Hemingway and Steinbeck in translation so popular with young French writers in the 1940's."[13] Although much can be said about the direct and indirect influence of Faulkner and others on *Le Tricheur*, it suffices here to indicate in what ways these "prefabricated" techniques serve as the point of departure for the long process of textualization that is Simon's work.

In commenting on this process, Simon has said that the one principle of composition that has remained constant in his work is precisely the system of internal reflections: "The idea that the novel must be a play of internal mirrors has not changed, it is the writing that has changed."[14] In *Le Tricheur* these reflections are created primarily by the disruption of conventional chronology and causality, and by the use of multiple points of view. Because of the general ambiguity created by these devices as well as by the author's withholding of information, the reader is forced to order the work reflexively. The order emerges, in part, from the relationships put into play among the structural divisions of the book and among the characters, who come to mirror one another. Thematically, the order emerges from the numerous interrelated motifs and images which form a group of oppositions: oppositions between wakefulness and sleep, between light and darkness, between mobility and stasis, between the horizontal continuum of fate on the one hand, and the vertical polarity of volition and passive submission on the other, all of which serve to relate the basic problems of the fiction and the experiences of the different characters to the central experience of the protagonist.

In thus breaking down the conventional metonymic axis of the narrative and replacing it with a reflexive, metaphoric order, *Le Tricheur* fell into the mainstream of modernist developments of the novel. Considered from the perspective provided by subsequent works, the first novel reveals the problems for which so many of Simon's later technical developments were the solutions. Simon's work, like much of modern literature, can be seen as an ever more radical contestation of the representational function of writing. In *Le Tricheur* Simon attempted to represent a human struggle with an experienced reality; what he did, in spite of his modernist devices, was to write *about* that struggle rather than write the struggle itself.

In *La Corde raide*, where Simon further developed the notion of *truquage*, or counterfeiting, man's response to the world is divided into two existential categories: authentic and inauthentic. According to that division, the inauthentic person, or the cheater, deceives himself with logical systems, formulas, and faiths, while the authentic person accepts contingency and rejects all fictions. The world of *Le Tricheur* is not "the multiple infinity of realities, all equally possible, all equally true", described in *La Corde raide* (p. 122). Behind the fragmentation of the novel there is a fictional objective reality that remains uncontested. And although the reader must order the work reflexively, he can, at the same time, reassemble the pieces of the puzzle in a reductive manner and end up simply with a conventional story about conventional characters. The problem with *Le Tricheur* is that there is no void at the core of the work, no lack of a stable point of reference for the play of internal mirrors. In Simon's own terms, this retrievable, stable fictional reality is inauthentic.

In *The Wind* Simon was still concerned with representation and still dependent on episodic invention, but for the first time in his work he abandoned an uncontested, objective fictional reality. To do this, he adopted the device of a single narrator with a restricted viewpoint. Whereas *Le Tricheur* relates Louis's search for an act that will impose order on experience, *The Wind* is the narrator's effort to order remembered and imagined experience, the reality of which is too complex and protean ever to be seized. In *Le Tricheur* the meaninglessness of Louis's act is reinforced by a hiatus in the narrative. Three times the events surrounding the murder are related from different points of view. The first two times, the actual scene of the murder is omitted. The third time, the reader witnesses the scene from Louis's point of view, but the instant of the

murder itself is absent, contained, so to speak, in the interval
between two paragraphs and in a shift of tenses: "Then I pick
up the brick./ I struck downward . . . with all my might" (p.
248). In *The Wind*, where the quest becomes an
epistemological one, this absence becomes the enigma, the
unanswered question that torments all of Simon's narrators
and serves as the fictional correlative of the moment of immanence which they cannot seize because they are already
reflecting on it.

From *The Wind* through *Histoire*, a number of the narrative and linguistic devices in *Le Tricheur* and the two novels
that follow it are abandoned. The multiple points of view of
the early books are replaced by a single narrator who struggles
from his limited perspective to make sense out of the multiple
versions of reality available to him. The structural fragmentation is replaced by a continuous flow of narration, which corresponds to the continuous workings of the narrator's consciousness. The associational operations of memory and imagination, already used extensively in *Le Tricheur*, are fully
developed in the narrator's search for a past or lived experience, with the difference that in the later books the operations of memory and imagination are explored along an un-
broken metonymic axis. The language, already somewhat
freed from conventional syntax in parts of *Le Tricheur*, [15] expands into the abundant, profuse language of *The Flanders
Road*, a language that continually circles, continually tries to
close in on the fixed point of certainty that the narrator can
never capture. The present participle, already in evidence in
Le Tricheur, becomes the principal tool of Simon's
"hypothetical" mode of writing, "the mode of striving, that is
to say, of impotence."[16]

From *The Wind* on, the main subject of Simon's novels is
man's struggle to create meaning. A number of the motifs
through which the struggle is metaphorically described—particularly in those novels through *Histoire*, where Simon is still
concerned with the phenomenological activity of an ordering
consciousness—are already present in *Le Tricheur*. Among

these motifs are the window, the small rectangular opening which serves as a correlative for the characters' limited perspectives on the world; separation symbols, such as the clinging integument which evokes a womblike barrier between Louis and the world he wants to control; vehicles that carry characters through a world they can only passively and partially register; snapshots, paintings, postcards, and posters, all of which are both literal representations of fragments of the world and metaphoric representations of mental images of reality; and interplays of light and darkness, which evoke man's cognitive possibilities and limitations. It is significant that the mirror, which in the later works becomes the central metaphor of the experience of the narrator and of the internal reflections of the novel, is used only minimally in the first book.

In exploring the ways in which the fictional consciousness experiences his reality, the novels from *The Wind* through *Histoire* increasingly examine and expose the operations which generate the text itself, the text that constitutes the reality of the narrator. This autorepresentation is found only to a limited degree in *Le Tricheur*. Certainly the breakdown and fragmentation of the conventional narrative structure is an important element of this process, but the exposure of the novel as novel is effected not internally, but rather by reference to the stable fictional reality that the reader can construct from the fragments. The one important exception is the first part of the fourth chapter, where the novel incorporates into its own fiction this same activity of reconstruction. In that section, Ephraim Rosenbaum, a watch salesman, tries to fit together the pieces of Belle's and Louis's story.[17] It is this process, by which the novel tells the story of its own activity, which is developed in the later works.

In the movement from representation to autorepresentation (to use the terms of Jean Ricardou), the tensions between the fictions of phenomenological realism and the actual activity of writing are gradually exposed and lead to the abandonment of those fictions in *The Battle of Pharsalus*. In the course of this movement the role of "description" in Simon's work gradually encroaches on that of narration until *Histoire*, where the whole experience of the narrator is generated fictionally by the description of postcards. Finally, the role of the referent itself diminishes until, in Simon's most recent texts, "it is only in the process of writing that something produces *itself* in every sense of the word."[18]

In a 1952 review of *Gulliver*, Roger Kemp complained that "Mr. Simon has a mania for description."[19] This same preoccupation is already evident in *Le Tricheur*. Although the descriptions in the first novel are fully integrated into the fiction, they tend to expand into independent blocks that interrupt the flow of the narrative. Rather than camouflaging their analytic nature for the sake of the progress of the narrative, such descriptions deliberately halt it, creating the effect of movement in place, an effect reinforced by the use of incomplete phrases, the absence of action verbs, and by the use of present participles. The result is an impression of two-dimensional artificiality, which is underlined by the mythical and theatrical content of many of the descriptions.[20] The general flattening contributes in the course of Simon's work to the emergence of a fictional world that tends to become the theater of the whole play of language.

More than thirty years separate *Le Tricheur* from Simon's latest texts, yet in some very superficial ways the first novel appears closer to the more recent works than it does to a novel such as *The Flanders Road*. The external structures of the latest works again emphasize the play of contiguous elements; the sentences have again been shortened, and the syntax and punctuation have become conventional, more conventional than that of much of *Le Tricheur*. However, there is a great distance between the first book and the most recent ones, and this distance can be measured by the evolution that has occurred in Simon's notion of *truquage*, or inauthenticity in writing.

From the earliest novels, where the concern for phenomenological authenticity is largely thematic, through *The Wind* and the four novels that follow it, where thematic and formal concerns more completely coincide, there is a

human figure at grips with an experienced reality. In every
case this figure fails in his effort to order the fragments of his
experience, "which is a little like trying to stick together the
scattered, incomplete debris of a broken mirror . . . getting
only an incoherent, ridiculous, idiotic result" (*The Wind*, p.
10). Incorporated within this fiction of defeat is the most important fictional failure of all: that of language itself. As early
as *Le Tricheur*, where the rational interpretations of events
seem to be nothing more than a few "words plastered on the
absurd" (p. 213), where words are no more than "an agreable
dead sound . . . accompanied by the reassuring and inoffen-
sive odor of cadavers" (p. 108), one finds a profound distrust
of language as counterfeit, as a distortion of lived experience.
In *The Flanders Road* Georges rejects his father's reverence
for language and has only contempt for the uselessness of
words; in *The Palace* the words of journalists kill the nascent
revolution; and in *Histoire* a girl's youth is transformed into
the dead messages of dusty postcards, and the power of events
into empty words.

In abandoning the fiction of the narrator, a narrator who is
unable to read intelligibly the text of his own production,
Simon relinquishes a last form of inauthenticity and affirms
the activity of writing. For with the fictional narrator goes his
distrust of language and his perception of his textual experience as a vertiginous play of signifiers around a void. In
La Corde raide Simon described the world as "an incoherent
and disjointed gibberish, without consistency" (p. 105), which
man could only painfully try to reconstruct and decipher. In
his most recent books the reading of the world coincides with
the reading of the text produced, for what is involved "is not
the decipherment and recognition of a code or a series of
codes . . . but the grasping of the code of writing itself
(language) as an area of activity (transformation) in the
demonstration of its play (limits).[21]

In works such as *Triptych* or *Leçon de choses* one finds this
play of writing a play in which lucid operations metaphorically and literally govern the text. And in the play of articula-
tion that is the activity of writing, the human struggle con-

tinues, a struggle summed up by Philippe Sollers: " 'To write is to impose one's will.' 'To write is to pursue fortune.' To passivity and resignation we must thus always oppose will and fortune, will as fortune.'"[22] Here, at last, may be the distant response to the dilemma of *Le Tricheur*.

BROWN UNIVERSITY

Notes

1. Maurice Nadeau, "Un nouveau roman de l'absurde," *Combat* 15 (February 1946).

2. Jean-Luc Seylaz, "Du *Vent* à *La Route des Flandres*: La Conquête d'une forme romanesque," in *Un Nouveau roman?: recherches et tradition*, ed. J. H. Matthews, special edition of *La Revue des lettres modernes* 94-99 (1964): 225.

3. Cited by Simon in *Le Monde* (26 April 1967), p. v.

4. Stephen Heath, *The Nouveau Roman: A Study in the Practice of Writing* (Philadelphia: Temple University Press, 1972), p. 157, citing Simon, "Qu'est-ce que l'avant-garde en 1958? Réponse à une enquête," *Les Lettres françaises* (24-30 April 1958), p. 1.

5. *Le Vent* (Paris: Minuit, 1957), p. 10. Subsequent references to Simon's work are to the following editions: *Le Tricheur* (Paris: Sagittaire, 1945); *La Corde raide* (Paris: Sagittaire, 1947); *Le Sacre du printemps* (Paris: Calmann-Lévy, 1954); *L'Herbe* (Paris: Minuit, 1958); *La Route des Flandres* (Paris: U.G.E., Collection "10/18," 1960); *Histoire* (Paris: Minuit, 1967); *La Bataille de Pharsale* (Paris: Minuit, 1969); *Orion aveugle* (Geneva: Skira, Collection "Les Sentiers de la création," 1970).

6. The relationship between Louis and the priest is also the first of a number of such relationships in Simon's work in which, as Ludovic Janvier says, the question-response dialectic appears "sous la forme du couple questionneur-révolté/questionné-soumis," in *Une Parole exigeante* (Paris: Minuit, 1964), p. 91n.

7. See Heath, *Nouveau Roman*, p. 171.

8. Janvier, *Une Parole exigeante*, p. 91.

9. Ibid., pp. 90-91. The interplay between wakefulness and sleep, a major metaphor in the modern novel, occurs throughout Simon's work, most notably in *La Corde raide*, *The Flanders Road*, and *Histoire*.

10. See Janvier's discussion, *Parole exigeante*, pp. 91-96.

11. Jonathan Culler, *The French New Novel* (London: Oxford University Press, 1969), p. 81. Significantly, the only time Louis indulges in a game, it is billiards, a game of skill.

12. Serge Doubrovsky, "Notes sur la genése d'une écriture," *Entretiens: Claude Simon* (1972), p. 58.

13. Jacques Guicharnaud, "Remembrance of Things Passing: Claude Simon," *Yale French Studies* 24 (Summer 1959): 102.

14. *Nouveau roman: hier, aujourd'hui* II (Paris: U.G.E., Collection "10/18," 1972), p. 108.

15. Incomplete phrases, some trailing off into three staccato dots, unexpectedly truncated phrases, verbs with no subjects, and phrases with no verbs are all common.

16. Janvier, *Une Parole exigeante*, p. 109.

17. There is also a passage which reflects *en abyme* the whole story of the *tricheur*; in it Louis watches a group of children who are concerned only with cheating at the very game they invented (p. 237).

18. Introduction to *Orion aveugle*. Anthony Pugh has summarized well Simon's simultaneous contestations of the narrative and descriptive functions of the novel in *Claude Simon: Analyse, Théorie* (Paris: U.G.E., Collection "10/18," 1975), p. 118.

19. Roger Kemp, "Jeux d'imagination," review of Gulliver in *Les Nouvelles littéraires* (12 June 1952), p. 2.

20. See, for example, the descriptions on pp. 42-43, 127, and passim.

21. Heath, *The Nouveau Roman*, p. 64, in the context of a discussion of Nathalie Sarraute.

22. Philippe Sollers, citing Georges Bataille, "Le Roman et l'expérience des limites," *Logiques* (Paris: Seuil, 1968), p. 249.

2
Life's Illusions: Patterns of Initiation in *Le Sacre du printemps*

Philip H. Solomon

Most of Simon's critics routinely divide his novels into three distinct periods: the early novels (*Le Tricheur*, *Gulliver*, *Le Sacre du printemps*); the novels from *The Wind* to *Histoire*; the later novels, beginning with *The Battle of Pharsalus*. Regrettably, the works belonging to the first group have been systematically ignored, virtually deleted from Simon's literary production. At the Colloque de Cerisy, held in July 1974, which brought together specialists on Simon from several countries, there were no papers devoted to this first phase.

There was, however, a brief paper given on *La Corde raide*, a kind of journal, published by Simon in 1947, two years after the appearance of his first novel, *Le Tricheur*. The paper's author, A. B. Duncan, while noting that the early works were of an "inferior quality," linked their neglect at the colloquium to a reductionist reading of Simon's novels. One obviated, he remarked, an examination of "Simon's slow and magnificent evolution" by attempting to "cast all his novels in the mold of *Conducting Bodies* and *Triptych*."[1] Duncan's critique, directed against the formalism of Ricardolian analysis, and its imposition at the colloquium, raises some fundamental questions concerning that methodology.[2] Simon has himself abetted the neglect of his earlier works by dismissing them, on several occasions, as too conventional in plot and structure.[3]

Yet at this same colloquium Simon, echoing Duncan, defend-
ed the necessity of his "progressive evolution" against those
critics all too eager to ignore those early works lest they not
provide enough grist for their critical mills.[4]

My point here is not to deny the greater relevance and interest
of Simon's mature works but to contend that certain considerations of modernity need not eliminate pluralistic
readings of those works or *any* reading of the earlier ones. My
examination of patterns of initiation in *Le Sacre du printemps*
will attempt to reveal their thematic and structural function in
Simon's depiction of the human condition. In so doing, I hope
to demonstrate that this novel has an intrinsic interest and
constitutes as well a rich inventory of material that will reappear in Simon's subsequent production. Although this last
perspective has in many ways shaped my analysis, I have left
matters of intratextuality to those readers familiar with the
corpus of Simon's writings rather than disperse my attention
over many novels.[5]

Bernard Mallet, the protagonist of *Le Sacre du printemps*,
is a nineteen-year-old engineering student. His father having
died two years after the liberation, Bernard's mother has been
remarried, to a middle-aged man who is a dealer in used furniture. The stepfather, who remains nameless throughout the
novel, is considered by Bernard to be "useless and a failure"
(p. 55).[6] There is an older brother, a student in medicine, as
well as a number of other relatives—Bernard treats all of them
with sarcasm and contempt.

Bernard's family constitutes a burden that he would like to,
but cannot entirely, reject. Not having been able to escape
what Schopenhauer (quoting Calderon, *La vida es sueño*) has
termed the "major sin" of having been born,[7] Bernard attempts to escape the disorder of contingent reality (of which,
among other things, his family ties are a constant reminder)
by leading an ascetic existence whose order, ideally, would
approximate that of mathematics or logic: "The algebra of
logic, in which our visions, anguish, hesitations, choices are
reduced to a formula" (p. 26). Ironically, it is while serving as
a tutor in mathematics that Bernard will encounter, in the
very household in which the lessons take place, the presence of

an overwhelming "anarchic force," that of sexuality, which will undermine and, eventually, destroy the mode of existence to which Bernard aspires.[8]

Indeed, Bernard has already perceived, at least superficially, the anarchy of sexuality and has sought to protect himself against it. He has even contemplated what his life would be like were his sexual organs to be removed. Sexuality was responsible for his coming into the world and its agents are women—"mouvante, mystérieuse, perfide . . . instabilité féminine (p. 21). But when Bernard offers to sell a ring that Edith, the attractive sister of the boy he is tutoring, has stolen from her mother, the disparity between his deeper feelings and his philosophy of life begins to manifest itself. Although Bernard seems convinced that his motives are altruistic—he is helping the girl raise some desperately needed cash—it is obvious that he is sexually attracted to her and probably in love with her as well. No more aware of his own motives than of Edith's, Bernard does not suspect that Edith might be pregnant and need the money for an abortion. The voyage that Bernard will undertake to assist her will force him to discover the truth about himself and, concomitantly, about Edith as well. It will be his initiation into reality.

The title of the novel recalls the Stravinsky ballet of the same name, in which one finds the conjunction of primitive rites and modern life. Its music, T. S. Eliot noted in *The Dial*, "metamorphosed the rhythm of the steppes into the . . . barbaric cries of modern life."[9] We shall see a mingling of primitive and modern in *Le Sacre du printemps* as well. Specifically, the title of the novel refers to the religious (in the larger sense of the term) significance of the coming of spring, that segment of the cycle of the seasons traditionally associated with fertility and rebirth. Isomorphic to that cycle are the initiatory ceremonies typical of so-called primitive societies, the *rites de passage*. These rites consecrate "changes in status or social position undergone as a person passes through the culturally recognized life phases of his or her society."[10] The most exemplary of these changes is the transition from adolescence to manhood. The traditional scenario of the *rite de passage* is divided into three principal phases:

separation, (symbolic) death, rebirth and reintegration into
society.[11] A structuring device in the architecture of the novel,
this tripartite organization corresponds to the three days (10,
11, 12 December 1952), each constituting a chapter of the
novel, that Bernard's adventure will occupy.

Amply documented by studies of primitive cultures, this
scenario has also been discerned in a great number of myths
throughout the world. Whereas ritual is essentially preverbal,
myth is the narrative that renders the ritual communicable in
the form of traditional plots. In this context Joseph Campbell
refers to the *rite de passage* as a "monomyth"—"the standard
path of the mythological adventure of the hero."[12] The evolution from myth to realistic fiction is effected, according to
Northrop Frye, by "displacement"—the movement toward
plausibility (mimesis or empiricism) as opposed to the im-
probable actions of the divinities or semidivinities found in
myths. The intermediate step in this evolution would be
romance—an "idealized world dominated by a powerful
mythico-poetic impulse."[13]

In *Le Sacre du printemps* we find explicit references to
romance, by means of which Bernard is compared to the
knight-hero engaged upon a quest. For example: "Like the
pure and shining paladin of love, jeered at" (p. 126); "the one
with the silver armor has caught his feet in the stirrups and
has fallen flat on his back" (p. 208). These references suggest
a reading of *Le Sacre du printemps* that would complement
my own. Such a reading would transcode—establish
equivalencies—Bernard's adventure (the variant) into the
secondary modeling system (the invariant) constituted by the
conventions of quest-romance rather than those of ritual or
myth.[14] The passages just quoted also reveal a self-conscious
process of displacement which casts Bernard's initiation in an
ironic mode.

The first phase of initiation is separation, from parental
protection and, in a broader sense, from those societal structures which have hitherto oriented the initiate. In the case of
Bernard, his decision to assist Edith is perforce a separation in
that it obliges him to forsake the moral values with which he
has grown up. That separation is prepared by yet another,

which takes place before Bernard meets Edith—the departure from his mother's house and the acquisition of his own apartment. That break is announced by Bernard to his mother at a subway station, "that subway entrance, one Sunday evening, it served as a railway station or something like that, in sum, perfect for a separation" (p. 47). That this event should take place at a subway entrance—in French *bouche* (literally "mouth") *de métro*—anticipates subsequent elements of the initiation scenario. Mouth connotes swallowing, and in this context the swallowing by the monster typical of the second phase of initiation. As we shall shortly see, it is into the viscera—subway tubes—of the city of Paris as symbolic monster that Bernard will descend as he searches for a buyer for the ring. The mouth of the subway connotes as well an entrance into the earth as womb and thus suggests rebirth—the final phase of initiation—by which the initiate's birth (the original separation from the mother) will be reenacted on a different plane of existence.

The swallowing by or descent into a monster is a widespread initiatory symbol. A well-known example is Jonah's entry into the belly of a whale. Indeed, one often finds associated with the monster (frequently a marine creature) the elements of darkness and water. Here the initiate undertakes a return to the womb and beyond by means of which he (re)enters a "preformal embryonic state of being," is plunged into "nocturnal chaos."[15] It is by dying to his profane existence that the initiate can acquire wisdom, a knowledge of the real through the sacred, and thus be reborn spiritually and take his proper place in the community. His rebirth signifies a recreation of the cosmos.

The greater part of Bernard's adventure takes place at night and in the rain. Paris is the monster whose bowels are not only the subway lines as previously noted — "the stairways and corridors from which emanated the breath of a lower and dirty world" (p. 92)—but the sewers as well. These sewers carry away, amid the other forms of detritus, the remains of aborted existences. And it was only "a misunderstanding, a chance, a careless moment" that saved Bernard, to his regret, from such a fate: "Hastening noisily into the entrails of the city, bearing me into the visceral labyrinth, into the visceral darkness . . . the visceral knot . . . entangled in the depths where sewers carry at every instant thousands of lives, thousands of deaths carried off to the roaring noises of toilets flushing" (p. 76). One can readily discern from the imagery of the passage just quoted other ritualistic patterns of symbolic death, homologous to the swallowing by a monster—the voyage to the underworld and the descent into the labyrinth.

Associated with the initiate's symbolic death, as part of his metamorphosis, are suffering and mutilation (beatings and scarification,for example). These ordeals are often inflicted by demons or monsters — in primitive cultures by elders wearing frightening masks. The temptation of Saint Anthony would be an example of an initiatory trial in the Christian tradition.[16] Bernard's torturers are young people, like himself, whose monstrous nature lies in the visible disparity between their youth and their "mask" of maturity. It is as if, having been initiated, they have attempted to exteriorize an internal transformation that had not as yet manifested itself physically. Having once been the tormented, they are now the tormentors.[17]

The first of these monsters is Abel, one of Bernard's acquaintances, whom he meets on the fringes of the city. Consonant with the place of their meeting and his role as an intermediary — he gives Bernard the address of a potential buyer for the ring—Abel is less disquieting than his successors. He is a self-designated political organizer who cultivates a perpetually rumpled appearance which, with his balding hair and somewhat older features, gives him the look of a man "ripe before his time" (p. 80). But when Bernard penetrates farther into Paris and encounters Jacky, the receiver of stolen goods designated by Abel, he is genuinely disturbed by his presence: "Lost in the vast and velvety overcoat, which fell to his heels, with his delicately featured face, his curly hair, his voice with its somewhat common inflections, he had the appearance, at once ridiculous and troubling, of one of those kids dressed in the castoff clothing of adults, roaming in empty lots" (pp. 98-99). Bernard is also introduced to Josie, Jacky's fiancée. As with the others, Bernard is troubled by Josie's efforts to appear older than she is. She employs makeup to create a mask: "almost a child despite her tweezed eyebrows, her foundation cream, and the arc of her mouth . . . traced in thick lipstick so as to copy the sophisticated, bitter, and tired curve of a movie star's pout" (pp. 99-100). However, her role as monster will transcend that of the others.

Josie is linked to Edith in several ways. Both radiate an intense, self-centered sexuality. They are compared to a cat awaiting its food, "hardly bothered by external contingencies, attentive only to [their] feminine satisfaction, [their] feminine desire" (p. 29). They are also connected by the obscene graffiti on the walls of the telephone booth in the café from which Bernard, in the company of Josie, calls Edith to inform her of his progress. These drawings are viewed by Bernard as "symbols of a priapic and barbaric cult" (p. 112). He will participate in that "cult," despite himself, for he yields to Josie's charms and makes love to her, even after discovering that she is little more than a prostitute. It is not so much that Josie seduces Bernard but that she causes him to manifest those very proclivities which he had sought to deny and which had begun to emerge in his decision to sell the ring for Edith. Sexual pleasure is both an escape from and an affirmation of man's essential discontinuity, the individual, alienated, mortal self: "pleasure which is the faithful and symmetric reflection of that which one fiercely attempts to deny: loneliness, suffering, and death" (p. 120). Woman becomes a man's momentary salvation from the terrors of contingent existence; he finds in her, through sexual release, an atemporal continuity with the Other, a provisional death.[18] Simon compares this salvation to the thread Ariadne gave to Theseus so that he could escape from the labyrinth after slaying the Minotaur. But that thread has now become an "umbilical cord leading to a symbolic woman, to the warm, black womb from which all life has emerged and for which a yearning, moaning flesh longs, haunted by the desire and, more than the desire, the need, the necessity to return there, to die there anew" (p.122). That "symbolic woman" is Josie, for she is the figure in which the symbolism of this second phase of Bernard's initia-

tion converges. Her womb lies at the center of the monster
that swallows Bernard, at the center of the earth to which he
returns, at the center of the labyrinth into which he descends.
One aspect of swallowing should be added to this convergence. Not only has Bernard been swallowed by the
monster that is Josie, he has in the process become a
swallower. Having descended into the labyrinth of his own
psyche and having discovered there the sexuality inseparable
from the human condition, he has had to swallow his pride —
those beliefs, and attitudes and aspirations with which he
began his initiation.[19] Thus Josie, virgin (child-woman), prostitute, idealized woman (movie star), womb and tomb,
becomes, in her manifold aspects, Quintessential Woman,
Supreme Temptress, the mythological Great Mother (of
which Diana, Hera, and Isis are types).[20] Through his encounter with Josie, Bernard dies to a former mode of existence
and attains a knowledge of the real that is inseparable from
self-knowledge .

I have already noted that the initiate must undergo, in this
phase, pain and suffering and mutilation. Bernard has lost his
pride, but there is an additional price to pay. When Bernard
leaves the hotel room where he has slept with Josie, he
discovers that the ring is missing and assumes that he has been
the victim of a conspiracy between Josie and her fiancé to steal
the ring from him. A confrontation with Jacky leads to a fight
in which Bernard is soundly beaten. Jacky and Josie disappear, and Bernard is left to nurse his wounds. After washing
his facial bruises with some water from the Seine, he heads for
home. That symbolic washing would seem to indicate that
Bernard is now ready, as the third phase of his initiation, to
return to society, regenerated by the experience and
knowledge he has acquired. However, at this point the text
describes Bernard as a "phantom-like personage" who, having "survived the underworld", is informed by the gods that
his "dossier is incomplete" and hence he must return for "additional trials" (p. 131). Bernard's further education will take
place after he has returned home and will not only consist of
discovering the truth about Edith and the ring but also, and
more important, reevaluating his experiences with respect to

the particular view of time, history, and, finally, language that is Claude Simon's.

In opposition to its more "primitive" models, Bernard's initiation has taken place within the context of a desacralized society. Mircea Eliade remarks: "In the case of modern man, since there is no longer any religious experience fully and consciously assumed, initiation no longer performs an ontological function; it no longer includes a radical change in the initiate's mode of being or his salvation. The initiatory scenarios function only on the vital and psychological planes."[21] We can interpret Eliade's remarks to mean, that, whatever kinds of initiatory experiences modern man may undergo, they are set within a radically different historico-temporal framework from those of primitive men, or indeed from the authentically religious man within the traditions of higher religions. Sacred or mythical time does not flow irreversibly but is cyclical in that it repeats the eternal time of the gods, and in so doing it creates and recreates the cosmos. In the Judaeo-Christian tradition, time is valorized or sanctified, and the historical event becomes the revelation of God's presence. In all these cases, sacred time may enter profane time through festivals, rituals, and ceremonies—and death is but a transition to another phase of life.[22] Simon's conception of time and history is, as we shall see, profoundly pessimistic.

The continuation of Bernard's trials takes place within an atmosphere of sickness and death. It is the third day of his adventure, and he and his stepfather are in a hospital awaiting the medical report on Edith, who has been brought there after having been struck by an automobile. To pass the time Bernard relates his experiences to his stepfather and as he and the older man discuss what has happened, Bernard begins to enlarge their meaning.

The "fragility," "insignificance," and "solitude" (p. 238) that Bernard had discovered to be characteristic of the human condition are recalled and reemphasized by an awareness of their temporal dimension. "I have time" becomes the childish and absurd protest of the uninitiated. Forty hours of Bernard's life have disappeared along with the ring, and their passage, seemingly accelerated, puts into sharper relief the

flow of time as a "continuous hemorrhaging . . . of a supply
stingily allocated, measured" (p. 238). This concept of time as
a linear progression toward infirmity and death must be linked
to a view of history as cyclical in nature. Bernard's progress
has been "seen" by "millions of eyes . . . resigned to seeing the
succession and repetition, to the rhythm of their circular
course, of the same tiring and insipid episodes of a tiring and
insipid life" (p. 102). Such a view of history—at least on the
scale of the individual—promises neither the renewal nor the
transcendence that would obviate the deleterious flow of time
but only the devaluation of individual existence as one's identity merges with those of countless others. Bernard does not
repeat what the gods have done *in illo tempore* but what men
have done on the road to death. The emblem of this circularity
is the band of the ring.

Bernard's education continues by means of the reflection of
his experiences in the mirror of those of his stepfather. The architecture of the novel anticipates as it reinforces the relationship that will develop between the two men, a development
that will cause Bernard to revise his earlier, naïve opinion of
his stepfather. *Le Sacre du printemps* is divided into four
chapters: the first two and the last focus on Bernard; the third
chapter, framed by the others, describes three days in the life
of the stepfather during the period in which he participated in
the Spanish Civil War. These events had been related to Bernard prior to his initiation. That they should be inserted in the
novel as an overture to Bernard's "supplementary trials" indicates that he can now comprehend them in the light of his
own discoveries and that this comprehension is an integral
part of those "trials."

Just as Bernard had been naïve and idealistic, so too his
stepfather as a young man engaged in the glorious enterprise
of fighting the fascists in a war that seemed clearly to oppose
the forces of good and evil. He has returned to France to assist
in the vaguely clandestine (given the attitude of the French
government at the time) activity of shipping arms from
France to Spain. Three men are involved in the operation re-
counted by the stepfather: Ceccaldi, a boat captain seemingly
of Italian origin, Suñer, a Loyalist official, and the French

student (the stepfather). There are also two shadowy figures, never identified, who seem to be spying on the three men. The two men may be French policemen, fascist agents, or, indeed, Loyalist guards. Suñer, crippled by the war and perpetually morose, and Ceccaldi, a middle-aged but still handsome and virile mercenary, quarrel repeatedly over the details of the operation and the payment that Ceccaldi, who has hired the crewmen of the boat on which the arms will be shipped, is to receive. The student, whose principal function is to deal with a reluctant French bureaucracy, attempts repeatedly to reconcile his two companions. After the student and Suñer depart for Spain with the arms, Ceccaldi, who has remained behind, is found shot to death in his hotel room.

These events set against the eventual defeat of the Loyalists serve as an initiation of sorts for the stepfather, one that bears certain resemblances to that of the stepson. The stepfather had become a participant in the war as if he had been "something like a boyscout" (p. 187) off to perform a good deed, unlike Ceccaldi, who was in the war for money, and unlike those who had no choice but to fight. The stepfather begins to perceive the naïveté of his idealism when, during a visit to a brothel, a prostitute with whom he has spent some time (but not actually partaken of her services) refuses to accept money from him because she believes he is a hero of the war. As for the death of Ceccaldi, a man whom the stepfather admired, it remains a mystery and, finally, becomes an illusion.

Ceccaldi's identity—he had false papers—disappears along with whatever significance his death may have had. What is left is a yellowed newspaper clipping in which the murder is attributed to a settling of accounts among arms traffickers (at least, the stepfather remarks, the author of the article did not mention a communist conspiracy) and the impressions of the stepfather. These impressions are mental images torn from their original spatiotemporal context and floating in the "gelatinous transparent time" (p. 202) of the stepfather's consciousness. They become an illusion of the real, a fiction the maintaining of which is a vain struggle against time's destruction, and to "lose" the reality of Ceccaldi's death is, for the stepfather, to lose a part of the war's reality, his own identity, inextricably bound up with the murder.

Ceccaldi's death is no less illusory than the war itself. The stepfather discovers that men do not make history but are made by it. And war, another "anarchic" force, emphasizes man's fragility as well as the cyclical nature of history. The soldiers in the Spanish Civil War are like all soldiers have been in all wars, repeating the same time-worn attitudes and gestures: "as on every front, in every war . . they remained there, no longer so much in the hope of winning but in order not to be defeated" (p. 142). Ultimately, the war itself becomes an illusion as the real disintegrates into the deceptive re-presentations of memory. The early days of the war, the father explains, were "too dazzling for the human eye to capture for any length of time" (p. 142). Perceptions are transformed into mental images which, mingled with other mental images by various processes of associaton, blur the distinctions one wishes to maintain between fact and fiction—"ephemeral . . . fleeting visions whirling in our minds, having no other life but that and disappearing as soon as we think we've seized them" (p. 142).

That the two men's experiences tend to converge serves to demonstrate once again Simon's conception of history. All men, it would seem, undergo similar initiations, share similar deceptions and illusions; all are trapped in time. It is with this sense of community that Bernard will be reintegrated into society, reborn through his realization of what it means to be born a *human being*. The two men's professions, J. A. E. Loubère has remarked, symbolize their situations. Bernard is a *répétiteur* (a "tutor" but, literally, a "repeater"); the stepfather is a *revendeur* (a "reseller" of old furniture, but, in this context, of old and worn ideas).[23] However, these roles are not necessarily fixed. The stepfather, as Bernard discovers, has become a *répétiteur*.

Despite his disillusionment and cynicism, the stepfather had sought to escape time's destruction, to deny his forty years, by having an affair with Edith. He had negated her reality and by virtue of what he sought, transformed her into a myth, a Tellus Mater in whom he could find renewal, as the earth is renewed every spring. She is linked "to springs, to grass, to the soft and fragrant earth: in the shredded green light of springtime, something faunlike and pagan" (p. 254). The stepfather's delusion lasted long enough for him to make Edith pregnant. In the hospital he informs Bernard that Edith is carrying his child. But Bernard, no doubt as the result of the new awareness he has acquired, had already been able to piece together the truth. Chance accomplishes what Bernard was unable to provide for when, after a final confrontation between the stepfather and his young mistress, Edith runs out into the street and is struck by a passing car, causing her to lose the baby. This happenstance anticipates another: while in the hospital Bernard draws out his handkerchief and finds, hidden in its folds, the ring he had thought stolen. The recovery of the ring reveals once again, this time with devastating irony, the seeming vanity of imposing an order upon an elusive and chaotic reality.

One should note here the problem of language. Part of Bernard's new awareness is his consciousness of the disparity between his acts and the words he uses to relate them. At times he has the impression that a second Bernard emerges from this divorce of word and thing. But he is equally aware that, to quote Beckett, he "only knows what the words know."[24] And thus, like so may of Beckett's protagonists, he finds himself obliged to continue speaking, searching for the words that might seize the real and, perforce, creating fictions: "But I am not telling the truth, he thought, without ceasing to speak, without being able to stop speaking" (p. 244).

"It was not because he ate the apple that Adam was expelled from Paradise," the stepfather remarks, "but for having tried to draw it" (p. 263). As we have seen, Simon has used patterns of initiation drawn from ritual and myth as a means of delineating what is eternal in the human condition and what distinguishes contemporary man. Concomitantly, he has also used them to give a shape and an order to the chaos of modern existence and, in so doing, to create a fruitful tension between order and disorder. The narration, be it assumed by Bernard, the stepfather, or the anonymous narrator, self-consciously struggles to circumscribe the true nature of experience. And one already finds in *Le Sacre du printemps*, though to a relatively limited extent, many of the stylistic traits that will become typical of the writing through which that search is conducted: proliferation, digression, accumulation, rectification, among others. These contrasts and tensions with their texture of themes, symbols, and images give *Le Sacre du printemps* a fascination and interest that merit our attention.

SOUTHERN METHODIST UNIVERSITY

Notes

1. Alastair B. Duncan, "A propos de *La Corde raide*," in *Claude Simon: Analyse, Théorie*, Jean Ricardou et al., eds. (Paris: U. G. E., Collection "10/18," 1975), pp. 367-68.

2. See Fredric Jameson, *The Prison-House of Language* (Princeton: Princeton University Press, 1972).

3. For example, "Réponses de Claude Simon á quelques questions écrites de Ludovic Janvier," in *Claude Simon: Entretiens*, ed. Marcel Séguier (Toulouse: Subervie, 1972), pp. 15-23.

4. "Claude Simon à la question," *Claude Simon: Analyse, Théorie*, pp. 419-20.

5. See Karen L. Gould's study of mythological and archetypal imagery in *La Route des Flandres, Histoire*, and *La Bataille de Pharsale*. "Mythologizing in the *nouveau roman*: Claude Simon's Archetypal City," *French Literature Series* 3 (1976): 118-28.

6. Page numbers within parentheses in my text refer to the edition of *Le Sacre du printemps* published by Calmann-Lévy (Paris, 1954). All translations are my own.

7. Arthur Schopenhauer *The World as Will and Idea*, trans. R. B. Haldane and J. Kemp (London: Oxford University Press, 1969), p. 79.

8. According to John Sturrock, the three "anarchic" forces in Simon's fiction are sexuality, war, and exchange of wealth. *The French New Novel* (London: Oxford University Press, 1969), p. 79.

9. Quoted by Herbert Howard, "*The Wasteland* and the Modern World," in *A Collection of Critical Essays on The Wasteland*, ed. Jay Martin (Englewood Cliffs, N.J.: Spectrum Books, 1968), p. 20.

10. David Hunter and Phillip Whitten, *Encyclopedia of Anthropology* (New York: Harper Torchbooks, 1967), pp. 190-228.

11. See Mircea Eliade, *Myths, Dreams and Mysteries*, trans. P. Mairet (New York: Harper Torchbooks, 1967), 190-228.

12. Joseph Campbell, *The Hero with a Thousand Faces* (New York: Meridian Books, 1970), p. 36.

13. See Northrop Frye, *Anatomy of Criticism* (New York: Atheneum, 1966), pp. 186-201. Robert Scholes and Robert Kellogg note the "separation and interaction and recombination of the two great modes of narrative." These are "fictional" and "empirical." Romance is a division of the "fictional." See *The Nature of Narrative* (New York: Oxford University Press, 1968), pp. 12-14.

14. *Système modélisant secondaire* and *transcodage* are taken from Yuri Lotman, *La Structure du texte artistique*, trans. H. Meschonnic (Paris: Gallimard, 1974). See William Beauchamp's excellent discussion of Lotman's work in "From Structuralism to Semiotics," *Romantic Review* 67 (May 1976): pp. 230-36.

15. Eliade, *Myths, Dreams and Mysteries*, p. 122.

16. Ibid., p. 207.

17. René Girard explores the theme of the *double monstrueux* in *La Violence et le sacré* (Paris: Grasset, 1972), pp. 201-34.

18. See Georges Bataille, *L'Erotisme* (Paris: U. G. E., Collection "10/18," 1957), pp. 111-19.

19. For the theme swallowed/swallower see Campbell, *The Hero with a Thousand Faces*, p. 108, and Gilbert Durand, *Les Structures anthropologiques de l'imaginaire* (Paris: Bordas, 1969), pp. 230-35.

20. See Campbell, *The Hero with Thousand Faces*, pp. 109-24.

21. Mircea Eliade, *Birth and Rebirth: The Religious Meanings of Initiation in Human Culture*, trans. W. Trask (New York: Harper and Brothers, 1958), p. 128.

22. See Mircea Eliade, *The Sacred and the Profane*, trans. W. Trask (New York: Harvest Books, 1959), pp. 68-113.

23. J. A. E. Loubère. *The Novels of Claude Simon* (Ithaca and London: Cornell University Press, 1975), p. 54.

24. Samuel Beckett, *Molloy* in *Three Novels by Samuel Beckett* (New York: Grove, 1965), p. 31.

3

The Faces of Language in *The Grass*

Karen Gould

> It is language that tells us about the nature of a thing, provided that we respect language's own nature. In the meantime, to be sure, there rages around the earth an unbridled yet clever talking, writing, and broadcasting of spoken words. Man acts as though *he* were the shaper and master of language, while in fact *language* remains the master of man. Perhaps it is before all else man's subversion of *this* relation of dominance that drives his nature into alienation.
>
> Martin Heidegger, *Poetry, Language, Thought*

Since Claude Simon's first affiliation, in the late 1950s, with the *nouveau roman*, his use of language, particularly syntactic patterns, analogical forms, and generating principles, has been the subject of considerable critical review. Recently, critics of Simon appear to be focusing more and more of their energies on charting and analyzing the "process of language" as it develops within the text, primarily because the author has, himself, become increasingly fascinated with the creative potential of linguistic signs as generators of fiction. But language as a human issue, that is, as a central thematic consideration, has received relatively little critical attention despite its fundamental role in Simon's fictional constructions. A close look at the differing attitudes toward language in *The Grass* is, in one sense, a method of pointing out leitmotifs that can be found in most of Simon's novels. However, it is also apparent that *The Grass* is, in some measure at least, unique, since it seems to lay greater stress than do either earlier or later novels on the tensions created among its characters through the use, misuse, or outright abandonment of language. This tension is markedly present in *The Flanders Road* as well.

In a brief essay on *The Grass* in the Cerisy volume,[1] Joan Stevens notes that Simon's principal imagery falls into two distinct and opposing subject groups, the first emphasizing the oppressive presence of aggression, hostility, and anguish, and the second reflecting, for the most part, aspirations of purity and immortality. Within this rubric language plays an important, if sometimes obvious, role as transmitter of aggression, hostility, and anguish in *The Grass*, but it is also intimately linked with a desire for permanence and transcendence. In fact, the problems posed by language are clearly traceable throughout what appears to be the novel's three major centers of thematic tension, which emerge time and again throughout Simon's texts: sexuality and impotence, disclosure and concealment, being and nothingness.

The story told in *The Grass* hinges on a few simple but emotionally potent events as they are recalled in the mind of Louise, a young woman living in the southern French countryside, near Pau, with her husband, his parents, and an ailing aunt, Marie. Louise's recollections cover a period of about ten days at the end of summer a few years after World War II. Her fleeting memories are obsessively organized, mulled over, and rearranged throughout the narrative in an apparent attempt to discover some meaning amid scattered impressions of family arguments, infidelity, and death. This mental odyssey conjures up haunting images—whether real or imagined—of the last days of Georges's dying aunt, Louise's in-laws in their burlesque and futile fight against aging, the young woman's isolation from Georges, as well as her sexual rapport and emotional ties to an unnamed lover.

The backdrop for all of Louise's flickering glimpses into the past is an unrelenting series of omnipresent sounds: the gasping voice of Marie, Sabine's whiney lamentations coupled with her husband's curt responses, the repressed but notably bitter voice of Georges, the lover's distant, inquisitive speech, the noise of the comings and goings of occasional cars and trains and, above all, the continual, though oftentimes barely audi-

ble, sounds of nature. Hence, the act of hearing, of listening
and deciphering, takes on particular prominence in Louise's
reconstruction of past events. But what she remembers hearing
is not merely a mass of modulated sounds or a medley of
noises made by man, nature, or mechanical device. Instead,
the recollected sounds constitute an intricate network of com-
peting languages that, in Louise's mind at any rate, *speak* to
her, which is why each series of emitted sounds acquires a
symbolic quality for the narrative consciousness. And
although there are instances in the text when Louise appears
overwhelmed by the persistent reverbations of sound, sooner
or later she makes an effort to unveil the significance of the
audible phenomena recreated in her mind. Like Beckett's
wandering Molloy, Simon's protagonist lends an unconven-
tionally attentive ear to the sounds—human and otherwise—
of the world.

Initially, language may be thought of as one of the fundamental vehicles facilitating human interaction. Through
the exchange of learned sounds, human beings participate in
one another's worlds, share each other's feelings, and identify
with phenomena outside themselves that would otherwise remain distinctly foreign. Ideally, of course, the medium of
language brings its speakers closer together through mutual
understanding and the interchange of differing world views.
This is not the case, however, for the characters in *The Grass*.

Language as a potentially unifying force that ultimately
fails, particularly between men and women, is a highly
developed motif in *The Grass*. Louise places strong mental
emphasis on reconstructing the discussions she has had with
her lover and her husband as well as those which she
overhears between Pierre and Sabine. The individually articulated words per se have relatively little significance for her,
but the form of the oral presentation, the tone of the delivery,
and the emotional messages behind the spoken words are subjects that challenge her attentive nature and continually demand further reflection.

Because language is, in principle, outwardly directed, while
aggressively seeking the attention of the other, it may well har-
bor strong sexual motivations that are only vaguely percepti-

ble in everyday speech. In his recent book, *After Babel: Aspects of Language and Translation*, George Steiner asserts that "eros and language mesh at every point. Intercourse and discourse, copula and copulation, are sub-classes of the dominant fact of communication." Moreover, he goes on to say that "semen, excreta, and words are communicative products. They are transmissions from the self inside the skin to reality outside."[2] Such established parallels between coition and dialogue are readily apparent in the thematic development and imagistic patterns found in *The Grass*. Indeed, language often takes on forms that Louise construes as offensive sexual assaults, which both fascinate and horrify her.

The mother-in-law's (Sabine) seemingly endless and frustrated harangues with her monstrously overweight husband, Pierre, are clearly the most forcefully sexual, verbal jousts in the novel. Each time they have a verbal encounter of sorts, Louise recognizes that it is, more profoundly, their bodies that confront one another through their respective voices: "the two people, then, reduced to only their voices, to their principles, so to speak, their essentials, the voice with the prima donna's doleful and pathetic inflections colliding with the other's pachydermous, exhausted, patient and unshakeable opposition" (*Grass*, 140-41).

More often than not, Pierre refuses to respond to Sabine, since silence affords him an insurmountable position of strength. Susan Sontag has argued that "silence remains, inescapable, a form of speech (in many instances, of complaint or indictment) and an element in a dialogue."[3] In the case of Pierre, silence is just that, an inaudible indictment that is nonetheless powerful because it is left unstated. Humiliated by Pierre's persistent silence, Sabine finds herself unable to restrain her language, in much the same way that she is incapable of bridling her own sexuality: "The woman with the vermillion hair and the breath smelling of cognac harked back with her lamenting, desperate voice to her eternal grievances, like a comic parody of love, in a kind of one-note aria, obstinate and pathetic" (*Grass*, p. 84). Through the thin partition separating Louise from her grotesquely aging double, Sabine's indistinct words drown in a whining intensity, a

receding female voice, which is slowly submerged by male
silence. But the cadence, speed, and intonation of her soliloquy disclose only too well Sabine's eager emotional and
physical intent.

Sabine wants so desperately to be noticed, acknowledged,
and desired by the other, the male other in particular, that her
ceaseless flow of words, like her ostentatious jewelry and flam-
ing colored hair, requires that she be *physically* recognized.
"For the function of language," as Jacques Lacan points out
in his study of language in psychoanalysis, "is not to inform
but to evoke."[4] What Sabine seeks in a few words from Pierre
is the *response* of the other, not to her questions but to her being. Thus, she prods her husband into verbal struggles but is
repeatedly rebuffed. Eventually, Sabine and Pierre's
dialogue, which often sounds more like a female monologue
addressed in the void, takes on all the attributes of physical
combat, resembling the sexual encounters in Simon's later
novels, which are frequently referred to in hostile, warlike imagery where javelins, swords, wounds, and blood prefigure
the cries and fury of an amorous physical encounter: "the
words not exchanged but dealt and accepted in the same way
(that is, like two mortal adversaries exchanging blows in
silence . . .)" (*Grass*, p. 154).

For Louise, the verbal contact between her in-laws, which
is sought and thwarted time and again, becomes one of the
key narrative episodes around which her own search for a sexual identity and emotional commitment is centered. These
overheard encounters are, to be sure, erotic in nature since
each one underscores the friction/attraction established between two bodies located in an intimate space, whose failures to
communicate are invariably accompanied by the exasperating
but nonetheless constant desire for fusion. Hence love spells
suffering for Simon's characters because it seeks to affirm an
impossible union. As Louise's mental images progress, the impact of Pierre and Sabine's verbal-sexual contests appears
more incisive. Louise gradually realizes that her own ex-
changes with Georges have taken on dangerously similar
characteristics: "then the dialogue again, the two alternating
voices not mingling now, but somehow confronting each

other, a kind of give and take, like an exchange of blows"
(*Grass*, p. 133). With this recognition, the young woman's
disappointment necessarily increases. Neither couple has
managed to construct a unifying language that encompasses
and consoles. Words are spoken at times offensively,
pleadingly, or in defiance, but no verbal or physical consum-
mation seems possible.

Yet, if human beings speak to communicate sexual impulses, to fuse with another, Steiner assures us that they speak
to conceal as well, to leave hidden.[5] As in the works of
Lawrence and Proust, language used to withhold and hide
behind is a predominant motif to which Simon gives considerable weight, particularly in *The Grass*. Throughout
Louise's intermingling recollections of verbal interactions,
there runs a sense of perplexing concealment, whether conscious or not, and a disquieting air of deceit. Language appears to serve as a kind of cloaking device, superficially protecting both the self and the other from coming to terms with
uncomfortable thoughts and feelings.

Aunt Marie, around whose lingering death much of the narrative continually turns, seems to have lived an unusually in-
sulated life, where the potency of words, along with the
power of sex, were never probed. Like the bride and groom in
an old family photograph, Marie's steadfast choice to remain
a virgin was a matter of seeking "an exemption, not from
pleasure but from suffering" (*Grass*, p. 59). In the same way,
the control that Marie had always exercised over her own
language and that of others sheltered her from inflicting pain
or hearing anything that might cause personal suffering: "she
whose voice had never wavered, had never permitted itself to
waver or even to say things that might have made it waver"
(*Grass*, p. 48). A disturbingly mysterious martyr figure in
Louise's eyes, Marie divests words of their power in order to
strip life symbolically of its joys and sorrows. As her
fastidiously kept records disclose, Marie's written words listed
all events, the most trivial along with the more commonly
significant, in the same fashion, thereby denying life any
hierarchy of meaning: "as if . . . some secret knowledge, that
rigorous experience which needs neither books nor eloquence,

had led the hand through all these pages, had taught it not to make distinctions between the fact—the obligation—of decorating graves, of wearing a dress, or of dying" (*Grass*, pp. 103-104). Marie's controlled language is indicative of her closely controlled environment, but it also reflects a refusal to deal with the intensity of human situations.

While Marie's speech is restrained, Louise does not view her as consciously evasive. Georges, Pierre, Louise, and, to a lesser degree, Sabine, on the other hand, frequently employ words to screen their intent in the same way that actors make use of masks to disguise their identity. At times, we are reminded of Nathalie Sarraute's subconversations or internal dialogues, which her characters' external gestures and poses may suggest but cannot completely divulge. Such is the case, for example, in the following passage, where Georges and his father, Pierre, find themselves sidestepping their real dialogue or subconversation with inauthentic babble; as Louise imagines them, both men appear conscious of their veiled speech but are equally unwilling to risk an honest verbal encounter: "and between them the last words that had been spoken, although they knew perfectly well (both knowing they both knew) that they were not talking about money, that it was not money the older man was discussing but something neither one would mention" (*Grass*, pp. 124-25). Françoise Van Rossum-Guyon has argued that, in the eyes of his narrators, Simon's characters are perceived as heavily made-up "personnages," affecting theatrical or clownlike poses, and playing fictitious roles.[6] If this is, in large measure, true, the element of verbal masquerade is at least partially responsible for the unreal, "fictional" quality of many human interactions in Simon's texts.

Along with the general mistrust that seems to permeate much of the novel's dialogues between father and son, the theme of infidelity, found in the majority of Simon's other writings as well, gives an added reason for the nagging, untold suspicion and intentionally deceitful responses that exist between Georges and Louise. Like Hélène and the unnamed narrator in *Histoire*, their exchanged phrases only serve to distance one from the other more fully, despite their acute awareness of the inexpressed: "the limit, the line of demarcation between the formulated and the unformulated consisting only of this porous, clumsy and fragile barrier of words" (*Grass*, p. 126). In their dialogues, Louise and Georges carefully measure their choice of words since both feel compelled to suppress their most earnest thoughts. Because of Louise's infidelity and Georges's gambling habits, each partner fears dealing with the other, and their words, like their emotional and physical contact, are usually monitored in order to avoid discomfort and pain. But even when they do, at last, verbally confront one another, the words spoken cannot transmit their mutual anger, alienation, and despair: "the sounds pronounced, the words rolling over each other, that is, showing their various faces, their various combinations, then (the words, the assemblage of words) fraying out, falling apart, dissolving in the night air" (*Grass*, p. 131).

When the novel first opens, Louise has already ceased expecting or even hoping for any kind of authentic communication between Georges and herself. Her expectations, although unspoken, hinge on what can be learned from and with her lover. It is because Louise is indeed searching for something else that she speaks to him at great length about her in-laws and the dying Aunt Marie. Yet, while desperate to *articulate* her inner preoccupations, Louise also worries about saying too much to her lover. For, in the final analysis, language is dangerous because it reveals. Thus, like many of Simon's protagonists, Louise is caught in the trap of wanting to unmask herself, both verbally and sexually, and fearing eventual deception and abuse if she does so. It is not surprising, then, that Marie's symbolic abstinence, both sexual and verbal, provides an increasingly viable alternative to Louise's dilemma, since Marie reveals herself to no one and is therefore never abused.

With the progression of the narrative, we are alert to the direction of Louise's choice as she becomes more and more aware of the falseness of her own words—words that should expose in order to permit discovery but which lie instead, however reticently: "knowing (at the same time she heard her own voice saying it) that it wasn't true, that they were only

words, phrases to fool herself, blind herself" (*Grass*, p. 174).
The "implacable and absurd concatenation of all dialogue, all
language" (*Grass*, p. 129), which has long existed between
Georges and Louise, eventually undermines the exuberant intimacy shared by Louise and her lover. Their closeness
dissolves as her voice moves away, speaking not to "the indistinct face leaning over her but to the emptiness, the
darkness" (*Grass*, p. 171). In the end, she hears his voice as if
it were coming from a tremendous distance, "as if from
behind a sheet of glass" (*Grass*, p. 206), and her own words
tell him the lies he wants to hear but, like Louise, no longer
believes.

Besides serving as a sexual weapon or concealing personally
vulnerable areas from others, language in *The Grass*, as in
Beckett's works, becomes a method of asserting one's self in
the world. Simon makes it clear that his characters' most basic
motivation to speak stems from a pressing need to affirm their
own presence in the midst of life's impermanence and meaningless flux. Like Beckett's babbling Winnie in *Happy Days*,
as Sabine's awareness of old age and approaching death
heightens, her desire to *voice* her existence understandably increases: "Sabine's voice seemed to break suddenly, to twist,
rising in a cry, a desperate, furious (and even peevish, indig-
nant, stubborn protest, saying: "I don't want to die!" the old
man probably just looking at her without saying anything, for
after a moment the voice—the protest, the challenge—rose
again, though weaker . . .)" (*Grass*, p. 145). Sabine's compul-
sion to talk, often despite the virtual deafness of her listener, is
a futile but moving attempt to fill up the void with words so
that she can escape contact with its silence. Her effort to evade
the suffering that comes with a recognition of man's inevitable
fate creates a still greater gulf between Sabine's unreasonable
demands of life and the real nature of being in the world.

Psychologically speaking, Sabine cannot give up her stream
of words without giving up her existence as well. Even Pierre,
whose constant refusals to speak *to* rather than *at* Sabine gnaw
at the very core of her being, continues to indicate his presence
through garbled sounds and clumsy gestures: "the man-
mountain had long since stopped answering other than by

those vague, indistinct sounds uttered not as a response but as a kind of signal, and even more: a signal not of attention, of interest in what she was saying, but somehow merely as a manifestation (the sound, the guttural noise) of existence, a reflex provoked not by words but by silence" (*Grass*, p. 155). Like an increasing number of contemporary prose works, Simon's fiction often cultivates what Sontag terms "a kind of ontological stammer," which takes the form of "a discourse that appears both irrepressible (and, in principle, interminable) and strangely inarticulate, painfully reduced."[7] In this way, his protagonists rely on the potentially affirming qualities of language in order to elude, however momentarily, the quieting hand of death.

The soundlessness of the void that ultimately awaits all of Simon's characters is, to be sure, even more excruciating than the muteness of other people. Louise remembers anxiously recording the solemn weight of that silence when she overheard her in-laws arguing. The pathetic physical struggle that ensued, as their wildly gesticulating bodies tumbled to the floor, ended in an oppressive, deathlike stillness: "dragging down the towel rack and the chair in a crash, a cascade of noises echoing disproportionately in the still of the night . . . after that the silence not flowing back but falling in a mass, suddenly something absolute, crushing (a ton of silence) and total" (*Grass*, p. 199). Sabine's fear of being crushed and, as a result, silenced by her husband's massive body is a forceful metaphor, indicating a deep-seated dread of physical annihilation.

More realistic or resigned than his wife to the progressively debilitating stages of old age, Pierre has less difficulty accepting his physical condition. Yet he, too, battles to conquer the void, not with spoken words but by obsessively filling up one page after another with scribbled phrases. For Pierre's father, an illiterate peasant, written language contained secret meanings that could, if properly understood, reveal the mysterious complexities of life and, in so doing, lift man out of his ignorance. A university professor, Pierre apparently inherited his father's belief in the magic of words and trusts that by dispelling their mystifying qualities he will command their power. As the text here suggests, Pierre's success at taming those unknown words conjures up images of an ancient military victor: "having not only conquered them [words], assimilated them, but, as all conquerors deal with their conquests, pulled them apart, stripped them, emptied them of their mystery, that terrifying power that every unknown thing or person possesses when it is without antecedents or past" (*Grass*, pp. 37-38). But this need to master the written word and thereby uncover its secrets is overridden, in Pierre's aging years, by a still more urgent wish to prolong his own image through writing. Finally, Pierre's hopes of victory are oriented toward the menace of the future, and his frantically recorded verbiage points toward an adamant desire for transcendence.

Surely, one of the primary reasons for Georges's pervading sense of estrangement in *The Grass*, as well as in *The Flanders Road*, has to do with his disavowal of the supremacy of the written word, which, on a psychological level, undoubtedly represents the most effective way of challenging Pierre's paternal authority: "I wish I could not even know, I mean have learned, I mean have let myself learn, have been stupid enough to believe the people who taught me that letters lined up on white paper could mean something besides letters on white paper, I mean exactly nothing, except as a distraction, a way of killing time, and for people like him an excuse for showing off" (*Grass*, p. 127). Georges conveys a similarly bitter response about the uselessness of written texts in *The Flanders Road* when he remembers his father's distress over the bombing of the Leipzig library and glibly retorts that the library's great works must certainly have been worthless if they were unable to prevent the holocaust that destroyed them. But in both instances, the son fails to recognize the real basis for his father's persistent faith in the value of writing, which is Pierre's fervent conviction that words engraved in men's minds become, like those Latin words learned by school children, "rows of words, themselves cemented together, themselves like indestructible walls destined to outlast time itself" (*Grass*, p. 109). It is this desire to perpetuate one's thoughts into the future, even after death, that encourages Pierre to continue his obsessive scribblings, which represent little more than a frenzied attempt to alter the inevitability of his own destruction. By means of excessive caricature, Simon thus manages to ridicule the more naïve view of the artist's consuming struggle to achieve immortality. Rather than affirm a deeply personal, creative vision, Pierre's rapidly composed writings seek only to continue his own paltry existence.

As the crescendo of Sabine's obstinate lamentations and Pierre's harried writings mounts, the "Cyclopean death rattle" that issues forth from the withered aunt grows more menacingly inhuman. Louise realizes, furthermore, that this powerful noise of death has begun to reach through the walls, passing through the house like a remindful and haunting spectre: "arriving muffled but distinct, like the regular and terrible pulsations of some organ installed at the very center of the house" (*Grass*, pp. 112-13). Upon hearing the booming sounds of death, Louise's initial reaction, predictably, is to flee. Her desire to escape from the heavy, fermenting smell of Georges's rotting pears further underscores Louise's rejection of those deathlike surroundings. But Louise is also mysteriously drawn to this shriveled carcass of a woman who, even in her last agonizing moments, accepts her fate willingly and without remorse. Thus, Simon's protagonist gradually allows herself to become engulfed by Marie's bellows, "not in the presence of or in contact with, but so to speak inside the death rattle" (*Grass*, p. 137), and succumbs, little by little, to its influence.

No longer in control of her speech, in the same way that she no longer regulates her own life, Marie submits to the dictates of death, including death's "cavernous rumble." In short, Marie yields to that which Sabine and Pierre fear most: the loss of human language, which, in turn, signals the loss of self. Scenes of the dying aunt, which emerge and then linger in Louise's consciousness, are replete with mythological imagery, including descriptions of an attentive hunchback who understands Marie's feeble gestures and whose function as an intermediary between the living and the dead is, indeed, mythological in nature. Louise perceives this crippled woman as "a kind of bilingual interpreter able to translate a language no one else could understand, or, generally, not a language at all" (*Grass*, p. 96). The mythical motif of initiation that is suggested here seems clear enough: uneducated as to death's role in the human condition, Louise learns about the solitary nature of mankind's end through the language of death, which speaks of Marie's suffering as well as her impotence, and, especially, warns of the futility of all rebelliousness against *la condition humaine*. That being the case, Louise apprehends in the sounds of death what nearly all of Simon's protagonists also learn and what Simon himself asserted years earlier in *La Corde raide* (1947); "that every man is alone. It is irremediably alone that he proceeds, burdened with his past that belongs only to him, toward his death which must be confronted alone."[8]

The remarkable interplay of sounds and silences in Louise's mind leads her to still another, equally important discovery concerning the place of death in the larger pattern of things. In the face of Marie's impending silence, Louise remembers becoming more cognizant of the sounds of nature, which continued their vibrant discord despite Marie's agony. The chatter of birds and the rustling of leaves drew her attention, involuntarily, to "the fierce, exuberant and noisy explosion of life" (*Grass*, p. 68) that existed beyond the walls of her aunt's mausoleum-like room. On several occasions, the sharp contrast between the shrill sounds of chirping birds outside and the heavy silence emanating from Marie's room played on Louise's sensibilities to such an extent that she instinctively protected herself by sealing her senses off from the intense vibrations of the natural world: "Louise alien there, as if the light, the continual hissing of the wind in the leaves, the air itself were separated from her by a pane of glass, although she stood at the very center (but like a diver under his bell), the deafening racket of the sparrows in the clump of bamboos surrounding her without, somehow, reaching her" (*Grass*, p. 194). But the sounds of nature, like the gasping sounds of death, persist. And although she might well wish to do otherwise, Louise is compelled to listen to and decipher the "language" of her natural environment, which tells of "a kind of secret, exigent, imperious life" (*Grass*, p. 195) that continues its course in spite of human tragedy.

As the novel's denouement unfolds, human speech and human cries slip more appreciably into the background, leaving in their place the multiple sounds of nature, which endure even after man has been subjugated and conquered by his natural fate. The monotonous, all-encompassing murmurs of the rain, in particular, evoke the drowning force of Mother Nature, who is capable of liquefying the world and of submerging the human voice altogether—a powerful image that is also developed at some length in *The Flanders Road*: "thousands of countless, calm, keen drops soaking, corroding, eroding, surrounding the house with that terrible and majestic murmur ahead of which or rather at the heart of which the old woman's voice seemed to pursue some eternal and unappeasable complaint in the void, an agonized, insistent and yet languid litany" (*Grass*, p. 163). In the final analysis, Louise must accept the fact that the slow but piercing regularity of the rain drops will invariably silence Marie's weakening pleas. Like the last lingering ticks of a clock, the occasional groans of her dying aunt mercilessly run themselves out in symbolic recognition of the provisional, temporary, and therefore tragic character of human life.

Louise closes her reconstruction of past thoughts and memories with a profoundly sensorial description of the modulated exchange of sounds and silences in her natural environment. The image we are left with, as the novel ends, is one of Louise remembering how attentively she listened to the silence of nature after a rainfall, a silence broken only by the screeching, metallic noise of the train from Pau, the last few drops of rain, and the delicate shiver of a rain-drenched tree. Louise no longer appears frightened of the soundless void because she now understands or at least is willing to accept its role in the life cycle. The various languages spoken in the novel, by man and nature alike, have brought the young woman into contact with human sexuality, disguise or deceit, and mankind's inescapable mortality. With the extinction of an individual voice toward the end of the novel and the continual rehearsing of nature's chorus, Louise acknowledges the ultimate limitations of herself and others within the natural environment.

It has often been argued that Simon's protagonists repeatedly fail to learn anything about themselves, are unable to alter their perspectives on living in the world, and, as a consequence, do little more than roam, aimlessly, among their own obsessions. However, it is difficult to support entirely such conclusions about *The Grass* when Louise's lessons about the natural cycle of birth and death are so painfully clear and, so far as she is concerned, instructive. As the novel draws to a close we are aware that Louise has gained a new respect for the cruelly consistent way in which individual dreams of being-in-the-world and being-for-others are always eclipsed by the laws governing the physical world. Given the contradictory attitudes held by various characters in the novel as well as the thematic tensions that are manifestly present in *The Grass*, this kind of recognition would seem to be significant. Simon has, in effect, drawn our attention to Louise's new awareness by underscoring the silence that inevitably follows all articulated sounds. In the most general sense, this silence is the pause between the passing of one life, or lives, and the beginning of another, and it continues to insert itself into even the most recent of Simon's fiction.

VIRGINIA POLYTECHNIC INSTITUTE
AND STATE UNIVERSITY

Notes

1.   Joan Stevens, "L'évolution des images entre *L'Herbe* et *Les Corps conducteurs*," in *Claude Simon: Analyse, Théorie* (Paris: U. G. E., Collection "10/18," 1975), pp. 379-80.
2.   George Steiner, *After Babel: Aspects of Language and Translation* (New York: Oxford University Press, 1975), pp. 38-39.
3.   Susan Sontag, *Styles of Radical Will* (New York: Delta Books, 1969), p. 11.
4.   Jacques Lacan, *The Language of the Self*, trans. Anthony Wilden (New York: Dell Books, 1968), p. 63.
5.   Steiner, *After Babel*, p. 46.
6.   Françoise Van Rossum-Guyon, "La Mise en spectacle chez Claude Simon," in *Claude Simon: Analyse, Théorie*, p. 27.
7.   Sontag, *Styles of Radical Will*, p. 27.
8.   Claude Simon, *La Corde raide* (Paris: Sagittaire, 1947), p. 20. My translation.

4
The Road to Creativity: Eighteenth-Century Parody in *The Flanders Road*

Randi Birn

Through *The Battle of Pharsalus* Claude Simon's narrators are Janus-faced, their eyes turned simultaneously upon both past and future. Burdened by upbringing, education, and the weight of a literary heritage, they progress in painfully slow fashion. The narrator of *The Flanders Road* considers his past to represent "the heavy, rotten and stinking corpse of his disillusions" (p. 203)[1] and Simon himself refers to the remnants of inherited ideas and techniques within his work as "slag which I have endeavored to suppress little by little."[2] Elsewhere, Simon writes: "It takes time for one to rid himself little by little of his bad habits."[3] From *The Wind* through *The Battle of Pharsalus* each of Simon's novels brings the narrator a step forward in attempting to escape the past and establish himself as an independent creative artist. Each work illustrates, often in ironic terms, the struggle against forces frustrating this development. Old and new are locked in combat, and Simon notes the feeling of released tension and liberation once a novel is completed: "Totally detached. It is a turned page."[4]

Thematically, *The Flanders Road* is Simon's richest novel.

To convey its complexity the author employed a language that compares favorably to Proust's. Above all, *The Flanders Road* is a novel about its own genesis. It relates the story of George's struggle to become an artist; and as in the case of Marcel, Georges undergoes a mutation at the conclusion of which he evolves into the narrator.[5] One major factor, however, distinguishes Simon's narrator from Proust's. Simon's never stops to admire and cherish his creation—the novel just completed. As a matter of fact, in *The Flanders Road* the creative process is presented, not as a lifelong love affair, but as a single sexual act. Once climax is attained, desire abates, and passion is reduced to virtual indifference.[6] At the conclusion of *The Flanders Road* the narrator finds himself exhausted, empty, and cleansed—"as if a clean-up crew had passed through" (p. 314).

The drama of Georges's artistic development is played out within a setting suffused with eighteenth-century associations. The protagonist is an aristocrat who has been torn away from the family château and mobilized at the outset of World War II. He passes most of the war inside an enemy prison camp. Subsequently, while recalling his past in an effort to convert it into material for a novel, fragmented memories of his father and mother surface to mind. Eighteenth-century references—Rousseau, Mozart, as well as paintings, engravings, and miniatures from the château—accompany the parental recollections, forming a curious contrast to the horrible memories of war, defeat, and death. Frequently, the narrator compares his attempt at writing the novel to the staging of a play. Stylized sequences or isolated scenes associated with the eighteenth century function as banal family drama, vaudeville, or puppet show, vying for attention with the tragic scenes linked to the 1940 defeat in Flanders. The characters are customarily wooden caricatures, "Standing there, like those apparitions on a stage, those characters rising from a trap door at the tap of a magician's wand" (p. 81). For the narrator, however, they and the bloodied victims of the Flanders debacle are merely opposite sides of the same coin, "because vaudeville is always only an abortive tragedy and tragedy a farce without humor" (p. 201).[7]

Eighteenth-century associations occur sporadically in Simon's novels prior to *The Flanders Road* as well—a plaster statue of Rousseau graces the mantelpiece of old Herzog in *Gulliver*, Louis XV clocks form part of the decor in *Gulliver* and *The Grass*. The narrators associate the objects with decay and describe them ironically. In *The Flanders Road* the eighteenth-century material branches out into a comprehensive network. Associations, sequences, and fragments associated with the Enlightenment and pre-Romanticism as well as with "underground" art and literature, form a powerful leitmotif throughout the entire novel. They are significant in illustrating Georges's liberation from his parents, his gradual detachment from inherited ideas, and his unexpected discovery of a source of energy that inspires him to compose his novel. The scenes function in a way reminiscent of the play within a play of *Hamlet*, urging the reader to detach himself emotionally from the action, encouraging him not to suspend his disbelief. During his struggle to attain artistic liberation Georges frequently resembles Don Quixote, fighting windmills and ghosts, an absurd "hero" lifted from a puppet show. If *The Flanders Road* indeed relates the story of an artistic quest, it does so by means of ironic twists that are persistently undermining the novel's central theme.

The first step along the path that transforms Georges from a "jeune homme de bonne famille" into an artist involves a series of confrontations with his father, a peasant's son who had forsaken the soil for the scholar's life.[8] Presented are three basic scenes from a family drama. Having attained both professional and social success by virtue of his intellectual capacities, Georges's father incarnates the most optimistic of the *philosophes*: "Being the son of illiterate peasants, he's so proud of having been able to learn how to read that he's deeply convinced that there's no problem, and particularly no problem standing in the way of humanity's happiness, that can't be solved by reading good authors" (p. 226). Inside the small garden pavilion of his wife's château, the father spends the days before, during, and after World War II engulfed by papers and books, filling notebook after notebook with his tiny " pattes de mouches," commenting upon the wisdom of

his patron saint, Rousseau. Twenty-three volumes of
Rousseau's works crown the château's library; portraits and
engravings of Georges's eighteenth-century maternal
ancestors decorate the building's rooms; and the attic contains
the fruit of ancestral labors, a chest full of dusty, rotting
documents.

The initial meeting between Georges and his father takes
place on the evening of the son's departure for the front. The
father delivers a pompous speech derived from Rousseau's notions in the "Discourse on the Origin of Inequality" (1755), of
property as the source of both trade and war. Knowing only
that he will be leaving the next day for the inferno, Georges is
contemptuous of his father's faith in abstract ideas. Several
years later the son still hears the old man's voice ringing in his
ears: "heavy with the sadness, that intractable and vacillating obstinacy in order to convince himself if not of the
usefulness or the veracity of what it was saying at least of the
usefulness of believing in the usefulness of saying it, persisting
for itself alone—like a child whistling on his way through a
woods in the dark" (p. 36).[9] Georges's father chooses to
believe in the age of Reason *against* all reason. Rousseau's
works are his crutch against the nothingness he lacks the moral
courage to face. In Georges's mind the father's world is
associated with "the rotting summer where something was
finally going completely bad," "a corpse full of worms and
finally splitting open," "an insignificant residue," "a *longue
théorie*" (p. 36). At this stage restraint prevents Georges from
breaking with his father. The son simply leaves the stage, the
old man continues to address the empty chair in front of him.

Georges's disgust with his father's values is heightened by
the old man's reaction to the horrors of World War II. For
him the greatest tragedy of the conflict has nothing to do with
human loss. Indeed, it is on the Flanders battlefield, with the
agony of the dying surrounding Georges, that the second
scene of the drama is played out. The son reads a letter from
his father—the only one he receives from the old man during
the entire war. The missive laments the destruction of the
Leipzig library, the world's most impressive arsenal of
eighteenth-century books. Perusing the words, Georges again

feels the pangs of contempt for his father: "thinking constantly of you there and of this world where man strives to destroy himself not only in the flesh of his children but even in what he can best achieve and bequeathe: History will say later what humanity lost the other day in a few minutes, the heritage of several centuries, in the bombing of what was the most precious library in the world, all of which is infinitely sad, your old father" (p. 227). Surely, the son feels rejected, but even more importantly, Georges believes himself to have exposed the smugness of his father's attitude once and for all: "to which I answered in return that if the contents of the thousands of books in that irreplaceable library had been impotent to prevent things like the bombing which destroyed them from happening, I didn't really see what loss to humanity was represented by the disappearance of those thousands of books and papers obviously devoid of the slightest utility" (p. 228). More emphatic are the words of Georges's fellow soldier Blum: "Shit on the Library of Leipzig" (p. 229).

Returning to the château at the conclusion of the war, Georges finds his father encased as usual in the garden pavilion. The son is now determined to seal the break by crushing the old man's faith, and by extension, the reformist mission of the Enlightenment—that "idyllic and sentimental reign of Reason and Virtue" (p. 205). "Pachydermic, massive almost deformed," the father is monstrous. More fearful than ever of the reality of the contemporary human condition, the old man has become a hermit in a pavilion astonishingly similar to Rousseau's refuge at Ermenonville, where he nourishes himself on the myths and lies of the past, "where through the colored glass panes the world looked as though it were made of a single and simple material, green, mauve or blue, reconciled at last" (p. 248). Georges's decision to assume the life of a peasant, to enter the world his father had rejected years ago, breaks the fragile link. The son hears the rupture, "the imperceptible sound of some secret and delicate organ breaking, snapping" (p. 238). A shell of silence then separates the two men.

Achieving liberation from his father is a relatively easy process. The confrontations were direct, and Georges could crush

the old man's theories beneath the weight of empirical
evidence. However, the break with his father does not liberate
Georges from his heritage. His arguments against his father
echoed those of Voltaire against Leibniz; his decision to abandon idle intellectualism for work was fully in keeping with the
message of *Candide*—"We must work without reasoning, . . .
that is the only way to make life bearable,"[10] and, of course,
the idea of returning to the soil is consonant with the
Rousseauist rejection of the corrupt intelligensia of
eighteenth-century Paris.

The narrator illustrates Georges's idealization of the peasant by means of a particularly ironic tableau. While arguing
with his father in the garden pavilion, Georges observes a
tractor driver circling in the fields "like those characters sitting on a merry-go-round" (p. 34). As his respect for his father
diminishes, his admiration for the peasant grows. During the
first father-son scene, Georges had considered the peasant "irresistible," "invincible," "eternal" (pp. 34-35); during the last
one the peasant has become no less than a saint, his straw hat
transformed into "une noire auréole." However, the narrator
admits that the images had reached Georges through two sets
of distorting lenses—first through the colored window of the
pavilion, then as a reflection in his father's eyeglasses:
"Georges could see the tiny figure silhouetted against the setting sun reflected twice as it crossed (or rather slowly slipped
across) the convex surface of the glass undergoing the successive phases of distortion due to the curve of the lens" (p.
33). Georges's vision of the peasant is distorted. It is inspired
by Romanticism, "sliding, attached to nothing, ghostlike" (p.
35). It is particularly ironic that precisely at the moment when
Georges believes that he has sealed the break with his father's
philosophy, he unknowingly reveals himself to be an even
more faithful disciple of Rousseau than the old man himself.

While Georges's father transmits a heritage drawn from
schoolbooks and literature, that of his mother derives from
blood. For Georges the influence of Sabine—"a woman who
unfortunately for me was my mother" (p. 8)—is difficult to
cope with. Though Georges's attitude toward his mother is
consistently negative throughout the novel, the myths she had

instilled in him during childhood continue to exert a haunting influence. As if resenting her approval of Georges's decision to return to the soil, the narrator qualifies Sabine's attitude as "noisy, obscene, and uterine." After eight years as a farmer, Georges admits to not finding Candide's peace on the soil. As a matter of fact, in the best Romantic tradition, from his tractor-seat he contemplates his own shadow. Sabine's voice gives expression to Georges's dissatisfaction. Noticing that his fingers have remained long and fine, she informs him "that he had pianist's hands, that he should have been a musician, that he had certainly spoiled, wasted a gift, a unique opportunity" (p. 242).

Sabine is Georges's chief link to his familial heritage. A peripheral member of the aristocratic de Reixach family, lacking both *particule* and title, she nevertheless has acquired the ancestral château "following a succession of divisions and legacies whose intricacies she was undoubtedly the only member of the family to decipher" (p. 54). Quite naturally, the pure-blooded de Reixachs consider her a parvenu, an undeserving guardian of the mansion, its portraits, and historical paraphernalia. On the other hand, Sabine considers herself to be a well-equipped, well-informed purveyor of the heritage, and her stories of the de Reixach past, particularly its eighteenth-century past, are the most significant part of Georges's upbringing. In *The Flanders Road*, it is Sabine's interpretations of the heritage that stifle Georges. Literally and symbolically Sabine is a usurper. By imposing on her son her own interpretations of the past, she renders him impotent, incapable of orienting himself both in the past and in the present.

The very first scene of the novel recalls Sabine's guardianship of the family's aristocratic tradition. It occurs during the disaster in Flanders. George's captain, himself a de Reixach, is reading a letter from Sabine: "He was holding a letter in his hand, he raised his eyes looked at me then the letter again then once more at me" (p. 7).[11] The letter reminds the captain of Georges's heritage and requests privileged treatment for him. In this encounter Georges and the captain resemble a pair of actors playing out absurd forms of politeness on a stage set for tragedy: "we went on with our little ceremony standing there in the frozen mud" (p. 8). The exchange of clichés only increases the social and psychological distance between the two men.

The narrator associates Captain de Reixach with Sabine's favorite family tale, the story concerning an eighteenth-century ancestor whose portrait adorns her bedroom. What fascinates Sabine is a gruesome reddish stain on the painted face. Though the stain is nothing more than a crack in the surface of the canvas, it stimulates Sabine into inventing tales about violent death. The stories, subsequently referred to by the narrator as a "voluble and encyclopedic prattle" (p. 52), are the most significant part of Georges's upbringing.[12] He recalls how, as a boy, he would feel along the walls of the château, searching for the bullet which he believed killed the ancestor (p. 58); or else he would peer awesomely at the ancestor's pistols, exhibited in a case "wide open on the days when company came, closed the rest of the time for fear of dust" (p. 83). He even remembers having seized one of the weapons, lifted it to his temple, and pulled the trigger — the noise of the latch frightening a sleeping dog beside him. Like her husband, Sabine has wrapped herself in an eighteenth-century past, not that of Rousseau and the *philosophes* to be sure, but of a romanticized feudal nobility. Sabine's world, where time has no meaning, is literally a defense against the onslaught of her own physical decay.[13] She has dedicated her life to a gallery of ghosts. The few "modern" objects in the château—vases, some picture frames, an electric lamp—become vulgar intruders "picked up at the employment office to serve an assembly of ghosts" (p. 83). They undermine her attempt to become enclosed within a world of stultified permanence: "the same lacquered furniture, the same faded striped curtains, the same prints on the walls showing courtly or rural scenes, the same mantelpiece of white marble with pale gray veins" (p. 83).

In effect Sabine is an *artiste manquée* unable to muster the mental discipline that would give form to her stories. Her tales are gibberish, her aesthetic concepts confused; she considers art to be nothing more than a shield against time. Surely, it was Sabine who had stimulated Georges's artistic aspirations, but at the same time she had provided him with a set of misguided concepts as to the nature of art. For her, an artist is a person with delicate hands and God-given talent, his head forever turned toward the past.[14] Georges must struggle against his mother's pat formulas. In order to become an artist in his own right, he will have to be rid of Sabine.

Following her advice to leave the soil, Georges appears to undertake a quest to become an artist. His memories frequently focus on a series of dialogues he once had with his fellow captive Blum in the German prison-camp. The discussions centered upon Georges's childhood and particularly Sabine's stories. As it returns to the narrator's memory, the dialogue with Blum becomes a play in which a single actor assumes two roles. Blum's voice expresses the "liberated" side of the protagonist, while Georges's voice echoes the Romantic inheritance of Sabine. All too aware of this, the voice of Blum accuses Georges's of chattering like a book, and Georges responds: "a hereditary taint" (p. 226).

Restaging the dialogue with Blum helps Georges to find himself as a man and as an artist. It demonstrates how the Romantic, sterile vision of Sabine must yield to a healthier, more potent one, that will kindle Georges's creative energy and inspire him to write his novel.

The dialogue recalls Georges's aesthetic retreats into the eighteenth century in a particularly revealing way. Within the horror of the prison camp he would reflect upon the ancestor's portrait in his mother's room and accept both the artistic and literal value of Sabine's tale about him. According to her, Rousseau's writings had so fascinated the ancestor that he betrayed his class during the French Revolution. Not only did he voluntarily give up his feudal rights, but also won a seat in the National Convention, voted for the execution of Louis XVI, joined the revolutionary armies, and later suffered defeat with Bonaparte in Spain. The Spaniards, whom the misguided ancestor thought he had come to liberate, proved to be "absolutely rebellious apparently allergic to the tearful homilies on universal brotherhood the goddess Reason the goddess Virtue" (p. 318). Disillusioned, the nobleman returned home to his château and committed suicide.

A poverty-stricken Jew reared in the back room of a dry-goods store, Blum is the devil's advocate for Georges, casting doubt upon his friend's arguments. By recasting the dialogue within his mind, the narrator manages to purge the final remnants of Sabine from his own system. He recalls how Blum was terminally ill, while Georges's maladies were entirely cerebral. Blum assured Georges that ideas derived from books are divorced from reality and are a diversion for the rich. Contrasted with Blum's realism, Georges's behavior is exposed as shallow and emotionally immature. As misguided as his aristocratic ancestor, Georges had "evolved" from a youthful idealist to a disillusioned Romantic. In essence, however, he remained that little boy "so busy staring at the walls for the traces of a bullet that (if not glorious) at least was honorable, romantic" (p. 194).

In his unsuccessful efforts to become a narrator Georges would try to transform his mother's tales into a source of creative energy. However, Blum in turn would compare his restitution of the stories to the stream of cold air escaping from the mouth of their German prison guard: "But go on: after all there's no law against imagining that the air expelled by the bowels full of good German beer fermenting in the guts of that sentry produces, in the general concert a minuet by Mozart" (p. 190). The probability that Georges would succeed in transforming his mother's stories into a work of art was, according to Blum, as remote as the possibility that the German guard would transform his beer-stinking breath into a minuet in the tradition of Mozart. Such a metamorphosis would, in either case, require nothing less than a miracle. Georges would do well indeed to start looking for a new source of inspiration.

In order to emphasize his point, Blum transformed Sabine's tale about the ancestor into a myth of his own, and in so doing would indirectly contribute to Georges's development. Returning from the war in a sexually aroused state, the ancestor reached his wife's room. In bed with a servant, the wife heard the noise of her husband's horse in the courtyard, pushed her lover into a wardrobe, and tried to hide the pieces of clothing scattered about. When the husband entered she embraced him and in hopes of distracting him from the telltale surroundings, began to remove his clothing. To little avail. His suspicions now more aroused than his libido, the husband approached the wardrobe where the wife's lover was hidden. A shot rang out from it, and he fell dead.

Curiously, Sabine was herself the original source of this inglorious interpretation of her ancestor's death, but she would pass it off as untrue, "the scandal invented by his enemies" (p. 89). However, for Georges the alternate version is potent, fitting nicely with an eighteenth-century engraving in his mother's room, "something in the style of one of those prints called The Surprised Lover or The Seduction" (p. 87).[15] It also conjures up erotic images repressed by his mother and beyond his father's comprehension—the sensuality of Boucher, Crébillon, Laclos, a heritage of eroticism that would serve ultimately as aesthetic inspiration.

Georges was no stranger to eroticism. While his upbringing and education were intended to repress his sexuality, the frustrations of the Flanders defeat and the prison camp aroused it. Blum's notions of love contrasted markedly with the Rousseauist ideal, with the "gardens *à la française* making careful interlocking curves groves and nooks for marquis and marquises disguised as shepherds and shepherdesses" (p. 79).[16] The scene in which Blum attempted to convince Georges that Sabine's noble ancestor had craved nothing but "the act itself physical, naked, without emotional significance" (p. 194) is comic with Georges feebly and unconvincingly trying to defend his inherited world view. Lacking arguments, Georges would be reduced to correcting his friend's few facts. When Blum mentioned the ancestor's revolver, Georges would correct him, saying it was a pistol; when Blum referred to the twenty-five volumes of Rousseau's works, Georges, resorting to an obsolete eighteenth-century turn of phrase, would note that it was twenty-three: "Twenty-three tomes printed by a bookseller in The Hague for export and bound in full calf with the arms" (p. 197). Most of the time he would simply utter a weak protest: "no that . . ." (p. 195), "No. You're mixing it all up" (p. 198), and finally: "oh stop!" (p. 204).

The dialogue with Blum led Georges to the point where he would dispose altogether of Sabine's myths and, by extension, of the official Enlightenment heritage. Once more he would observe the heritage through the lens of eighteenth-century art. Inspired by Blum's rendition of his ancestor's homecoming, Georges would offer up a new descriptive tableau: "in that setting of a period print, stripping himself, tearing off, rejecting, repudiating those clothes, that ambitious and gaudy uniform which had now probably become for him the symbol of something he had believed in and now no longer saw any sense in" (p. 205). The Napoleonic uniform which the ancestor removed symbolized nothing less than the philosophy of the Enlightenment, that "idyllic and sentimental reign of Reason and Virtue" (p. 205). The narrator compares the stripping to a total purge, "a kind of terrifying diarrhea that fiercely emptied him of his contents as of his very blood, and not moral, as Blum said, but somehow mental" (p. 205).[17]

At this point Georges identified fully with the ancestor. After the historic defrocking, he too felt naked: "a kind of void a hole. Bottomless. Absolute. Where nothing had any meaning any reason for being—otherwise why take off his clothes, lying there that way, naked, unconscious of the cold, terribly calm probably, terribly lucid" (p. 217). Still addressing Blum, Georges compared the character in the tableau to an actor removing his costume, placing each piece neatly on a chair. Then, "stepping back to consider the effect, and finally knocking over the chair with the back of his hand, since in the print it was lying on the floor and the clothes" (p. 217). Having completed the elaborate process of liberating himself from his heritage, Georges himself in the end felt like a talentless actor who had played out a worn role.

The disillusionment provoked by his dialogue with Blum led inexorably to Georges's break with his father and eventual return to the soil. Once the term as a farmer complete, his recollection of the dialogue reawakened his desire for an artistic vocation. His quest led him to Corinne, a pure-blooded member of the de Reixach family and widow of Georges's commanding officer. Ostensibly, Georges desired to gain in-

formation about Corinne's marriage to de Reixach. Stories
had circulated about her faithlessness, and Georges believed
that de Reixach's death in Flanders was a suicide provoked by
it. Moreover, Georges believed that somehow Corinne might
be able to supply him with a factually correct version of the
ancestor's death as well. And finally, because Corinne represented the obverse of Sabine, visiting the cousin signified the
breaking of a maternal taboo.

Corinne is the catalytic agent of *La Route des Flandres*. In
Georges's mind she emerges straight out of Boucher or an
erotic engraving that occasionally adorned the officially pro-
hibited literature of the Enlightenment,[18] the side of the eighteenth century that Sabine had prudishly wished to suppress.
Corinne's links to the familial past are marked by a pair of
miniatures housed in Sabine's château. Both are of the wife of
the unfortunate ancestor. The first is an "official" portrait—bejeweled, dignified, and cold, the "virginal Virginie"
that represents Sabine's image of eternal femininity. The second
miniature is so different from the first that Georges could not
believe it to have been the same woman when he first beheld
it—"in that costume that was like a negation of costume, that
is, a simple gown, half transparent, leaving her half naked,
her tender breasts exposed, emphasized by a ribbon and spring-
ing almost completely out of the impalpable pale pink
stuff—something shameless, satiated, triumphant, with that
tranquil opulence of the soul and the senses appeased and
satisfied—and even gorged—and that indolent, candid, cruel
smile you can find in certain portraits of women of that
period" (p. 286). Georges will wonder at the versatility of the
eighteenth-century artist, "his trick of representing with the
same brush or with the same voluptuous pencil the matrons
and the lascivious odalisques lying seductively on the cushions
of Turkish baths" (pp. 286-87). Most important, he com-
prehends how his mother, a woman of slight intelligence, had
attempted to mold him in the image of her restricted fantasies.
By so doing, she has alienated Georges from the genuine
heirs: "not only Corinne and her husband, but the line, the
race, the caste, the dynasty of the de Reixachs—had appeared

to him even before he had ever come near one of them, haloed with a kind of supernatural prestige, an inaccessibility" (p. 52).

Having seen Corinne only once in passing, Georges would identify her with the woman in the second miniature, and the anticipated visit with her arouses his sexual fantasies. Blum's description of the ancestor returning home from the Napoleonic campaigns in Spain is appropriate for Georges's mood; equally appropriate is the narrator's description of a frustrated farcical hero lusting after an erotic princess: "and I the horseman the booted conqueror coming from the depths of the night from the depths of time coming to seduce to carry off the lily-white princess of whom I had dreamed for years" (p. 272). Georges learns nothing about Corinne's relations either with de Reixach or her reputed lovers; nor does she cast any light upon the eighteenth-century ancestor. However, the sight of her sends him into an erotic frenzy. She *is* the odalisque in the miniature, with her "dresses like nightgowns, pale mauve and a green ribbon around her" (p. 295). Deaf to her protests, Georges storms her body. The description of the scene resembles a reproduction of "la fille séduite," the language describing the sexual union both explicit and at times rhapsodic. Corinne has indeed become Georges's *madeleine*, stimulating his creative energies. During his night with her Georges conceives all the images that will become his novel, and it is at this point that he merges with the narrator. For him Corinne's vagina is the "wet mold from which I had learned to stamp pressing the clay with my thumb the soldiers infantrymen cavalrymen and cuirassiers climbing out of Pandora's box" (pp. 262-63). Once the narrator constructs the novel, Corinne's body dominates the imagery, often in the most unforeseen ways—her naked leg touching Georges's awakens visions of the bodies of the defeated soldiers transported by cattle train to their prison camp, her vagina recalls his protected hiding place on the Flanders road: "perhaps I was lying back there in the fragrant grass of the ditch in that furrow of the earth breathing smelling its black and bitter humus" (p. 261). While the seduction of Corinne emulates the creative process itself and is the culminating point of the novel, it is described in terms of self-irony. The scene is patterned on erotic, eighteenth-century art. Georges became a narrator by abandoning the role of the betrayed, disillusioned aristocrat, donning instead the costume of the unscrupulous, shrewd seducer. The prudishness of Sabine and the whole mentality which she represents, had rendered Georges impotent. Liberated at last, and at the height of his creative ecstasy, he resembles above all a small boy defying his mother: "I drank drinking all of her there (taking all of her into me) like those oranges that despite grownups telling me it was dirty that it was impolite noisy I liked to make a hole in and squeeze, pressing drinking her belly the globes of her breasts slipping under my fingers" (p. 265).

Thus, more than simply a source of erotic energy, Corinne's body rescues Georges from a universe of ghosts and catalyzes his artistic development: "what had I looked for in her hoped for pursued upon her body in her body words sounds" (pp. 279-80). Shortly after the publication of *La Route des Flandres*, Simon's interview with Madeleine Chapsal in *L'Express* revealed an aesthetic vision coinciding with the narrator's experience: "Such is the only role of the artist, his only chance to recover, as Proust said, *the eternal and universal substance* of reality. *To render not the meaning of the events, . . . but their weight, their flesh, their perfume.*" And Simon added, somewhat rhapsodically: "*I am in love with everything, everything, with a woman, with a blade of grass, with a pebble.*"[19]

In *La Route des Flandres*, Georges could progress as an artist only by overcoming interpretations of the past forced upon him by his parents' visions. In order to illustrate his struggle the narrator employed a highly ingenious descriptive technique—that of stylized theater, sometimes bourgeois drama, sometimes vaudeville, sometimes farce. Frequently, the quest motif was described ironically. Moreover, the stylizations often parody the historical era nourished by his parents—the French eighteenth century. Not even the novel's climactic scene, the liberation produced by the sexual encounter between Georges and Corinne, escapes fantasy and irony. Self-cast in the role of his cuckolded ancestor, Georges never-

theless plays a superbly vigorous lover. As the ancestor's unfaithful wife, Corinne does well as "the girl taken by
surprise." The episode concludes on a note of awakening, a
return to reality. His hunger satisfied, Georges dozes off.
Upon awakening, he discovers Corinne already dressed: "for
a second I saw her her (fragile) face too beautiful tragic two
shiny streaks on her cheeks" (p. 299). But Simon is not interested in social or psychological drama; his concern is with
the process of writing a novel. Her role in Georges's fantasy
finished, Corinne disappears, leaving the stage for the cleaning crew: "probably he would come by here along with the
ragpickers and the scrapiron men the garbage men picking up
the forgotten or outmoded props now that the actors and the
audience had gone" (p. 315). The erotic activity paralleled the
process of composing the novel—desire, striving, climax,
denouement, and indifference. Once Corinne's body has been
conquered (and the novel written), it is abandoned. For
the conqueror what remains is as unchallenging as "the soil the
whole earth closely inventoried described possessed in its least
features on the general staff maps" (p. 313). When the story
about Corinne's infidelities surfaces in the narrator's mind for
the last time, it produces nothing but indifference.[20]

One question remains. Why was the narrator so dependent
upon eighteenth-century motifs and associations? More than
likely the historical allusions developed according to
generative principles—one image providing a source for the
next, and so on. At the conclusion an entire fabric had been
woven together. Moreover, for Simon's narrator the textbook
Age of Enlightenment, with its pre-Romanticism, misguided
political idealism, unrealistic faith in Reason, and literary
sentimentalism, engendered a tradition inappropriate for an
artist in the modern world. Usurped by individuals with narrow minds and a spectacular lack of originality, the heritage
had become a dead weight indeed. Adhering to its values
would be as stultifying and anachronistic as dressing in
periwigs, knee breeches, or hoop skirts.

In order to grow as an artist and as a man, Simon's narrator
must break with the "textbook" past and locate new sources
of energy. Interestingly enough, in *The Flanders Road*,

Georges finds the source he needs within the heritage itself. The erotic eighteenth-century art and literature which had been suppressed by the "official" transmitters of culture (the nineteenth- and twentieth-century bourgeoisie), contained precisely that spark of vitality which would kindle his creativity and permit him to write his novel.

UNIVERSITY OF OREGON

Notes

1. Claude Simon, *The Flanders Road* (New York: Braziller, 1961). All subsequent references to this novel will be given in parentheses in the text.

2. Jean Ricardou and Françoise Van Rossum-Guyon (eds.), *Nouveau roman: hier, aujourd'hui* II (Paris: U. G. E., Collection "10/18," 1972), p. 107.

3. Claude Simon, *Orion aveugle* (Paris: Skira, Collection "Les Sentiers de la création," 1970), preface.

4. Josane Duranteau, "Claude Simon: 'le roman se fait, je le fais, et il se (sic) fait,' " (Interview) *Les Lettres Françaises* (13-19 April 1967), p. 4.

5. Georges is the narrator at an earlier stage of his life. Without discussing the problem at length, I nevertheless wish to emphasize that the individual who is learning in the novel is the narrator. It is by recalling his past and transforming his fragmented memories into a novel that the narrator is able to come to terms with his past and ultimately leave it behind. As Simon says: "The written world is not the perceived world. But through language one makes discoveries; one 'uncovers' himself, by the way, through writing, in every sense of the word, and it is a risk worth taking." Interview with Josane Duranteau, p. 4.

6. *The Flanders Road* could serve to illustrate Roland Barthes's statement that literature is a mode of Eros. *Essais critiques* (Paris: Seuil, Collection "Tel Quel," 1964), p. 14.

7. Dominique Lancereaux points out the importance of mime in Simon's work since *The Wind*. "Modalités de la narration dans *La Route des Flandres*," *Poétique* 14 (1973): p. 241.

8. According to Antony Cheal Pugh, "In neo-Freudian doctrine, the desire of each man, and particularly the creative artist, is to become 'his own father.'" See "Du Tricheur à Triptyque, et inversement," *Etudes Littéraires* 9, no. 1 (April 1976): p. 146.

9. Refusing to face up to the responsibility of the present, Georges's father is living his life in "mauvaise foi."

10. Voltaire, "Candide," in *Romans et contes*, ed. René Pomeau (Paris: Garnier-Flammarion, 1966), p. 259.

11. According to Raymond Jean, the first lines of a novel frequently contain the whole work in germ. As one of his examples, he discusses *Histoire*. He could have used *The Flanders Road* as well. "Commencements romanesques," in *Positions et oppositions sur le roman contemporain*, ed. Michel Mansuy (Paris: Klincksieck, 1971), pp. 129-36.

12. Simon told Claude Sarraute that, while *The Flanders Road* is above all a story about war, it deals with other things as well: "Here the complementary material is above all the story—it soothed my whole childhood—of that ancestor who killed himself with a pistol shot, and whose portrait I had before my eyes." In "Avec *La Route des Flandres* Claude Simon affirme sa manière," (Interview) *Le Monde* (8 October 1960).

13. In her effort to assure herself a place within a great historical lineage, Sabine would qualify as a Sartrian *salaud*.

14. Her aesthetics are diametrically opposed to Simon's own. Simon likes to think of himself as an artisan rather than an artist. See, for instance, Bettina Knapp, "Interview with Claude Simon," *Kentucky Romance Quarterly* 16, no. 2 (1969): p. 183. He is suspicious of the word "don" used by Sabine. See "Réponse à une enquête: Pensez-vous avoir un don d'écrivain?" *Tel Quel* (Spring 1960), p. 40.

15. Innumerable eighteenth-century engravings treat the themes of seduction, lovers hidden in closets, and cuckolded husbands. See, for instance, Honoré Fragonard's "L'armoire," Nicolas De Launay's "L'épouse indiscrète," Philibert-Louis Deboucourt's "La rose mal défendue." "La fille séduite" is the title of an engraving by François Boucher. It has been used to illustrate certain editions of *Les Liaisons dangereuses*. The stories surrounding Georges's ancestors are all inspired by eighteenth-century art.

16. The pastoral theme was very popular among eighteenth-century artists. See, for example, Boucher's painting "Pastorale."

17. The description of the aristocrat removing his Napoleonic uniform functions as a "mise en abyme," which Stuart W. Sykes does not mention in his article, "'Mise en abyme' in the Novels of Claude Simon," *Forum for Modern Language Studies* 9, no. 4 (October 1973): 333-45.

18. Fragonard, Boucher, and Gabriel de Saint-Aubin all painted alternately "official" portraits and erotic scenes.

19. Madeleine Chapsal, "Le jeune roman," (Interview) *L'Express* (12 January 1961), p. 32. Chapsal's italics.

20. Dominique Lanceraux notices the erotic structure of *La Route des Flandres*, and the mood of indifference conveyed through the style of the novel's final pages. "Modalités de la narration dans *La Route des Flandres*," p. 247.

5

Histoire: The Narrative as a Bio-Graph

Tobin H. Jones

Claude Simon's *Histoire* (1967),[1] like most of his novelistic work, manifests a tension between authorial control and the autonomy of the narrator's vision of the fictional world in the creation, disintegration, and subsequent re-creation of a literary universe. In *Histoire*, however, Simon has gone considerably farther in exploring the thematic and formal implications of this tension than he had in his earlier work. Like *The Wind* (1957), *The Grass* (1958). *The Flanders Road* (1960), and *The Palace* (1961), *Histoire* belongs to the tradition of the interior monologue. Its narrative form evolves in a process of thematic association and the projection of memory as an unidentified narrator plumbs the depths of his past in response to the emotional needs and material stimuli of the present. *Histoire* also has close ties with Simon's other novels with which it has similarities in both theme and story. Its dramatis personae and many of the events that its narrator remembers either recall those of *The Flanders Road* and *The Palace* or prefigure those of *The Battle of Pharsalus* (1969). Most important of these common elements are the characters, Corinne, Paul, and Uncle Charles, who make up the de Reixach cycle, which occupies the center of Simon's fictional universe, and who play major roles in both *The Flanders Road* and *The Battle of Pharsalus*. Despite Simon's clear intent to make *Histoire* a part of a larger fictional conception, however, the novel remains a self-contained fiction with a narrative system having its own limits, conceptual underpinnings, and aesthetic unity. The reader consequently need not be familiar with the de Reixach cycle or Simon's earlier works to appreciate the novel's rich and complex orchestration of themes.

Simon's epigraph to the novel ("It submerges us. We organize it. It falls to pieces. We organize it again and fall to pieces ourselves.") forewarns of the instability characteristic of the narrator's complex subjective vision of reality. The composition of *Histoire* proves to be an intricate poetic fabric woven from threads of imagined, remembered, and perceived events intertwined in the narrator's consciousness during an eighteen-hour period. Clear references to the physical reality of the day's events only intermittently punctuate the flow of memories and imagination. Throughout the novel, which begins and ends with the narrator lying in bed, only a few of his actions and even fewer of his motivations and intentions are ever explicitly revealed; and these moments— a visit to a bank for a mortgage and to his cousin Paul's villa, a visit by an antique broker to the narrator's house, and the time he passes in a restaurant and a bar—serve not only to localize his physical movements but, most important, serve as resources in the generation of thematic associations derived from a chronologically fragmented reality.

Histoire opens with the narrator in the early stages of waking. A center to an expanding constellation of images, he slowly begins to recall his reality around him, gradually structuring his world in the image of his psychology. The bulk of the historical and thematic material composing the narrator's monologue evokes the years of his youth when, after the death of his father, he and his mother lived with his maternal grandmother and his Uncle Charles and cousins. But he also recalls episodes from his later life, episodes such as Corinne's amorous adventures and her engagement to the Baron de Reixach, the narrator's own marriage to Hélène and their honeymoon in Greece, and his participation in the Spanish Civil War. Simon has intercalated episodes from these events with a number of other scenes, such as Uncle Charles's affair with a painter's model, Corinne's affairs with a coiffeur and her husband's jockey, Iglésia, and the deaths of de Reixach, the narrator's mother, and Uncle Charles, to develop the themes of adultery, disillusionment in love, and death—themes which, becoming the basis for the novel's psychological undercurrents, evolve unstated, beneath the surface of the narration.

Of all the thematic developments in *Histoire*, it is death which provides the clearest example of the implicit attitudes underlying the narration. Although a major part of the novel describes the narrator's struggle to overcome or suppress thoughts of death, the theme continues to dominate the narration. This is particularly true of the allusive references to Hélène and the narrator's apparent fear of her impending death (see p. 89) or suicide coupled with the frequently recurring theme of guilt. An obsessive interest in headlines to newspaper stories about a suicide leap from a fourth-floor window and veiled reference to the dangers of sleeping pills further suggest his morbid interest in suicide. But they do not reveal what personal experience, if any, lies at its source. What they do achieve is to evoke death and bring it to the fore as a thematic function of psychological motivations. By reason of certain compositional relationships such as homologous situations, the theme of death gradually evolves as a suspected cause of events on the level of plot.

Simon renders his subject's obsessive concern with suicide and his ever-present sense of guilt through a series of suggestive parallels between situations in the narrator's and his uncle's experiences. The narrator's sympathy for his uncle stems in part from his awareness of the similarities he sees between their respective lives. His unsuccessful marriage to Hélène, his travels to Spain, and, far less clear in its implications, his affair with another woman which may have precipitated his wife's departure all find echoes in the passages describing Uncle Charles's affair with a model and his wife's subsequent death by suicide. The narrator's emotional identification with his uncle's affair becomes most evident in the repetitions of two scenes, one depicting

Charles with the model, the second depicting the narrator with his mistress. The similarities between the two scenes are sufficiently great to cause confusion. In fact, following one of the scenes describing Uncle Charles, the narrator assumes a role in which he imagines the incident as though he were his uncle (pp. 311-14). The parallel situations and the merging of identities strengthens the suggestion of guilt and points to the possibility of the parallels even including a threat of his wife's suicide. If Charles's wife did commit suicide in despair, as the grandmother's allusion to an overdose of pills suggests (p. 334), the narrator's obsession may well be grounded in the fear that Hélène too may die or take her own life or in the guilt he feels because she has already done so.

Breaking the chronology of their occurrence, Simon has woven a thematic pattern from the events of his narrator's past—a pattern which implies the existence of a suppressed content, a moral knowledge and an emotional attitude which only briefly surface in the guilt-ridden allusions to Hélène, her sudden departure, the threat of suicide, and the apparent extramarital affair. Simon has conceptualized this pattern in the form of a mathematical model which he represents graphically as several intersecting sinusoidal curves of varying wave lengths along a linear development A———A' (figure 1).

Figure 1

The "positive" segments of these curves (shown as solid lines above A———A') correspond conceptually to the expressed and "readable" elements of the narration. The "negative" segments (shown as interrupted lines) correspond to the unexpressed, implicitly suppressed subconscious knowledge underlying the expressed. According to Simon's description of the novel's structure,[2] the linear development represented by the line A———A', along which the sine waves intersect in a pattern of decreasing wavelengths, ultimately turns upon itself to form a large circle represented in perspective as an ellipse (figure 2).

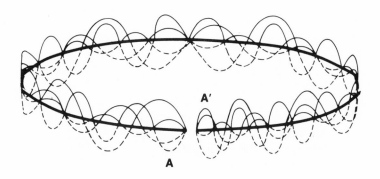

Figure 2

This pattern figuratively brings the narration to a close where it had begun—in the narrator's bed—and imposes upon the novel an artistic format whose regularity suggests an authorial control not directly related to the narrator's psychology.

Simon's comparison with the homologous relationships of a geometric model helps to schematize the principles underlying the composition of *Histoire* and certainly makes it more accessible conceptually. At the same time, however, as a representation corresponding to the novel's thematic relationships and the poetic function of its narrative structures,

Simon's mathematical equivalent raises some interesting questions pertaining to the way in which we experience and conceptualize the narration as a system of harmonies and conflicts in the expression and suppression of knowledge.

Simon uses only the positive portions of the intertwined sine waves to represent the "readable" episodes which the reader experiences as the textual realization of the narrator's consciousness. Their recurrent cyclical pattern represents the discontinuity in the narration of events and their casual relationships, a discontinuity we conceive of as a series of breaks in the threads forming the novel's action from which events are suppressed. Meanwhile, we do not perceive the negated segments of the curves corresponding to those attitudes and events in the consciousness which, because of their temporary "submergence" by another more dominant content, are absented from the narrative stream. Simon has insisted that all of the elements of a text are at all times present whether temporarily submerged or not. "Even though they are not in the foreground, they continue to be there, running as an intricate filigree beneath or behind that which is immediately readable and which, by its constituent parts, itself contributes incessantly to call the others to mind."[3] According to this conception, the readable text of a narrative becomes an explicit alternate for the "invisible," suppressed text of what is neither said nor read. Moreover, as the readable text evolves to become one term on what might be considered an axis of expression and suppression, it tends increasingly to suggest the existence of its unexpressed counterterm and thus reflects a potential for meaning never explicitly stated. The phenomenon has a clear conceptual homologue in Simon's mathematical model, but the reader's experience of its relationships as they emerge in the process of reading the novel as a fiction prove to be much more complex than its theoretical terms would indicate.

The clearest cases of suppressed episodes and knowledge in *Histoire* occur as allusions to the narrator's experiences which evoke his sense of guilt. This is especially true of his crumbling relationships with Hélène which tend to evolve in a form of ellipsis that leaves gaps in the narrative's chain of casual relationships. The "suppression" of content which supposedly determines the development of plot is not new with *Histoire*, of course. In *The Voyeur*, Robbe-Grillet avoided telling Mathias's involvement in the rape, torture, and murder of Jacqueline Leduc and made the absented events the object of a form of narrative conjecture. *Histoire* presents us with a somewhat different case, for it is not only the event which demands clarification but the attitudes as well. The suppressed knowledge in *Histoire* tends to emerge as an arcane emotional or subjective attitude which we infer in our reading on the basis of what we feel is not being said. The submerged elements of plot in the narrative thus serve as hidden resources implied by the visible narration which they underlie and at the level of which they occasionally surface in the form of thematic motifs. As such, they are the implicit thematic correlatives to the creative impetus behind the novel's composition as a record of a consciousness in the process of formation.

In *Histoire* Simon has created a narrative language which evolves according to the conflicting principles of a need for continuity and the open-ended character of thematic generation based upon a form of free association. Narrative technique remains generally consistent throughout the novel. However, by reason of a thematic density uncharacteristic of later chapters, the first chapter reveals more clearly than others the principles underlying the narrative movement. Beginning midsentence in a temporal ambiguity, the novel's first line describes how a tree branch, rustling in the wind, nearly touched the house in its movement, "When I worked late into the night sitting in front of the open window I could see it or at least its farthest twigs in the lamplight with their feathery leaves trembling faintly against the darkness beyond . . . and behind you could discern transmitted by degrees a mysterious and delicate murmur spreading invisibly through the dim tangle of branches" (p. 1). Following the analogy between leaves and feathers in movement, the tree becomes a source of sound and animation hidden in the darkness where are imagined birds "stirring trembling moaning in their sleep" (p. 1). The evocation of birds—their cries, appearance, and behavior—introduces a second movement that recalls the *vieilles dames* who visited and filled the house during the narrator's childhood. The third and fourth paragraphs of the novel further develop the analogical relationships between the old ladies and birds. They also extend the relationship to embrace the house through a comparison between the penetrating odor of mildew and rotting plaster and the stale smell of mummified flesh which the narrator associates with the abandoned rooms in a house that now evokes phantoms from a past long dead.

Further developing these associations, Simon expands the context of the tree to include historical connotations, "As on that Orleanist caricature reproduced in the History textbook and which represented the genealogical tree of the royal family whose members hopped among the branches in the form of birds with human heads" (p. 2). The genealogical tree and the tree outside the house, of course, have much more in common thematically than the expression of the narrator's link to his past and his family. The textbook's schematically chronological representation of history by means of the genealogical tree does have the principles of generation by association in common with the narrator's own subjective history. But as the narration takes form in the ramifications of his memories, it evolves an order vastly different from the distant temporal and causal relationships recorded in his school textbook. From the metaphorical perspective, the image of the tree's branches partially obscured in the darkness proves a particularly suggestive paradigm of the potential and still invisible relationships in the past. For instance, the development of the word "they," at first connoting the branches, then the rustling leaves visible in the light, and ultimately signifying those in the darkness effectively becomes a conceptual model of the thematic opposition between the expressed and the suppressed knowledge of a past which continues to whisper and rustle about in the recesses of the narrator's house and mind.

This insistent analogical pattern continues throughout the novel, attesting that any element in Simon's narrative language has the potential to provoke and generate the analogical development of the interior monologue on several levels. However, since its generative character depends upon the existence of similar or homologous elements in the reality momentarily evoked or upon the repetition of like syntactic structures to establish equivalence,[4] the narrator's associations are most easily understood or "readable" as psychological phenomena. In moving from outside to inside, from the material reality of the tree to the immaterial aura of the past, associations reflect the dynamic, generative potential of an active imagination recreating experiences from the past. Such a reading emphasizes the representative function of the narrative language. However, while we may more readily explain the fictional narrator's need to express and organize experiences in the flux of his mental universe according to psychological causes, the motivations that they represent may be extended on an aesthetic level to embrace the artistic principles underlying the novel's composition as an affective poetic form.

The narrative of *Histoire* thus gives rise to a tension between two seemingly incompatible functions: on the one hand the evocation of a fictional world through linguistic and thematic associations; on the other the creation of a language that tends to be self-referential and responsive to formalist concepts. Many of the linguistic and thematic associations serve to bring together the two opposing functions since they result from verbal expansion by the homonymic or paronymic generation of individual words' connotative values. For instance, the proper name Cerise evokes the color (p. 4) which eventually leads by association to the colors of riding habits, to jockeys, to the horse races at Pau, and to the mania of the Baron de Reixach for the equestrian life. In this particular context it may be related to Corinne de Reixach's affair with the jockey Iglesia and to the baron's death. The word also leads to *cerisier* (cherry tree) and back to the narrator's childhood, to a raid on the cherry orchard with his cousins Paul and Corinne, and to the wild cherry tree whose bitter fruit he tasted with Hélène on their honeymoon trip to Greece (p. 322). This second context develops the theme of guilt. Still other associations evolve from situation and action. As the narrator washes his face, the flow of water through his cupped hands suggests the concept of an "enchanted cup," which in turn generates *cupula* and by further distortion *culpa mea*, followed by an unexplained allusion to the narrator's sense of

guilt and unworthiness (p. 32). Thus, even as semantic change
occurs in a subjective process that calls upon experience in an
emotionally inspired response to unforeseen linguistic openings, the elements of the narrative language which evolve in
constantly changing contexts serve simultaneously as verbal
epicenters in the development of the novel's major themes of
love and death, integration and disintegration.

The narrator's interior monologue is a moving collage of experiences and imagination of which most of the moments narrated belong implicitly to a prior chronology. However, other
moments such as mythic visions, extended analogies, and
scenes of pure imagination are clearly functions of the narrator's cultural and emotional attitudes. For instance, when
the narrator fully awakens, his conscious perception of a bird
first seen upon opening his eyes soon gives way to hallucinatory
images, and he appears to lose all deliberate control over the
analogical processes of his association. Thereupon follows a
vision of mythical Stymphalian birds which evokes the narrator's sense of guilt through an association between the lake
Stymphalus, "that lake haunt of bronze-beaked, bronze-
taloned, bronze-feathered birds," and the tear-filled eyes of
Hélène at the time of her departure, "her wide enormous eyes staring at me but no tears only lakes" (pp. 27-28), a
motif reappearing later in the context of conflict and self-
reproach (see pp. 318 and 322). The mythic images drawn
from the narrator's aesthetic and cultural background contribute to several thematic developments. But perhaps most
important, they permit Simon to suggest his narrator's motivations without explicitly stating them. The author is thereby
able to weave allusive thematic patterns from mythic, religious, and material motifs whose relationships both mask
and simultaneously suggest the nature of those incidents
which the narrator seeks to suppress.

An understanding of the narrator's temporal and spatial
situation with respect to the fictional universe plays an important formative role in the reader's experience of the novel's
text as a problematical form expressing an almost ritualistic
quest for self-definition. In the process of the quest, the
various scenes which constitute the fictional universe tend to
oscillate between a referential function designating an original

a priori "historical" situation which is opposed to the scenes' function as narrative events localized in the contextual present of the interior monologue. In the latter case, the temporal situation of a scene is no longer chronological. It is aesthetic or psychological. In either case, whether we read *Histoire* as a story or as a poem, since each scene and each moment are pure subjective functions, a form of tension develops between our reading the narrative as a formalistic and poetic rendering of a lyrical, psychological development and our reading it as a form of interior monologue belonging to a broader historical context of which it is but a moment. This tension between our desire to read *Histoire* as a novel with a chronological development and our reading of its form as a pattern of constantly changing analogical relationships underscores the thematic opposition of integration and disintegration announced in the novel's epigraph. It also has the effect of interrelating the various meanings of the novel's title, *Histoire* (whose French form has been retained in the English translation for this very reason). The narrative is at once a history having cultural and psychological implications, a story, and, in recognition of that tendentious hidden reality we conceive of underlying the narration, a scandalous incident which the narrator seeks to suppress from his memory.

Our sense of the structural complexity and thematic richness in *Histoire* depends to a large degree upon our speculative association of contents as we seek to fill in the gaps in our understanding of the novel as a unified narrative whole. In attempting to give form to the events that are not narrated and in attempting to situate them in a plausible chronology, we enter into the aesthetic realm of the puzzle, where operations (interpretations) are tentative and the sequences of our decisions (represented by the associations we make in our reading) no longer exclusive.

The ultimate criterion determining the viability of our interpretations of the novel's composition lies in the satisfaction of our expectations. In opposition to the disintegration of events and the historical chronology within the fictional world of the narrator, our "need to know" becomes an integrative force. Encouraged by the novel's thematic and formalistic associations and finding passages which suggest conceptual parallels

in our activity of reading,[5] we tend to make our experience of
the text symmetrical. For each unexpressed reality, we find
we are encouraged to hypothesize the existence of its plausible
context and hence of its logical place in our evolving vision of
the fictional universe as a system. For each positive value, we
find ourselves invited to infer the existence of its counterterm;
for every "unreadable" text, an interpretation of its context
which makes it readable. Ultimately *Histoire* brings the attentive reader face to face with himself, with the problematical
nature of reading as an integrative but speculative process of
discovering meaning, and with the nature of the novel as a formal mode of expression reflecting the associative processes by
which Man creates meaning in his own image.

COLORADO STATE UNIVERSITY, FORT COLLINS

Notes

1. Claude Simon, *Histoire* (NewYork: Braziller, 1968). Future references to this
novel will be included parenthetically in the text.
2. Simon described *Histoire* in these terms at the colloquium on the *nouveau roman*
in July 1971, at Cerisy-la-Salle. See "La Fiction mot à mot," in *Nouveau roman:
hier, aujourd'hui* II, ed. Jean Ricardou (Paris: U. G. E., Collection "10/18," 1971),
p. 89.
3. Ibid.
4. Maurice Merleau-Ponty has argued that prior experience is essential to the play
of subjective association, thereby denying the possibility of a purely creative act in the
generation of images by association. "Association . . . never comes into play as an
autonomous force; it is never the word suggested which 'induces' the replay in the
manner of an efficient cause; it acts only by making probable or attractive a
reproduction intention; it operates only in virtue of the meaning it has acquired in the
context of the former experience and in suggesting recourse to that experience; it is ef-
ficacious to the extent to which the subject recognizes it, and grasps it in the light or
appearance of the past." See Maurice Merleau-Ponty, " 'Association' and the 'Projection of Memory,' " in *Phenomenology of Perception*, trans. Colin Smith (London:
Routledge and Kegan Paul, 1963), p. 18.
5. There are numerous instances where the text seems to allude to the characteristics
of the novel's composition or to the problems related to the activity of reading inter-
pretatively. The metaphorical use of the tree is a case in point. Another is the description of violin music, where the text suggests a conceptual parallel both for the novel's
apparent structure and Simon's mathematical model. "The violins weaving an invisible network of cords stretched to the breaking point, intersecting drawing closer
mingling parting diverging again" (*Histoire*, pp. 69-70).

6

Announcing the World: Signs and Images at Work in the Novels of Claude Simon

J. A. E. Loubère

In *The Battle of Pharsalus*[1] a dilapidated machine sits disintegrating in a Greek field. Around it, the long grass and flowers spring luxuriantly, A detailed description of the machine's complicated anatomy requires extensive use of geometric and mechanical terminology ("horizontal," "cylindrical cone," "trapezoidal," "pully," "sprocket wheel," "chamfered sprocket," "frames," "beams," "plates," "bolts," "pins," "perpendicular," "motor axle," "cables," etc.). Parts of the machine are broken or missing, its paint has rusted off, and broken cables and lines are festooned about it like strange, parasitic vegetation. The proliferation of metallic limbs sticking out at all angles makes it resemble a many-legged, armored insect. It is a McCormick harvester-combine, and its decaying presence in the ancient field links it in time with a tremendous past, filled with the skeletons of all the armed men, animals, and machines that ever plowed through Greek soil. In space, it calls up a vast, distant continent, where other men work constantly on the production of new machines.

The contemplator of the machine has come to this particular juncture of time and space because of a text, or rather, several texts, written by Plutarch, Lucan, Livy, and others,

describing an event that took place nearly two thousand years
ago. The exact spot where the Battle of Pharsalus occurred is
not to be found. Instead, the dusty Greek countryside offers
the observer fragments of memory, suggestions from other
texts, scenes from elsewhere, historical events reconstituted
and re-presented many times by painters, sculptors, and
writers. Everything that the narrator sees is intimately connected with the structure of his own existence—an unhappy
love affair, life among art students in Paris, family incidents,
classical studies with an uncle whose life he doubles, scenes
from combat in World War II, people, paintings and other art
forms observed during travel all over Europe; but individual
memories broaden into a wider scene in which time and space
expand continuously to include most of man's creative and
destructive activities. The abandoned machine proposes, in
fact, elements for the reconstruction of a world far greater
than that implied by the personal concerns of the narrator. If
we wonder that a broken mechanism can be so prolific in suggestion, we are enlightened by a quote from Heidegger: "The
tool turns out to be damaged or the material unsuitable . . . .
When its unusability is thus discovered, equipment becomes
conspicuous. . . . The context of equipment ("le système de
renvois") is illuminated, not as something never seen before,
but as a totality constantly sighted beforehand in circumspec-
tion. With this totality, however, the world announces itself"
(p. 129).

This *système de renvois* connecting a broken-down
harvester with the damaged emotional life of the narrator can
be discovered through a single word in the text. At the base of
the machine is a round metal part called a *"cocotte,"* a word
used variously in French for a cylindrical pot, for a woman of
easy virtue, for a chicken, and for addressing a horse (*Dictionnaire Petit Robert*, p. 296). All of these meanings are present
and intricately connected in this novel, but also refer beyond it
to many other preexisting texts. The horse is a central figure
in Simon's work, and its reappearance in the war scenes of
Pharsalus where the narrator recalls a headlong flight on
horseback during the breakdown of the French armies in
World War II, takes us back as far as *The Flanders Road*

(1960). The bird is another constant motif, appearing as the omnipresent pigeons in the Civil War setting of *The Palace*, the birds in the trees of *Histoire*, the pigeon, divine dove, roosting chickens, and winged Eros in *Pharsalus*. The cylindrical metal container is related to battle gear, particularly armor and helmets, numerous in the war scenes, ancient and modern, of *Pharsalus*. It is also, as Françoise Van Rossum-Guyon has brilliantly demonstrated,[2] evocative of various passages from Proust's *Le Temps retrouvé* which Simon inserts into his own novel, in particular one concerning the strange "cylindrical turbans" which women wore in Paris in World War I. Proust, war (physical contest[3]), and the cylindrical forms in turn connect with the *cocotte* or professional courtesan, recalling Swann's Odette, and the narrator's faithless lover who bears the same name later in *Pharsalus*. Finally, the term, combining the notions of exhaustive service and breakdown, refers back again to the harvester and all the other useless mechanisms that, like "ancient fallen courtesans," bestrew the landscape (p. 104). Once aware of the fragments of Proust scattered through Simon's work, the reader perceives that they are reused to form different texts, just as the dismantled parts of the machine are salvaged by farmers and mechanics for other purposes. The text itself is thus related to the machine, and the proliferating images within it form geometric patterns, and act upon one another like the mechanical parts so carefully described by Simon. Following the directions suggested by the single word *cocotte*, we return once more to the abandoned harvester. This does not imply final closure, however: sections of the machine still stick out at unexpected angles; new models wait on a siding in the United States (p. 184); another waits in the station at Pharsalus (p. 171).

    One small part of the machine provides us with an excellent example of the way in which the word in Simon's text works[4] to generate images and group them into motifs (e.g., cylinder—women's and soldiers' headgear) merging into themes such as sex, change, war, destruction. This generative work has been carefully studied by a number of critics in the case of individual novels.[5] A further step is necessary,

however, for a fuller appreciation of the weight and momentum
communicated to the text by such combinations of images: only as we trace their passage from series to series—converging
and diverging—throughout the ongoing process of Simon's
writing, do we realize to what extent the most commonplace
forms become charged with a transformational dynamism that
literally "announces" the world.

The extraordinary density of a text such as "Machine" is
obviously not the result of purely accidental or un-
premeditated development. It requires the preliminary
storage of a large number of forms which return incessantly in
the text, carrying with them a wealth of established relationships, to be still further enriched by additions from the writer's
store. The building up of these complex arrangements is a
lengthy procedure, during which simple associative clusters,
present in Simon's earlier work, combine as text follows text
into ever more intricate designs, without the least suggestion
of prospective finality. These preliminary clusters depend on
variable criteria. They may be formal—a category of round or
curving objects (rings, bracelets, necklaces, arabesques, or-
namental flourishes, as in *The Grass*; color-based (shades of
pink and red in clothes, bricks, blood, in *The Flanders Road*;
typographic (posters, headlines, banners, in *The Palace*);
semantic and orthographic (as in the cluster of images deriving from "Frascati" in *Histoire*). The images grouped by
Simon then acquire extra significance from cross-reference and
intratextual usage: for a second—not secondary—effect of
their multiplicity is that any image and its neighbors in a series
assume new relationships and change according to the sequence in which they are found; so that there is no one,
definitive way in which they can be interpreted, only a
cumulative, intensifying process in which they play their role.
Simon, trained as a painter, an admirer of Cézanne, and later
of artists in montage such as Rauschenberg, Nevelson, Ar-
man, early recognized the transformational force of juxtaposition. In his essay *La Corde raide* (1947), he observes: "the
same forms can change, inflated with their own substance and
with the substance absorbed through ceaseless osmosis from
their near and distant neighbors, a perpetual obscure gesta-

tion, blind and ardent . . . the multiple infinity of realities, all equally possible, all equally true, driving upwards, their presence an erection."[6] Unlike the symbol, which in normal usage is fixed in content and maintains a constant relationship with the world it implies, the phenomenon in Simon's work continually modifies its connections with the world of other phenomena, and its significance proliferates, spreads in unexpected directions, attaching itself to forms not originally perceived in the writer's choice of material. This proliferation is the most important feature of Simon's prose.

In the earlier novels, two or more objects or events are often found repeatedly in close association with one another. For example, in *Le Sacre du printemps*[7] the adolescent hero, after sleeping with a girl whom he later suspects of stealing a ring (the book's emblem) from him, discovers his loss in the Paris *métro*, and the roar of the underground train accompanies his emotional crisis. In *The Grass* the sound of the departing car follows the union of Louise with her lover in the woods. She also hears the train entering and emerging from a nearby tunnel. In *The Flanders Road*, Georges, while making love to Corinne whom he characterizes many times as a *moule*, or hollow, reproductive mold, recalls being crushed among prisoners of war in a railroad cattle car. If we are not attentive to the fact that these events are juxtaposed in the fiction, we will not give them undue significance. In later novels, however, the three elements—sex, the mechanical vehicle, the hole—are repeated and multiplied in a more and more insistent fashion, but no longer as simple, apparently realistic parts of a "story." In *The Battle of Pharsalus* the protagonist obsessed with sexual jealousy is seated in a train which travels through a narrow valley. From the train he observes men digging a hole, people engaged in erotic actions, and a fellow traveler reading an exotic love story, while he himself meditates on the foolishness of finding any single object more significant than any other (p. 165). The encounter with the dismantled harvester-combine, with its connotation of plowing, insemination, harvesting, and destruction, calls up an episode in Paris where, at the time of his mistress's betrayal, the narrator watches people coming up from an underground exit of the subway, people of all kinds, male, female, black white, old and young. The hole in the ground has an obvious erotic connection and the people suggest the seeds of procreation. The machines and the various hollows and cavities therefore have related connotations, and consequently the two sets of images become inextricably linked, the occurrence of one provoking the reappearance of the other. It is no longer necessary to offer explanations each time that they occur in the text: they refer immediately to the lover's experience of betrayal. Singly, such images might be insignificant, but by agglomeration they provide a cumulative effect that is denser and richer than any bald, expository narrative. Around all the images in the book connected with orifices and mechanisms (there are many more) cluster references to eroticism, jealousy, and failure (breakdown, death) in an increasingly close weave that makes it impossible to pull one thread without pulling the others along with it.

The procedure goes still further in *Triptych*[8]. Here we are no longer dealing with associations in any protagonist's experience. Simon uses the momentum of previous novels to carry the images of mechanisms along with all their weight of implication. *Triptych* is filled with vehicles: cars, trucks, trains, streetcars. Whenever one appears it triggers a scene of sexual activity. Even the sound of the squeaking wheels of an old perambulator is sufficient to set off a repeat of such a scene. As this activity increases in intensity, the various vehicles involved become faster and noisier: the truck that was stationary roars off, the train picks up speed, the streetcar decorated with a poster advertising a product for "Hommes-Femmes" clangs up and down the road. The image of the object is now independent of any story line, it serves itself as a release mechanism for any number of possible stories, told or untold. The process of simple association in which lovemaking in the woods is followed by the departure of a car has been transformed into an operation whereby the associated objects generate an increasing variety of scenes. The mechanism evokes sex; it also summons up the theme of failure and breakdown, and, again in connection with the "orifice" group of objects, death: for the hole is not only the mold-womb, but also the ditch-grave in which the doomed soldier of *The Flanders Road* hides, and the river hollow in which the child in *Triptych* supposedly drowns.

The photograph or reproduction offers an equally remarkable example of a regrouping of the hole and mechanism complex. Photographs appear in almost all of Simon's novels. In *The Wind* they are potentially present, implied by the expensive camera that Montès, the Innocent, carries slung over his shabby raincoat. Montès takes photos, but we do not see them, although we understand that his camera eye is the one that sees a world different from the daily logical one that we construct for our own purposes. It is, in fact, the single eye peering *through* the hole, perceiving things spasmodically and one-sidedly (like the boys in *Triptych* for example). Montès sees the world in flashes that he is unable to piece together into a coherent whole. The narrator of this story conveys to us the thought that this is the way the world is perceived by most of us. In succeeding novels Simon presents us with specimens of these flashes, old photos that immobilize people caught in the "gelatinous" substance of time, photos that, instead of helping the observer to discover what happened in the past, only confuse him more. In *The Grass* the young woman, Louise, tries with the help of a few photographs to guess at the secrets hidden in the life of a dying aunt; but the photos only give partial information and can be interpreted in several fashions. In *The Palace* the yellowing snapshot of a group of comrades in the Spanish Civil War does not help the man who is recalling his association with the group to rediscover his own past. On the contrary, it underlies his distance from those comrades and from that past, the "hole" in memory.

The photograph in *Histoire*, however, has a new dimension. A painter taking a shot in his studio of a group comprising his model, his wife, and a visitor tries to include himself and sets off a mechanism that will allow him to pose with the group before the photo is taken. The mechanism fails and a blurred picture results in which the photographer's movements are traced over the shot, "restoring to the event its density, postulating . . . the double series of past and future instants" (p. 226). Here the mechanism combines with the photograph to carry the message of sexuality and jealousy, which is essential in this section since the model's infidelity is the cause of the narrator's (or his Uncle Charles's) unhappiness. It also combines the idea of failure (its failure, his failure) with the thought of time, which a photo fails to record, yet suggests because the photo itself is a failure. In *Triptych* the motifs of mechanism, eroticism, and photography are even more closely intertwined, through the presence of the movie camera that intrudes continually, interrupting stories of high erotic content, showing that they are, in fact, productions of its own activity. It even breaks down, on one occasion, in the middle of an erotic scene, setting the film on fire. In *Triptych* we also find the photograph combined with another important motif. A "bird-headed" man has moved during a snapshot, so that in the finished photo he appears to have two heads pointing in opposing directions. Here the idea of the flight of time conveyed by the photo registering movement fuses with the thought of another group of flying objects—birds, which in turn are linked with various new categories of objects, and are very important parts of Simon's "inventory."

The role of the photo is sometimes played by other forms of representation such as the ancestral painting in *The Flanders Road*, and the postcards and posters that appear in almost all of Simon's novels. The postcards are, so to speak, nobody's photographs. They show objects and scenes that relate only to the impersonal outside world, "fragments, flakes torn from the surface of the enormous earth" (*Histoire*, p. 10). The postcards received by the mother of the narrator in *Histoire* from her future husband arrive from the farthest, most exotic areas of the world, "the fabulous sumptuous variegated inexhaustible world" (p. 13). Nevertheless, they depict objects and forms—lakes, villages, women carrying buckets, boats—that can be linked with already known series, pictured on cards received from sources close at hand. At the same time the reader is conscious of the postcards as postcards, accumulations of images spilling chaotically out of drawers in the furniture of the house where the narrator recalls his past. The confused and varied origins of all these images suggest that they may be organized into groups of different types (for example, according to dates, places, correspondents), and yet be scattered again and reorganized into other patterns.

The postcard, like the photo, provides only fragmentary and uncertain information about the past or present. At the beginning of *Triptych* we see a postcard representing a contemporary scene that is remarkable for its crude coloring and poorly printed figures. In fact, its function is not to document reality. The postcard, and even more surely the poster which appears so frequently in Simon's writing, offer a program for possible future combinations of images on various levels in the work. In *The Palace* torn fragments of posters that announce victory—*VENCEREMOS*—proclaim physically the defeat the entire book presages. In *Conducting Bodies*[9] the poster combines with the diagram to announce the very structure of the novel. In addition, the diagram of a new building, with its rectangular divisions,[10] that is to replace an old skyscraper being torn down relates closely to the anatomical model of the human body that the protagonist perceives in the doctor's office, also to the map of the subway and to an engraving of zodiacal signs. Each of these diagrams relates in turn to a new series of structures—the anatomical model and the subway map, for example, to the body of a woman with whom the protagonist has sexual relations. The tattered posters on the hoardings call up a picture of the torn scraps of flesh in the beak of a condor, a South American bird whose form is carved into the wood of a lectern at a meeting of Spanish-speaking writers. The first syllable of condor reminds the protagonist of South American names such as Áconcagua, Anaconda, and places that he may or will visit (or has already visited) by means of a mechanical bird, the airplane, from which he will see the constellation of Andromeda. The first syllable of *condor* also has an erotic meaning in French. Each of the images spawned in this way fragments into others that seem as endless as the stars the airplane traveler watches as he flies; but like the stars they will resolve themselves into diagrams, patterns, and mythological symbols.

The fusion of the poster with the schema or diagram returns

in *Triptych*, this time to announce not what will be, but what may be deduced from the elements of the design. Here a number of movie posters offer pictures of what could be events in forthcoming movies: a young man stares sulkily at a bride in tears, two men fight, an older woman wearing pearls seems to be pleading with someone. From these diagrammatic elements several stories are built up in the course of the novel. A man gets drunk and leaves his bride on their wedding night while he is out with a girl friend, and subsequently (?) has a fight. An older woman pleads with a friend to use his influence to save her son from a drug charge, and so forth. The stories are destroyed as soon as they appear when we discover they are parts of other stories which themselves are contained by one another. A circus poster causes the apparition of several scenes which may or may not be taking place within the framework of the other tales. All we can be sure of is that the poster no longer announces a certain program, but only the schematic form of a number of possible programs, no one of which annuls or guarantees the others. The picture, whether film, still photograph, painting, postcard, poster, or any other form of representation, no longer proposes something that happened or is happening, but endlessly offers something that might happen, that may go on happening in an undetermined number of ways in the future of writer and reader. The purpose of the representation has therefore been inverted.

The bird motif is both erotic and martial: the birds singing "arabesques" in *The Grass*, the peacock on the curtain in *The Flanders Road*, the twittering birds in *Histoire*, the swirling curtain of pigeons in *The Palace*, all belong to groups connected with love and death. The pigeon is the feathered arrow that reappears in *The Battle of Pharsalus*, where the epigraph from Valéry's *Cimetière marin* speaks of "la flèche qui tue," the mortal dart of war, or time, or the quill that writes and, writing, transfixes. The shadow of the bird that crosses the first pages of this work refers to all these motifs and many more, the divine dove of peace and religion, the Holy Ghost, paintings depicting war, arrows, religious themes, other feathered and hairy things. The passage of the bird sets in motion all the themes and motifs in this novel and inaugurates the quest of the protagonist, who, consumed by a bitter erotic memory, travels in various types of mechanical vehicles seeking for a lost battlefield in Greece. The pigeon is no longer a simple reminder of the past, its role is now one of active stimulant, setting off more and more metaphorical movement in the text, combining in an infinitely variable fashion with all the other motifs, yet never leaving the circle of the protagonist's preoccupations. In *Conducting Bodies* the bird similarly fuses with the objects described. We have seen how the condor is connected with the posters, the buildings, the Spanish-American meeting,[11] the sexual encounter, and also meets its mechanical equivalent in the airplane that soars over mountain ranges.

The motif of the continuously circling object is closely linked with the concept of the novel as Simon sees it. The reason for the quest in *Le Sacre du printemps* is a ring. We find numerous aspects of the circle in *The Grass* (where most of Simon's motifs begin to acquire strength); for example, in the curves and arabesques of ornaments, jewelry, and birdsong, and in the image of insects turning incessantly in the warm air. The swirling insects reappear in *The Flanders Road* as a metaphor for the continuous conversation of Georges's mother, and the curling, repetitive movement is mirrored in the construction of the novel, built like an ace of clubs or clover leaf, in which all the threads of narration continually pass through the same points along slightly different paths each time. This process is continuously exemplified in *The Palace*, where the epigraph from the *Dictionnaire Larousse* defines "Revolution: the locus of a moving body which, describing a closed curve, successively passes through the same points." In *The Battle of Pharsalus* the circle motif and the (w)hole meet, at a given point 0, in the undefined personage O.:

> Let O be the position occupied by the eye of the observer (O.) .
> . . . . . O. moving rapidly from one place to another the world appears at no moment identical with what it was in the immediately preceding moment, so that, taking into account the multitude of points of observation, reflections, virtual images and distortions,

the alternations which the latter can undergo depending on the reflecting surface . . . and also taking into account that in the foregoing exposition we have simplified the figure by choosing a single cross-section in a vertical plane and at a given moment (and that we might conceive of a number of other schemas, other cross-sections, either in space (horizontal or oblique), or even in time), we must represent the totality of the system as a moving body ceaselessly altering around a few fixed points. (pp. 123, 127)

In all the displacements of things and protagonists in Simon's work, the paths traced about a given "epicenter" are never exactly the same, yet never entirely out of orbit. It is this "varying about a few fixed points" that accounts for the diversity of appearance and the similarity of function of Simon's objects. Many other examples might be followed up, beside those already given: the grass-jungle-Nature combination, the horse-mutation-sex-death variation,[12] the currency-bank-exchange motif, and so on. For all of these arrangements, combinations, and permutations[13] three characteristic steps may be noted. In the first place, there is change, development, and diversification in the image itself, since it tends to attract and assimilate other objects in its category. Second, the role of the object is modified from simple illustration and descriptive association in the earlier novels to one of stimulator and generator in the later ones, so that an originally subordinate function becomes an essential one. Third, each motif tends to be "contaminated" by others in different categories, to enrich itself with the wealth of connotations contributed by its neighbors; until we find the accumulated groups of motifs concentrated around three great themes: Battle (war, love, sport, all forms of contest); Change (revolution, exchange, transmutation); Time (movement, repetition, death, and rebirth). These three, in their turn, can easily fuse to form one "epicenter" which is a man's view of life.

The progressive "charging" of each motif can, of course, be observed within the framework of each separate novel, but the intratextual spread and fusion of all the motifs in the course of Simon's writing has a far greater scope. Such textual activity suggests not only the past and present production of novels, but an illimitable future one, since the development of motifs and themes composed by motifs is no longer ended with the last page of one completed (published) work. Each book, on the contrary, is made up of elements capable of unlimited expansion into succeeding novels.

Expansion of this kind is particularly interesting since it brings into focus an object that is so close to the reader as to become almost invisible to him: the text itself. Traditionally, the printed text has been considered as an immovable whole, congealed once and for all into a final form. By his bold reuse of textual material, his own and the work of others (for example, the passages from Proust in *Pharsalus*, the fragments of print from posters and newspapers inserted into his narrative, quotations from Latin authors, translations from modern writers such as John Reed), Simon shows us how an already constituted work can itself be regarded as a set of images generating new sets intersecting at varying points, like the orbits of the circling insects about a given center. The text, or *ensemble du système* then behaves according to the same rules as the single image, proliferating, stimulating new versions, and interacting with other texts without restriction, beyond that of its own potential. No passage, seen in the light of possible development, can be closed within one meaning, or refer for ever to something fixed once and for all in the past. Writing now becomes an everlasting source of writing, not as commentary or explication, but true re-production.

The reader who has followed these developments is not surprised by the title of Simon's latest novel, *Leçon de choses*.[14] In this work, the process we have described continues unabated. Series already well known to us, for example, those included or suggested in the passage from *Pharsalus* selected as illustration, the mechanism, the bird, the geometric shape, and many others, reappear and continue to expand (the second section of the book is, in fact, entitled *Expansion*), demonstrating revised possibilities of reference and relationship. As Simon explains in the opening *Générique*: "The description can be continued (or completed) more or less indefinitely, depending on attention to the details of execution, the 'pull' of the metaphors proposed, the addition of other objects visible as a whole or fragmented by wear, time or colli-

sion (or also because they only partly appear within the
framework of the picture), not to mention the various
hypotheses that the spectacle may suggest" (pp. 10-11).[15]

The book is built around the themes of demolition (houses,
living beings, nature, anecdote) and construction (houses, living beings, nature, anecdote), and the reality of every object
built up in the text is dismantled, as it were, through the selection among its characteristics of those which can be successfully inserted into other groupings. Much more than mere
linguistic ingenuity is involved, however. This text, more insistently than any other, reminds us that the dismantling and
reconstituting is nowhere more pronounced than in what we
consider natural processes, where material such as earth,
rock, minerals, vegetable matter, flesh, blood, and bone are
continuously broken down and reassembled into other
substances and forms. The coincidence between Simon's
thematic material, its functioning, and the common preoccupations of mankind is most poignantly stressed in the
monologue of the fleeing cavalryman, in the two "Divertissements" which break up the text. He perceives the whole
process of destruction-reconstruction in terms of his own
desperate efforts on the battle front to avoid death and obtain
sustenance in the face of all the impinging forces that surround him (pp. 59-70, 119-29). Such a text, far from being a
sterile inventory or an idle intellectual game, demonstrates
how the least object of our attention, through its links with
everything about it, with its "close and further neighbors" is
inseparably bound up with our most intimate and gravest concerns.

These concerns, and the objects associated with them are,
we must recall, not the models, but the stimuli for the production of images in the text. *Leçon* is one more reading of these
images, reminding us that their expansion is inevitably accompanied by the dissolution of the series in which they appear
momentarily immobilized. The stability of the text is illusory;
like the hovering seagull in this novel, it embodies the
possibility of being *other*, elsewhere: "it remains there, proud-
ly existing, borne on nothingness, like a sort of challenge not

only to the laws of gravity, but also to the impossible conjunction of immobility and motion" (p. 98).[16]

In Simon's novels the process of proliferation and fragmentation appears, however, to be balanced by a tendency toward the formation of persistent groups, or repeated constellations of signs and images. Each of these groups exercises a power of attraction on the others, conferring on them its own accumulated attributes, and receiving theirs. Their function then is not to be applicable to a specific case, or referential reality, not to distinguish the object in the epiphanic sense as apart and unique of its kind, nor even to provide the metaphor and serve the design of one given work; but each displays itself as a fragment announcing the imminence of other fragments, themselves implying varying systems. The most pervasive example is perhaps the circle-hole conjunction, which, in its various combinations throughout the novels, becomes part of a vast ever-developing series that includes sex—birth (the womb)—the isolated and anonymous self (O.)—revolution (the circle)—zero, absence—the circular container (the *cocotte*, the head, the helmet, etc.)—death (the hollow grave)—imperfect memory—the circular text—the (w)hole (*tou[t]*, *t[r]ou*).

Reinstated in such a series the humble cylindrical pot at the base of the machine finds its immediate, apparent insignificance transformed by the imminence of all the possible other systems to which it may belong. In this perspective also an entire novel can itelf be an announcing fragment, ready for juxtaposition with or inclusion in the systems evoked. By ensuring that each combination works at the optimum rate and volume of conjunction and exchange, Claude Simon develops a tension between the elements furnished by the "fabulous sumptuous variegated inexhaustible world," and the configuration of these elements in his texts. This tension is dependent on the balance between the distributive and the integrative activity of each group of images, so organized that at all times a developing pattern can be perceived, not as the installation of a fixed, immutable design, but as the "multiple infinity of realities" in a "perpetual obscure gestation." It is in

this sense that we may discover, as Simon himself insists,[17] the
world in and through writing.

BUFFALO, N.Y.

Notes

1. *La Bataille de Pharsale*, trans. Richard Howard (New York: Braziller, 1971).
Other translations of Simon by Howard, quoted in this article, are *The Wind* (*Le
Vent*), 1959; *The Grass* (*L'Herbe*), 1960; *The Flanders Road* (*La Route des Flandres*), 1961; *The Palace* (*Le Palace*), 1963; *Histoire*, 1967.
2. "De Claude Simon à Proust: un exemple d'intertextualité," *Les Lettres Nouvelles*,
September 1972, pp. 107-37.
3. Simon quotes Elie Faure, "slaughter as well as love is a pretext to glorify the
body," in *Pharsalus*, p. 81.
4. Sylvère Lotringer calls it "une certaine *besogne* du mot." *Claude Simon:
Analyse, Théorie*, Jean Ricardou et al., eds. (Paris: U. G. E., Collection "10/18,"
1975), p. 326.
5. Examples: S. Lotringer, *Claude Simon: Analyse, Théorie*.; F. Van Rossum-
Guyon, "De Claude Simon à Proust"; Jean Ricardou, "La Bataille de la phrase," in
Pour une théorie du Nouveau Roman (Paris: Seuil, 1971), pp. 118-58; Ludovic Janvier, "Sur le trajet de ces corps," *Entretiens: Claude Simon* (1972), pp. 69-80.
6. *La Corde raide* (*The Tightrope*) (Paris: Sagittaire, 1947), p. 122. My translation.
7. *Le Sacre du printemps* (*The Rite of Spring*) (Paris: Calmann-Lévy, 1954).
8. *Triptych*, trans. Helen R. Lane (New York: Viking, 1976).
9. *Conducting Bodies*, trans. Helen R. Lane (New York: Viking, 1974).
10. An extract from *Conducting Bodies* was published in *Tel Quel* 44 (Winter
1971), 3-16, under the title "Propriétés des rectangles."
11. The French form of Columbus, "Colomb," is another obvious connection between the bird motif, *colombe* (dove), and the American motif.
12. A combination of these motifs has been studied by Christiane Makward in
"Simon: Earth, Death and Eros," *Sub-stance* 8 (Winter 1974), 35-43.
13. A favorite expression of Simon's referring to a course in mathematics. See *Entretiens: Claude Simon*, p. 67.
14. *Leçon de choses* [*Lesson of Things*] (Paris: Minuit, 1975). Translations from this
novel are mine.
15. "La description (la composition) peut se continuer (ou être complétée) à peu près
indéfiniment selon la minutie apportée à son exécution, l'entraînement des
métaphores proposées, l'addition de'autres objets visibles dans leur entier ou
fragmentés par l'usure, le temps, un choc (soit encore qu'ils n'apparaissent qu'en
partie dans le cadre du tableau), sans compter les diverses hypothèses que peut
susciter le spectacle," pp. 10-11.
16. "Il reste là, existant et superbe, porté par rien, comme une sorte de défi non pas
seulement aux lois de la pesanteur mais encore à l'impossible accouplement de l'im-
mobilité et du mouvement," p. 98.
17. "Découvrant à tâtons le monde dans et par l'écriture." *Orion aveugle* (Geneva:
Skira, Collection "Les Sentiers de la création, 1970), preface.

7

Simon Citing Simon: A Few Examples of Limited Intertextuality*

Karin Holter

Although the term "limited intertextuality"[1] is of recent invention, the phenomenon itself is not at all new. On the contrary, these intertwining relationships among texts bearing the same name seem to lie at the very foundation of our notion of the "novelistic world." Intertextual references or the recurrence in the text being written of characters, themes, descriptions, and techniques from texts already written, have been used by Balzac, Proust, and Beckett alike—although not in the same manner. Even though we have known for some time (at least since the Russian formalists and especially since Ricardou) that "a technique is at the disposal of everyone" and that it must be analyzed within the plan of specific texts to determine its precise function, still the concept of "limited intertextuality" (or the more or less synonymous notion of "self-quotation" which sometimes replaces it) remains so vague that it is relatively difficult to work with. The references from one text to another may be more or less explicit, the "quotations" more or less word for word, the effect of the comparison resulting from the juxtaposing of passages more or less easy to determine.

* Translated by Jane Carson.

133

Rather than attempt a definition based on formal criteria, it
would undoubtedly be better to relate it to some sort of "activity" in the text: the play of limited intertextuality may be seen
anywhere there is "reactivation" (the possibility of a new
reading) of a text already written by the text being written,
and where the earlier text serves as a comment on the new one.

It is not the purpose of this article either to define or to
discuss exhaustively the problems of limited intertextuality in
Claude Simon's novels. Its aim is quite limited: to take
specific examples and see how this phenomenon works in
several texts by Simon. My working hypothesis and long-term
objective affirm that an analysis of the specific functioning of
the play of limited intertextuality in Simon's various novels
will allow us to define more rigorously what constitutes this
development in Simon's writing about which one speaks so
glibly.

Indeed, the relationships among Simon's texts form a particularly interesting case study. Simon is the only one of the
New Novelists who—until the composition of *Conducting
Bodies*—seems to sanction a "classical," and reassuring, concept of the "novelistic world." From book to book we find the
insistent recurrence of the same characters, the same events
narrated and referring back to a lived experience that is all the
more recognizable because it is *collective* (it is the lived experience of Europe in 1936 or 1940), the recurrence of scenes
and "privileged" images, the textual recurrence of sentences
describing these scenes, the recurrence of devices and methods
of description (such as the present participle or tripartite constructions), finally, the recurrence of a certain discourse on
Time, History, War, Woman. This discourse is delivered
from book to book always by the same voice "saying . . . with
a kind of vehemence, an impotent despair . . . "[2] This ever-
recognizable voice, the very hallmark of the "Simonian
universe," allows the reader to find his way as he progresses
from text to text.

This is true precisely until *Conducting Bodies*, where this
voice is neutralized by a new writing practice which, after a
long period of gestation, now establishes itself permanently.
Consciously utilizing the creative power of the "word for

word" procedure and from this point on placing complete faith in the internal dynamics of writing itself, the author no longer needs to draw on the inventory of Simonian themes to make his narrative progress. Temporarily put aside in *Conducting Bodies*, these themes will reappear beginning with *Triptych*, but it is through a totally different flow of movement that they will be bound to the Simonian "intertext."

Let us now examine more concretely what kind of relationships may be found among Simon's texts. The reader cannot fail to notice the close textual ties between *The Grass* (first published in French in 1958) and *The Flanders Road* (first published in French in 1960). First of all, these novels present a very "Balzacian" use of the recurrence of characters: the same names, the same family situation, the same characteristics are present in both novels. Furthermore, *The Grass*, while written before *The Flanders Road*, describes a *later* period in Georges' life. As a matter of fact, *The Flanders Road* includes a two-page summary of the story told in *The Grass.* The following passage, referring to a scene from *The Grass*, furnishes its antecedent:

> the scene occurring like this: Georges declaring that he had decided to work on the land, . . . and no more, in other words not a word, not a remark, not a regret, the heavy mountain of flesh still motionless . . . instead of which or rather under which lay something that was like a part of Georges, so that . . . Georges heard perfectly . . . [the] deafening prattle, the imperceptible sound of some secret and delicate organ breaking, snapping, and after that nothing else, nothing except that carapace of silence when Georges would sit down at the dinner table in his filthy smock, with his hands not dirty but somehow encrusted with earth and grease. (*Flanders*, p. 238)

Here is the corresponding scene from *The Grass:*

> And: the man-mountain . . . the stare diminished, waned, fixed now not on Georges but on the hands with the long, thin, tapering fingers, a pianist's hands, his mother said, and paradoxically sunburnt, soiled grease-stained, darkly silhouetted against the white tablecloth . . .
> Contemplating then . . . (outside the monstrous prison of flesh . . .) this person he probably had to admit he had engendered . . .

therefore, ultimately, a prolongation of himself, even if it was apparently his negation, his adversary, and so, again, forced to recognize himself in it. (*Grass*, pp. 119-22)

Two novels—two intersecting points of view providing the reader with a privileged standpoint from which he has the impression of being able to see simultaneously, by superimposing the texts, two points in time and from which he holds "the totality of the enigma" of Georges's history (as Georges the narrator and the assassin behind the hawthorn hedge together hold that of de Reixach's death).[3] However, if from *The Grass* to *The Battle of Pharsalus* the reader—even the "alerted" one—often submits to the temptation of a synthesizing, more of less univocal reading, focused on a gallery of Simonian characters and themes, he will always be blind to the specificity of each text. Let us now look at another example of limited intertextuality linking *The Grass* to *The Flanders Road* while at the same time separating them by the work of writing. Here are three examples in which a very fertile comparison from *The Grass* is picked up again in *The Flanders Road*.

The Grass:

> . . . and between them [Louise and her lover] the sky was once again *like a plate of glass*.[4] (p. 14)

> (. . . Louise . . . separated from them the people in the old family photograph less by the impassable thickness of time than by the barrier of the *invisible, deceptive glass*, like an *aquarium* where it seems you need only hold out your hand to touch what is behind the glass, which in fact is as *hard* and as cold as a marble slab).

> Louise now lying *inert* in the grass, motionless, . . . above her the sky that had become like a *sheet of glass* . . . on which seemed painted the little heart-shaped leaves, in a *green* that was almost black.

Here are the same passages as they are written in *The Flanders Road*:

> ...and she [Corinne, Georges] still staring at him as if she were looking at him *through a sheet of glass*, as if she were on the other side of a *transparent partition* that was as *hard*, as *impenetrable*

as glass although apparently as *invisible* and behind which, ever
since he had come, she kept herself sheltered or rather out of
reach. (p. 235)

. . . so that now all that separated him from her [Georges from
Corinne] was that glass . . . exactly *as if* he had been standing *on
the other side* of the aquarium glass. (p. 246)

. . . and then standing there [Georges] *without making a move*,
without daring to *move . . . , the green [vert] and transparent
May twilight* like glass [*verre*] too, and . . . (p. 244)

Replaced in their context, these extraordinarily similar
passages all point to the same theme: glass (plate, partition,
sheet) indicates an invisible but impassable obstacle rendering
any communication impossible. Louise for her lover, Aunt
Marie's life for Louise, and Corinne for Georges are all equally "out of reach." Also, in both texts the green glass (*le verre
vert*) describes a certain perceptible texture of the twilight sky.

However, if one compares the functioning of these similar
comparisons in their respective texts, their dissimilarity is immediately apparent. In fact, the comparison "like [through] a
plate of glass" in *The Grass* generates numerous analogous
separation metaphors.[5] The marks left by these metaphors[6]
are mere pinpoints in the text; they have no effect on the
description of the characters involved, nor do they cause the
fiction to change course. And yet, this is exactly what happens
in *The Flanders Road*; Corinne is transformed, changing from
one "realm" to another, before our very eyes, just as the
Princess of Guermantes's guests entering her box (*Baignoire*)
at the opera became the victims of a transsubstantiation
brought about by the intrusion in the text of a word with
aquatic connotations[7]:

. . . and she—that is, her flesh, stirring imperceptibly, that is,
breathing, that is, dilating and contracting as if the air
penetrated her not through her mouth, her lungs, but by the entire surface of her skin, as if she were made of a substance like
that of sponges but with an invisible texture, dilating and contracting like those sea anemones those denizens of the deep
halfway between the transparent water. (*Flanders*, p. 241)

Not only Corinne, but also the setting of the story is
transformed by this intrusion:

> . . . he himself able to see himself in the cloudy depths of the
> glass behind her. (p. 241)

as is the subject matter:

> . . . and she still saying whatever came into her head: "How tan
> you are: *Have you been on the beach a lot?*" (p. 241)

and even the narrator himself:

> . . . then his own hand coming into his field of vision, that is, *as
> if he had thrust it into the water.* (p. 242)

The Grass plays on such homonyms as *verre* (glass) and
vert (green), but *The Flanders Road* goes farther. For example,

> The *green (vert)* and transparent May twilight like *glass (verre)*
> too, and in his throat that kind of nausea he had tried to choke
> down, swallowing thinking between two deafening rushes of air:
> it's from running too much, thinking: But maybe it's all that
> *alcohol?*

Glass acts here as a clutch, provoking a shift of sequence in
the fiction by a semantic slip from container to contained,
which permits the resumption of a former scene—Georges and
Iglésia escaping across the fields—which had been abandoned
and left fallow for six years and a good twenty-five pages.[9]

"Achilles Running Motionless"—The Pigeon or Description in Suspense

Every reader of Simon has noticed the insistent return or
rephrasing of certain favorite images; let us examine the
description of the pigeon which opens two of his novels, *The
Palace* (first published in French in 1961) and *The Battle of
Pharsalus* (first published in French in 1969):

> And all at once, in a sudden rush of air, immediately stilled (so
> that it was there—wings already folded back, perfectly mo-
> tionless—without their having seen it, as if . . . materialized by a

magician's wand), one of them landed on the stone balustrade . . .
strangely ponderous (like a porcelain pigeon* . . .) with its
speckled, dark-gray plumage . . . its coral feet. (*The Palace*, pp.
13-14)

Yellow and then black in the wink of an eye then yellow again:
wings outspread crossbow shape and shot between the sun and
the eye shadows for an instant across the face like velvet like a
hand . . . feeling them even smelling them that smell of dry-rot
cellar tomb . . . at the same time the sound of silk tearing the air
rustling or perhaps not heard perceived merely imagined bird arrow . . . like the one in that painting (where was it?) . . .

Dark dove aureoled with saffron

But white against the glass . . . surrounded by a sunburst of
golden rays . . . or painted in the background like the one in the
window of that pottery shop.

Vanished above the roofs . . . the vanishing unseen . . . (the
asphalt where two others are still strutting, gray with pink feet) . . .
between which it suddenly materialized for an instant. (*Pharsalus*, p. 3)

If bringing these passages together is justifiable because of
their use of the same vocabulary, down to the smallest detail,
there is at the same time a thematic return to a host of other
texts by Simon. Here the pigeon—elsewhere in Simon it may
be cats, horses, or young girls—embodies (like certain preferred paintings) the constellation of "lightning swiftness"
and "extreme slowness"

that you find only in those beings or things . . . capable not of
reaching but of becoming in the wink of an eye something not
released at a tremendous speed but which would be speed itself.
(*Flanders*, p. 167)

The two descriptions refer to one another by their method
of proceeding as well: emphasizing the consecutiveness of any
attempt to describe an object, the text progresses jerkily,
unveiling its object at the same time that it is kept in suspense.

*Richard Howard uses the word "dove." "Pigeon" is a more accurate translation of
Simon's "*pigeon*."

And when the pigeon is finally named, it is through an intermediary: *"Like* a *porcelain pigeon,"* "Dark *dove* aureoled
with saffron," *"Against the glass . . . or* painted . . . where
two others are still strutting, gray with pink feet." This device, which allows the writer to defer the appearance in the
text of the word "pigeon," creates the suspense at the beginning of *The Palace,* but it is in the novel which follows that
Claude Simon has drawn the consequences of it more radically. When he begins *Histoire* (first published in French in
1967) with "one of them" (*"l'une d'elles"*) he is explicitly
positing as subject of the text a *grammatical* personage or
rather a grammatical category: all feminine nouns and pronouns (and by dissimile, all their masculine counterparts)
could be used, one by one, to fill this potential space: "branches . . . old ladies paying calls . . . with their feathers . . .
chattering around Grandmother." But "they" (*elles*) is also
"El", that is, "wings" (*ailes*), which brings up birds, immediately bringing about in the text the merging of "old
ladies" and "birds in the branches": "imagining them, dim
and lugubrious, perched in the network of branches, as on
that Orleanist caricature . . . the women, their round empty
eyes perpetually filling with tears behind little veils between
the rapid fluttering of eyelids blued" (*Histoire,* p. 2). From the
"one of them" (*L'un d'eux*) in *The Palace* to the "one of
them" (*"L'une d'elles"*) in *Histoire,* a method has been
radicalized, as if the rules of the intertextual game allowed one
to reuse his own device on the condition that he develop it
systematically to yield greater profits. As Ricardou says of
"general intertextuality": he who makes the best use of a text
is its owner.

Despite the obvious similarities we have noted between
these two pigeon descriptions, it is their dissimilarity which
strikes us as significant. Indeed, whereas the description from
Pharsalus covers the one from *The Palace,* the reverse is not
the case. The lexical elements describing the pigeon in *The
Palace* are repeated, one by one, in *Pharsalus,* but distributed
over a wider surface. This is so because the words of the latter
description play a much more active part in the production of
the text,[10] for each element in the description indicates at the

same time a new direction for the fiction. The description from *The Palace*, while also containing fiction-generating elements,[11] is more "closed": it describes a *perception* linked to a privileged *theme* and introduces the *setting* for the fiction (Barcelona at the time of the Spanish Civil War). In *Pharsalus* the pigeon is still fully *perceived* (sight, sound, touch, odor) but then all at once "merely imagined," transformed into "bird arrow," into a stained-glass "dove," into a painted decoration from "chamber pots." Death, war, sex—all the thematic material which will be worked out in the novel "gushes forth" from the very first page.

Histoire represents a pivot in Simon's work around which all the rest turns, the center where all preceding and future texts cross, where a new style is forged while the old Simonian questions—the "How was it? . . . But exactly?" (*The Flanders Road*)—are stifled or reformulated.

With respect to limited intertextuality, *Histoire* provides a particularly rich field of study. It includes in summary the "stories" of *The Flanders Road* and *The Palace*, while presenting a first version of the story of the uncle (Charles) and the nephew, which is taken up again in *The Battle of Pharsalus*. *Histoire* also quotes, and spends entire pages expanding, the first descriptions of the photograph of the father and dying mother from *Le Tricheur*,[13] while providing material for *Triptych*, thus lacing together with textual relationships every segment of Simon's work.

It would be impossible in the context of a short article to attempt to analyze specific examples of the extremely tight play of intertextuality linking *Histoire* with other Simon novels of the 1960s. All the more so since the play of intertextuality is always accompanied by a play of *intra*textuality, whose action would have to be taken into account. Nevertheless, let us briefly look at the description of the "toothmarks" left in a chocolate bar from the "snack" scene, which appears in one of its variants in *Pharsalus*[14] and is repeated three times in *Histoire*,[15] where it assembles in the text three narrative sequences and thus three different *settings* and three *periods of time*: Corinne, cousin of the I/narrator, little girl at the beach with her grandmother—Van Velden's mistress-model with

Uncle Charles and/or the I/narrator in Paris—Corinne, Corinne's niece, in the country. One reason for and consequence of this "assembling" in *Histoire* is to question the solidity of the characters, as the fiction immediately attests (speaking of the studio photograph):

> their pale transparent forms mingling intersecting blurring each other so that finally nothing clear would remain except the setting of the studio . . . while the outlines of the figures are increasingly blurred, erased, no longer leaving anything but immaterial, increasingly diaphanous streaks like dubious vertiges (*Histoire*, p. 255)

The Battle of Pharsalus repeats and radicalizes not only the description of this scene, but also the character splintering,[16] for the O. in the last part of the book (where the quotation is found) marks the logical and theoretical culmination of the slow but persistent progression of Simonian practice. It is in fact in *Histoire* that we first encounter this "questionable" slipping from one fictitious character to another, where "his" (Uncle Charles's) adventure is at one moment confused with "mine" (the nephew's): the I/narrator taking the uncle's place "sitting in the wicker chair" in the studio photograph, and thus assuming the other's story.[17]

It is not by chance that criticism has dwelt on the *richness* of *Histoire*. Since the novel is peopled with characters and events the reader already knows, their assemblage (*mise ensemble*) gives the reader the vivid impression of being faced with a "novelistic mobile," a fictitious universe that is undoubtedly fragmented, but to which he seems to have found the key, the connecting thread or rather the privileged "conducting body": that, precisely, of Corinne, which ties the fragments to each other and to the narrator. She is the precocious child in the cherry tree, the Baroness de Reixach in the pink dresses (*Flanders*) the sceptical witness whose cousin runs off to join the Revolution (*The Palace*), finally the hypothetical presence "against backgrounds of palm trees and blue sea"[18] announcing retrospectively one panel of Simon's future work (*Triptych*).

But if everything ties together—or almost—it is already in a

completely different way. Until *Histoire* the reader could
manage with the tools at hand; after *Histoire* he too must
forge new ones. Moreover, from the standpoint of chronology
and verisimilitude, how are we to understand this Aunt de
Reixach, this Cherry Baroness who, at the beginning of
Histoire, stands with her "old cracked lips painted a red com-
ically evoking the freshness of the word *cerise*" (p. 4)? Surely
we must see her as a farcical counterpart to that other
"cherry" baroness, whose description in *The Flanders Road*
already seems to give us, implicitly as if by chance, a clue to
the reading:

> in that red dress the color of a gumdrop (but perhaps he had
> invented that too, that is the color, the harsh red, merely because
> she was something he thought about not with his mind but with
> his lips, his mouth, perhaps because of her name, because "Cor-
> inne" made him think of "coral"? (p. 239)

The "name . . . with multiple associations"[19] seems to be
placed at the beginning of this novel (whose epigraph posits
the problem of organization) as an ironic reminder to the
reader to be careful about his own standards.

While a retrospective reading of *Histoire* may reveal in the
description of the aging Corinne "against backgrounds of
palm-trees and blue sea" the foreshadowing of the "Riviera"
segment of *Triptych* (first published in French in 1973),[20] the
text of *Triptych* refers in turn explicitly to that of *Histoire*.[21]
Faced with a "character" ("this Lambert, this deputy")
reminding an aging baroness of a youthful encounter in the
house of "[her] best friend from school," the alert reader
declares (like Georges facing the dead horse in *The Flanders
Road*), "But I've seen that somewhere before, I know that."
And when he locates the reference, he can evaluate the clarify-
ing, if not subversive, effect of this textual encounter on his
first reading of *Histoire*, which tended to be referential and
synthesizing.

In *Triptych*, the baroness episode is presented like a *filmed
sequence* with "ambiguous" meanings: "The few words that
the ear catches (time, how much, eat, fortune, Reixach) being
pronounced with an interrogative and slightly ironic intona-

tion" (p. 40). The narrative is interrupted not only by other
fictitious sequences telling other "stories," but also by the intrusion into the fiction of technical problems involved in its
making: questions of sound and lighting, the way to lay out on
the bed the body of the actress playing the baroness, all of
which forestall any temptation to create an "illusory" atmosphere. Here Corinne is called—and insistently so—by no
other name than a *quartered* or *disjointed body* (*"corps
écartelé, désarticulé"*). And it is as such that it can be found
throughout the text, joining with every other "pink naked
body" in the novel. Corinne is then once again a "conducting
body" (*"corps conducteur"*) and has always been an essential
element (*"un corps"*) in the construction of the text.

It is impossible to conclude, even provisionally, without
saluting the passage of yet another de Reixach on Simon's
narrative roads. If, in *Leçon de choses* (1975) the central
metaphor for the writing of the text is the house—which is
either built or torn down to build others—it is not surprising
that the mason (the "makio," "he who makes") occupies a
privileged position. Indeed, it is he, alias the purveyor of the
"Entertainment" section of the book, who takes over and
rewrites once again *The Flanders Road*. The following
passage from *Leçon de choses* is a variation of the description
of the "High Society" scene which in *The Flanders Road*
precedes de Reixach's death:

> . . . engaged in talk all three of them standing at the side of the
> road very much the kind who make fashionable conversation
> after the horse races as still as if they had on corsets like some
> species of stuffed bird garden party at the Stirrup Club at the
> Spur Society and Dellahead sure did go over the triple bar well or
> Duspittle really faulted at the brick wall and this and that did
> you see the colonel's wife's hat all you had to have otherwise was
> the ladies with their parasols under the foliage gilded by the set-
> ting sun like you read about in books. (*Leçon*, p. 122)

As one reads more specifically early on in the "pre-text" book
in question—the passage receives a mocking salute from the
quotation's joking tone.

Nevertheless, it should be noted that in this entertaining
book where Simon plays so gaily with his linguistic material,

Reixach is brought into the text not by a reference to the circumstances of his death, but as a name, a play on consonances, supplying the purveyor with the material for fiction:

> you'd think you were reading a calendar or the wine list in a restaurant Saint Emilion Saint Estève Sainte Rose Saint Romain Saint Rémy Saint Michel Saint Eustache the chief what was his handle again hold it I can't remember his parish but the other one *it was like some kind of sauerkraut* something like Brissach or Ritmeister Reichenbach that's it now it's coming Reixach I got it. (*Leçon*, p. 123, my italics)

Sauerkraut ("*Ch*oucroute") *S. . .K* thus refers to and summarizes perfectly the first play on this name in Simon's work, reminding us retrospectively by this new textual milieu that it was a matter even then of minute, at times explicit, work with generative sounds: "and he: (Iglesia) Reishak good God haven't you learned that yet: shac the X like sh and the ch at the end like k God." (*Flanders*, p. 46)

It is well-known that the prefix *re-* before certain verbs has become ideologically suspect in the eyes of the New Novelists:

> I used to say it was possible to reconstruct things felt and experienced. Now . . . I don't believe one can "reconstruct" anything whatsoever. What is *constructed* is a text, and this text corresponds to one thing only: what is going on in the writer's mind at the time he writes.[22]

It is important, however, that the particle be kept and emphasized in places where it indicates not repetition but transformation. In *rereading* Claude Simon one realizes to what degree he is "absorbed by the problems of limited intertextuality," and to what extent, for him, the writer's work is precisely to *rewrite*, from "things felt and experienced," what he has already previously written.

UNIVERSITY OF OSLO

Notes

1. I refer to the definition proposed by Jean Ricardou and to the distinction he makes between "limited intertextuality" and "general intertextuality" in " 'Claude Simon,' Textuellement," *Claude Simon. Analyse, Théorie* (Paris: U. G. E., Collection "10/18," 1975), pp. 10-11.

2. *The Grass*, p. 15.

3. *The Flanders Road*, p. 319.

4. Of course, the intertextual play involving the comparison "like a pane of glass" is not confined to *The Grass* and *The Flanders Road*. For example, this passage selected from *Histoire* is related in an interesting way to the second quotation from *The Grass*:

> The voice reaching me as through plate glass, the words seeming to come from a great distance, perhaps because the speaker did not seem entirely real: . . . taken one might have said from one of those postcards with its old-fashioned figures . . . and conjured up now. (*Histoire*, p. 36)

5. Here are those which may be found in the immediate vicinity of the example quoted above: "separated from her by à pane of glass . . . (but like a diver under his bell)" (*Grass*, p. 194); "as if she were trying to understand, to remember what he was trying to communicate (. . . but separated from that knowledge as though by a pane of glass . . .)" (*Grass*, p. 196); "like those tiny creatures enclosed at the heart of one of those glass spheres or appearing, unreal, untouchable, in the fortune teller's crystal ball . . .)" (*Grass*, p. 197).

6. Here I use "metaphor" in the same way as Ricardou in *Problèmes du nouveau roman* (Paris: Seuil, 1967), p. 134.

7. " . . . the passage to which he was directed *after mentioning the word 'box'* and along which he now proceeded was moist and mildewed and seemed to lead to subaqueous grottoes, to the mythical kingdom of the water nymphs . . . " in Marcel Proust. *Remembrance of Things Past*. trans. C. K. Scott Moncrieff (New York: Random House, 1925), "The Guermantes Way," Part 1, p. 740 and following. The italics are mine.

8. My italics.

9. See *The Flanders Road*, pp. 208, 216-17.

10. For the textual yield of the pair yellow/black, for example, I refer the reader to Jean Ricardou: "La Bataille de la phrase" in *Pour une théorie du nouveau roman* (Paris: Seuil, 1971), pp. 118-58.

11. The most immediate result is: "the room with paneled walls or rather wall decorated with *plaster mouldings* that formed panels *painted Trianon-gray* . . . the magician's wand (*baguette d'un prestidigitateur*) having brought on the plaster mouldings (*baguettes à moulures*)" (*Palace*, p. 14)

12. See *Le Tricheur*, pp. 46 and 52.

13. See below.

14. *The Battle of Pharsalus*, p. 138.

15. See *Histoire*, pp. 196 and 254.

16. In *The Battle of Pharsalus* this process is caught up in a specific inter- and intratextual play with Proust as one of the privileged intertexts.

17. *Histoire*, pp. 241-45.

18. *Ibid.*, p. 129.

19. *Ibid.*, pp. 3-4.

20. Notice on the very first page the postcard which "shows an esplanade bordered by a row of palm trees standing out against a sky of too bright a blue, at the edge of a sea of too bright a blue."
21. *Triptych*, referring to *Histoire*.
22. *Kentucky Romance Quarterly* 16, no. 2 (1970: 182. The italics are Simon's.

II New Critical Approaches

8

Composition, Repetition, and Dislocation in Simon's First Three Novels*

C. G. Bjurström

Claude Simon's first novels have never been republished and the author has let it be known that he did not wish the critics to take them into account. Nevertheless, it is interesting and not necessarily indiscreet to examine them. A novelistic technique does not come into being overnight and even within works apparently completed, the author continues to feel his way along—sometimes he is groping for a quite different style of writing and will therefore later reject these works even more vigorously than a first book, which often keeps the freshness and innocence of a draft, without obscuring his real intentions. That is what has happened, for instance, with Claude Simon's second and third novels.

The purpose of tentative experimentation is to explore various directions and patterns before proceeding. He who attempts to follow those tentative paths will have to give his attention sometimes to the more obvious features—composition, internal divisions, repetitions, parallels—sometimes to what might seem to be details—verb tenses, the sonority of an adjective, a fleeting image. The importance of his observations will tend to be in inverse proportion to the size of the points observed: it is easier to point out a peculiarity in the composi-

---

* Translated by Jane Carson.

tion of a book than to account for variations in verb tenses, significant though they may be.

Claude Simon's first three novels are *Le Tricheur*, finished in 1941 but not published until after the war in 1945, *Gulliver*, published in 1952, and *Le Sacre du printemps*, published in 1954. No mention will be made here of *La Corde raide*, an essay containing autobiographical elements or a book of reflexion and discussion which appeared in 1947.

Le Tricheur

The first chapter of *Le Tricheur* begins with an evocation of the landscape where the action takes place and a dialogue between two characters, Louis and Belle, the protagonists of the novel. This opening contrasts with the often long and laborious descriptions that introduce the "Balzac" type of novel, where the author is not content merely to set the scene and specify the time period and circumstances governing the action, but also supplies the first elements for character analysis. If we are, therefore, dealing with a more "modern" novel, it is not yet showing us anything very original. It should, however, be noted that it is not particularly clear whether it is the author who is describing the landscape or whether we see it through the two characters' eyes: the narrative moves easily from "they" to "one" and back to the third person plural. But the narration slips soon enough inside the characters' minds. From the landscape and the characters' voices we move to their thoughts and memories. First in traditional fashion, by way of a "she thought," but a few lines farther on we slide, within the same paragraph, from the third person to the first, that is, toward a sort of interior monologue:

> She grimaced in disgust and turned away. If only I could have found out where Uncle Jacques hid the money, she thought. He counted the bills on the table. There must have been twenty-five thousand francs. (p. 11)

The quotation marks, which should ordinarily have signaled the moment of transition to direct speech and to Belle's interior monologue, do not appear until later, for the memories she is recalling continue with a retort by Uncle Jacques. But the somehow tardy quotation marks are not closed at the end of Uncle Jacques's remark: Belle's thoughts are directly linked up and it is not until several pages later that the quotation marks are closed and we are brought back to the present moment and to an "external" description of Belle's movements:

> She lowered her head and covered her face with both hands. (p. 13)

This gesture sparks a rejoinder from Louis, immediately followed by his interior monologue:

> Well if she starts crying like that over nothing, it's going to be impossible absolutely impossible! Ooooh!. . . If she didn't want to take off, why . . . (p. 13)

The chapter goes on in the same vein, alternating freely between what might be considered the account of the narrator—the famous "omniscient" author—and Louis's interior monologue, for he is in the foreground from now on, especially since Belle soon falls asleep. From this moment on the proportions are reversed: whereas in the beginning the narrative was interrupted by short interior monologues, it is now Louis's interior monologue that is occasionally interrupted by the notations of the author recording external events. This is carried out without difficulty, generally by starting a new paragraph, without any special punctuation. But there may also be more subtle gliding within the same paragraph by a simple change of pronoun:

> He felt her hard body under her dress. He clenched his fingers. He moved his hand higher, still keeping hold of her mouth, and tried to unbutton the top of her dress. He felt the pearly button under his nails. She kicked, but he held her fast. He squeezed her legs between his. And her mouth. . . I had kissed her behind the shooting-gallery. (p. 15)

Thus the three words "And her mouth" act as a sort of

pivot, since this unfinished sentence can just as easily be part of the *present*, described from the outside, as part of the *past*, relived in Louis's memory.

These few remarks, without being earth-shaking, serve to illustrate the intuitive ease with which Claude Simon moves from the account of an observer outside the events to the characters' interior monologue. This is not a theory put into practice, but simply an empirical step.

The second chapter takes place several years earlier and has no apparent connection with the scene just described. It introduces two other characters, Belle's parents, Catherine and Gauthier, and is told entirely in the third person and in the past tense. Everything is thus kept at a distance and, just as in any traditional novel, the characters' thoughts, like their movements, are described for us by a narrator who knows everything that is going on in their minds. There are passages that border on interior monologue such as the one where Catherine, in her anxiety, imagines what could have been happening to her daughter so vividly that we almost see it through her eyes:

> What could he be doing? The smashed bicycle lying on the side of the road, the man lying in ambush in the woods and Belle's stifled cries and her little schoolgirl's bookbag open and the white notebooks scattered on the green grass. My God! (p. 63)

But in spite of the question and in spite of the final exclamation, the passage remains part of the narration, largely because the verb is in the past tense.

With this exception, Catherine's thoughts are presented to us in the form of silent internal remarks accompanied by a "she thought" such as we find in traditional novels:

> She squeezed the flesh with her thumb. Her upper lip curled in an expression of fear and disgust.
> "No, it's nothing," she thought. "But look what's happened to my hands!" (p. 59)

Likewise, Gauthier's morose thoughts as he rides home on his bicycle are in the third person and the past tense and it is significant that the part of the chapter devoted to him begins with the pronoun "one," which makes it possible, in effect, to avoid the first person. Here again we are, for a moment, bordering on interior monologue, until a sort of communication is established between Gauthier's bitter thoughts and the external events happening at the same time—the noise of the bicycle, in this case.

> One ceased to be, and that was all. Ceased to be, ceased to be, ceased to be. The pedal crank shaft squeaked regularly in the late afternoon silence. (p. 81)

In contrast to this chapter, the third one starts right away as Belle's interior monologue, easily identified by its tone:

> Anywhat it's all the same to me, I'll ask the owner. She surely must have it. (p. 129)

But this is one of the rare moments when Belle "thinks" in the present tense: in fact, she usually rethinks the past, distant or recent, and consequently the verb is almost always in the past. Now it is well known that French uses both a simple and a compound past tense. The compound past, more colloquial, is used especially for *oral* accounts, while the simple past, more formal, is rarely seen outside a *written* narration. Most other languages do not make this distinction, and the subtlety is therefore lost in translation, but it is nonetheless important here since Belle, obeying a certain formal logic, recalls her childhood memories in the compound past and uses the simple past to speak of the events of the last few days: the chapter is thus torn between the interior monologue—which prefers a spoken style and the more natural form of expression in the present and compound past—and the written, even literary narrative, characterized by the simple past. Here the simple past constantly shatters the illusion of the "stream of consciousness" that the interior monologue is supposed to represent.

At this time we will not linger on the first two parts of the fourth chapter, since both are traditional accounts in the third

person and the past tense, the first devoted to Ephraim
Rosenblaum, the watch salesman who occupies the room next
to the couple in the hotel, the second to Armand, Louis's
friend. In the composition of the novel these two parts correspond to the parenthesis formed by the second chapter, also
split between Catherine and Gauthier.

The third part of the fourth chapter—which might have
formed a fifth chapter, stressing the symmetry of the novel's
composition, returns to interior monologue. It does not immediately declare its allegiance. In fact, we cannot know if the
author or one of his characters makes the following observation:

> One would have thought it was a sullen old man he had once
> again displeased. (p. 209)

Not until eighteen lines later do we realize that Louis is speaking:

> Then the little dog moves off beside the old lady, looking
> ludicrous as he wriggles and jerks on the sidewalk splotched with
> black shadows. As I raised my head, *I saw ("j'ai vu")* the cop
> coming, a little farther on. Armand *doesn't budge ("ne bouge
> pas")*. He *doesn't* even *stop* singing *("ne s'arrête même")* (pp.
> 209-10, italics mine)

This time—as the last quotation shows—the narrative
sways between the present tense and the compound past,
which is all the easier since the compound past has an auxiliary in the present. After "So I start walking" ("Alors je me
mets à marcher") (p. 217), and "At the news stand I *stop*
and *look* at the magazine covers" ("Arrivé au kiosque je *m'arrête
et je regarde* les couvertures") (p. 218), comes a sudden compound past: "I *bought ("j'ai acheté")* the machine and *looked
for ("j'ai cherché")* a restaurant" (p. 216), followed by a present
tense: "The waitress *comes ("vient")* and *takes away ("enlève")*
the dirty plate in front of me" (p. 219), followed by a compound past: "The waitress *came back ("est revenue")* with the
check" (p. 220). The same alternation appears at the dramatic
moment of the murder, which, after a long passage in the pre-

sent, takes place in the compound past—as if Louis wanted to put a distance between himself and his act:

> "Excuse me," *I say ("dis-je").*
> *And I stop ("je m'arrête")* as if to pee on the pile of bricks, while he goes on walking calmly beside the scaffolding. Then I pick up the brick.
> *I struck ("j'ai frappé")* from above. . . .
> *I waited ("j'ai attendu")* a while, listening, in case anyone came.
> . . . Then I go up and turn him over with my foot. (p. 249)

Once the crime has been committed, Louis returns to the present tense.

Now what is this present tense? Is it an authentic present, a "present present" corresponding exactly to the time it is expressing or recounting? Is it not rather—at least most of the time—a "historical" present, the equivalent of the simple past, used to accelerate the rhythm of the narration by making past events more "present," so to speak. Again we are faced with a hybrid form in the first person, hesitating between narration and interior monologue.

To make certain of this we need only compare Louis's monologue in this third part of the fourth chapter (pp. 209-250) with the scraps of authentic interior monologue found in the first chapter. There, Louis's observations and movements are glued to the text and move with it, even in some places that might appear to be awkward attempts to insert this present and these immediate surroundings into a "stream of consciousness" particularly concerned with the past. Such is for example the dramatic exclamation, "Watch out, someone's coming!" (p. 30), which for all we know may be ironic, or the little soliloquy:

> Hey, a snake? what was it that just took off over there in the grass? A lot of poisonous snakes around here, I bet. But probably more in the summertime. Let's toss a stone. Nothing. Probably slipped between the stones of that little wall, wriggling, crawling, sinuous. (p. 53)

In any case, these are the exceptions: generally Claude Simon does not hesitate to interrupt the "stream of consciousness" to

note "objectively" the characters' movements and observations and the events of the world around them.

Regarding its composition, *Le Tricheur* has a fairly clear
balance: The first chapter, "objective" in presentation, slides
gradually toward interior monologue and mingles the two
styles freely and to good effect. It provides a brilliant introduction, striking for its real dialogue and acute observations as well as for the duration of the interior monologue.

This introduction is followed by two traditional third-
person narratives, then a monologue or first-person narrative,
then once more two third-person narratives and a first-person
monologue. Only the two main characters, Louis and Belle,
who take turns speaking, use the first person. The other
characters are truly witnesses—this is particularly noticeable
in the case of Ephraim Rosenblaum, who spies on the couple
next door in the hotel—or parallels, such as Catherine and
Gauthier. By its very place in the novel, the Catherine-
Gauthier couple prefigures the Louis-Belle couple and
foretells its failure. Louis's resolution, "But I have decided.
An act" (p. 238), corresponds to Gauthier's repeated bluster-
ing, "Some day *he* would show them all" (p. 86), which is
even a caricature of Louis's statement.

Nor is this the only parallel, the only repetition. It is, for
example, the second time that Belle leaves "just like that" (p.
12) and through her escapade with Louis she remembers the
day she and her mother ran away from her father's house.
While Belle is asleep in the meadow, Louis goes to the railway
station and for a moment he is tempted to abandon her, but in
the end he returns for her and takes her back with him to the
station. Armand sees his friend Louis go by twice (p. 198 and
208), but he only manages to catch up with him the first time.
Lastly, when Louis arrives at the priest's house with a gun to
kill him, he is not able to carry out his plan (pp. 242-44), and
only when he meets the priest by chance, for the second time
in one day, does he achieve his purpose (pp. 246-48).

These recurrences and repetitions stress the ineluctable
nature of the events, and the fact that Louis can only complete
his action thanks to a "chance" meeting means that the

"gratuitous," and supposedly liberating, act has failed. Throughout this novel he is obsessed by the thought of an act of will that would break the bonds imposed by the world's absurdity and deny the role of chance. This is how Louis tries to *cheat*, in the sense of the epigraphy from the *Littré* dictionary: "To correct chance: to cheat" (*tricher*). He wants, as he says, "to be sure he had written it and not just been a puppet" (p. 32).

But the effect of his desperate eagerness to impose his will is to make the world around him abstract and flat, as can be seen a little farther on on the same page:

> A man was yelling and cursing somewhere. Two tranquil oxen, then the low cart they were pulling, emerged slowly from the bushy hedge hiding the road, the length of the field. Against the light, it was like a flat toy cut out of gray-blue cardboard, circled with light. (p. 32)

The doubling of certain scenes seems to be intended to combat this flatness by introducing a sort of stereoscopic element. Thus the scene where Belle vomits as a child because she is forced to drink out of a cup her idiot cousin has drooled in is told twice, first by her father (p. 97), then by herself (pp. 151-52). Ephraim Rosenblaum catches sight of Louis at the restaurant (p. 171) and the scene is related again by Louis (p. 219). The times Louis spends at his friend Armand's—another witness—are first related in the passage devoted to Armand (p. 204), then in Louis's monologue (pp. 222-31), and at that time we learn some details about the scene between Louis and Lydie, during which Armand was careful not to be present. More subtle is the repetition of the scene of Louis's return after the murder, which takes place on the last pages of the book (pp. 249-50). This scene has already been mentioned (p. 182) without revealing its actual importance to the reader; Ephraim is in fact the one who watches Louis's return from the room next door without suspecting—any more than Belle—what has just happened.

With this exception, the recurrences of the same scene, presented from different angles, finally add very little to the depth of time or of the events, undoubtedly because the two

versions coincide too closely or because the witnesses remain
too indifferent.

Thus *Le Tricheur*, despite the author's effort at composition, unfolds in a curiously flat time and it is perhaps no accident that Louis's first movement is to throw out his old watch,
which is simultaneously an inheritance from his father, a link
with the past, and an image for Time (p. 10), and that
Ephraim Rosenblaum is a watch salesman rebuffed by Belle:
"I don't need to know what time it is. I don't want to make
you waste your time" (p. 178).

Nevertheless, there are passages where time becomes
perceptible, especially in the first chapter, thanks to the interior monologue and the acuteness of the observations. And it
sometimes happens that it suddenly takes on depth in
passages such as the one we cited, where Louis observes the
little dog, then the policeman, finally Armand, in a perfect
movie-camera sequence, and especially in the following
passage:

> Catherine climbed up to the road along the canal, scaling the
> grassy flank of the embankment, her knees bent high, using
> her arms to help.
> Suddenly the shadow of the three walnut trees came out of the
> ground at her feet like a cloud of bubbles rising to the surface of
> the water. Blurred at first, it took shape, became sharp and blue.
> (p. 64)

Originating in the most elementary, the most concrete
observation, without the intervention of any literary plan, this
is here a startling zoom shot, an adjustment of vision momentarily disturbed by being out of focus, which makes time all at
once almost palpable. For the later works of Claude Simon
this is a crucial discovery.

Gulliver

For his second novel Claude Simon chose the unity of time:
the events take place in the space of twenty-four hours. The
structure is circular: chronologically speaking, the first

chapter takes place at the end of the story and the events that
are related in it are also found in the last chapter. Between
these two parentheses, the action unfolds chronologically, except for a few flashbacks indispensable for an understanding
of the plot and a longer account of the past life of the main
character: the past explains the present but does not enter into
it.

The novel consists of thirteen chapters divided into four
parts. The first part introduces the setting, the characters,
and the relationships between them. The second, which takes
place at night, describes the dramatic event that forms the
very heart of the novel. This part is perfectly balanced, with a
first chapter (chapter five in the book) which leads into the action and a last chapter (chapter eight in the book) which
describes the panic and despondency the characters experience after young Bobby's death. His death occurs practically in the middle of the book, 190 pages from the beginning
and 180 pages from the end. In the third part the thread of
events is interrupted by a flashback focusing on Max, the one
most affected by Bobby's death. In the fourth part the knots
in the plot are unraveled.

We are thus dealing with a carefully constructed novel told
in the third person, nearly as classical as a tragedy by Racine
and, like a tragedy, containing a certain number of "tales"
that support or explain the action. However, if there is unity
of time, there is scarcely any unity of action. It is more like a
sheaf of plots which unfold at the same time without any
parallel action and without always being well tied together,
other than by the movements of the characters who participate sometimes in one, sometimes in another. It might
even be said that there is a contrast between the apparently
clear composition of the book and the unrealistic complica-
tions of events.

In the same way the time in which the novel takes place is
not so simple as it first appears. The circular construction,
which gives the end before the beginning, somehow suggests a
need to recapture time, since the idea is to end at the same
place as the beginning; the coming and going of the characters

constantly pursuing one another, trying to catch up with one
another, is in a way the concrete image of this attempt to
recapture lost time.

Again in *Gulliver* we find the repetitions and doubling of *Le
Tricheur*, beginning with the first and last chapters, which recount the same event. One also notices, in one of the novel's
"intrigues" or in one of the plots forming it, a character who
belongs to a different story and who will be the subject of a
later chapter. For example, Herzog is glimpsed from a window before becoming the principal figure in the following
chapter, and Max's meeting with Eliane and Bert (pp. 80-81),
briefly described, is retold in a different mode, as background
noise in the middle of another plot (pp. 117-24): This device
almost reminds us of the famous recurring characters in the
Human Comedy, where characters are introduced now in the
foreground, now in the background, circulating from one
novel to the next and thereby producing a sort of stereoscopic
effect.

The most spectacular doubling is of course that of the twin
brothers Jo and Loulou. Oddly enough, the novel does not
exploit the pair, except in that their resemblance facilitates a
detective intrigue, which could just as well have taken place
without this peculiarity. Exactly alike, Jo and Loulou coincide perfectly and therefore fail to add a new dimension to the
novel: they are merely added together, appearing all the more
monstrous and gigantic. It is actually the doubling of Max
and Tom that is the most interesting, both of them equally
silent and enigmatic, both "returned" from combat, which
has left them solitary and disillusioned. It is perfectly logical
for Tom, the positive side of Max, to take charge of Eliane in
the end.

With the approach of Bobby's death, time gains a greater
consistency by slowing down. This slowing effect is felt not
only in terms of time: the images contribute effectively to it.
From the beginning of Chapter Six the accumulation of words
expressing wetness, softness, filth, grease, and drunkenness
prepare and explain Bobby's uneasiness and the bleary state
in which we find him. This nauseating softness culminates in
the portrait of the woman who keeps the inn, "a creature in

her fifties or so, large and puffy," thick-waisted, with rotten
teeth, a "gargle" for a laugh, she shifts "on her slippered feet,
the enormous volume of flesh that seemed, flattened by its
own weight, to slide like a stain" (p. 153), and she sways
"awkwardly, like the poultry she slowly stuffed with food,
dragging their distended bellies on their short legs like a
malediction" (p. 154). The room where Bobby is in this
passage is filled with the insipid and sweetish odor of the
meal; he feels caught in "something warm and poisonous
which was spreading out around him, enveloping him, protecting him in its suffocating and jealous folds" (p. 159). The
filth, the softness, the grease which permeate this preamble
lead imperceptibly to ideas of slowness, malediction, and suf-
focation: in this ogress's dwelling, Bobby is caught in the lime.

His drunkenness increases, space and time become blurred
and when, by abrupt returns to consciousness, he becomes
aware of what is happening—or rather of what has just happened—the sense of dislocation is obvious:

> He stopped, surprised, panting. Only then did he realize that
> his voice had been shaking. (p. 159)

He becomes "disinterested" in everything being said or done
around him, he has the feeling that everything is detaching
itself from him and that he himself is there "by mistake." If
he sees double—as a drunk man is said to do—it is because
he feels double: in fact, he experiences "a curious sensation:
he was himself and not himself all at the same time" (p. 161).
Finally, he tries to flee, but in the hall he bumps into the
enormous manager who absorbs and smothers his efforts,
reducing them to ridiculous gesticulation:

> he came up against a flabby and impenetrable barrier in which
> the shadows seemed to have formed, for the occasion, a sort of
> mattress in which all his impetus dissolved, disappeared, despite
> the willingness of his legs, which went on pedaling frantically on
> the floor. (p. 196)

This "frantic" running in place, which comes up repeatedly
in Claude Simon's novels, is an image that conveys so well a

sensation familiar to most of us that it is utilized repeatedly in animated cartoons. Like the fruitless waiting, the sudden return to consciousness, and the feeling of being late or of being outside of time, it reveals a gap between subject and events, between sensations and thoughts, between phenomena taking place at different rhythms, which thus give rise to the sensation of passing time.

Moreover, this sense of dislocation affects not only Bobby, but also Max, about whom we find such typical expressions as "Only then did he realize" (p. 177) and especially the future memory introduced in the narrative to explain a momentary unconsciousness—a device recalling certain common phrases from traditional novels such as "he was later to learn that" or "he was to remember that," phrases that generally play the role of epilogues, whereas Claude Simon's phrase designates the first dislocation in sensations and thoughts, later retrieved by memory:

> Only later did he remember that at the foot of the steps when his foot touched the ground, the sole had not slipped in the mud but had encountered instead a hard crusty substance. It was then he realized it must be below freezing now, but thinking of the cold as one happens to read a temperature chart in the newspaper. (p. 167)

In this short passage the "gaps" pile up: from a moment "later" (introduced in the present of the narration) Max returns to the moment when, contrary to what he expects (here the movement in time goes in the opposite direction), he finds not mud at the foot of the steps, but rather frozen ground: at this moment he realizes that it is "now" below freezing, but he immediately pushes this thought aside and holds it at a distance like the news one reads in the newspaper. It is clear what depth such devices can give to time in the novel.

But other methods exist as well, such as repetition, hesitation, marking time, which are often accompanied by hypotheses:

> They probably didn't need them for what they had to say.
> They probably needed no more than a hand placed on a shoulder. (p. 165)

And finally, the comparison between the individual, momentary gesture, and History, in a sort of ironic generalization, a flight of comic oratory:

> He lurched a little but held up. He crossed the room, walking straight, with his insolent bearing appropriate to the last representative of an acromegalic and fallen dynasty perpetuating in riotous living and car racing the lewd, bellicose traditions of an august line whose portraits strive one after the other to look like caricatures of themselves, each succeeding one offering an improved version, the last arriving in shape to appear in specialized magazines as a celebrity listed on the program for international festivities or charity balls. (p. 178)

Thus congealed in the great glacier of Time, the moment can be slowed down until it becomes nearly motionless, and this Time, immobile as well as resifted or repeated, takes on the shape of Destiny.

Compared to this slow-motion present, the past recalled in *Gulliver*—especially in the two chapters devoted to Max's past—seems strangely flat. This is partly because of the character, who is a perfect example of a mysterious character without mystery. Indeed, while the event of the death of Bobby in the middle of the book gives it the appearance of a detective novel, enriched by secrets and allusions spread about by small-town gossip, the enigma to be solved is not to find out who killed Bobby, but who is Max. Or rather, who killed Max. For despite the two chapters recounting his life, despite the information, gossip, and allusions, Max remains not a mystery but a blank. A flat blank, however, if such a thing is possible, just as for Bobby the darkness of the hall through which he tries to escape is "a false exit, a *trompe-l'oeil* painting on a panel" (p. 196). Max is actually dead long before he commits suicide, despite the novel constructed around him. And Tom, almost as elusive as he, will not bring him back to life. To see Max resuscitate in his opposite we must await Montès in *The Wind*.

Le Sacre du printemps

The structure of *Le Sacre du printemps* brings to mind that of *Le Tricheur*, in a simpler form: four chapters (divided into two fairly equal parts), the first an interior monologue which takes place on December 10, 1952, the second a third-person narration still focusing on the same character, Bernard, which has immediately followed the first, December 11. The third chapter presents an abrupt break in time, since it takes place sixteen years earlier, December 10, 11, and 12, 1936, and is divided into two parts: a third-person narration and a first-person narration spoken by a participant in the events of these three days in 1952 who turns out to be, as we learn from a comment at the end, none other than Bernard's stepfather, at approximately the same age as Bernard in 1952. With the fourth chapter we return to December 12, 1952, in other words, the thread of events continues after the 1936 parenthesis.

The very arrangement of the third chapter, the one that takes place in 1936, and the fact that the central character is not the one to whom the rest of the book is devoted, indicates quite clearly that we are dealing here with a parallel, similar to that of the Catherine-Gauthier/Louis-Belle couples in *Le Tricheur*, but in *Le Sacre du printemps* the educational aim is much more obvious.

In the first chapter Claude Simon has made every effort to write a true interior monologue, in the first person and the present tense, that is to say, a text exactly contemporaneous with the events and thoughts it reports. This requires the narrator to take note of daily actions with reflections that may appear contrived, as, for instance, "I've put the water on to boil for the noodles. When they're cooked, I'll put on the meat" (p. 43), or "maybe I should look and see if those noodles are done. No. But almost" (p. 56), or the following, though more amusing because of the association of ideas provoked by the objects:

> Oh fine, I'm not going to sing a canticle, am I? *Miserere. Amen.* Armed with the dishrag as with an aspergillum. *Asperges me, Domine*: a plate, a knife, a saucepan. And now the worst to clean: the frying pan. A wadded-up newspaper. There. (p. 72)

Bernard's interior monologue progresses by associations of ideas which sometimes connect so quickly and so abruptly that the sentence becomes almost incomprehensible, as for example:

> Hypocrites women hypocrites I could almost see her whining and delighted her opal belly, her open belly and the navel eye of the belly, and the one I came out of, blind, borne, enclosed in darkness, the visceral shadows only it wasn't in her but rather on her she should have received me dodging kicking mare then I never would have been as I watched what might have been a son die on her softest spot white death agony in the swaying shade of the ferns. (p. 70)

To interpret this passage, we must remember that Bernard's girlfriend placed herself "a little too easily on her back in the Fontainebleau forest" (p. 66), "abandoning herself in a sort of whining delight," and that he remembers her "stupid naked belly too white greenish-white," but also that he reproaches his mother ("on her back with someone not my father") (p. 58), for not moving away and causing his father's semen to be lost outside her.

Here the plays on words set off the associations of ideas. Indeed, it is because Bernard in his kitchen thinks about those who, rather than try to manage on their own, "prefer to have a family or a wife or a mother on their backs" (p. 58) that he starts thinking about his mother, "on her back with someone not my father," only to correct himself furiously a little farther on: "I should have said on their backs and not on her back. A nuance" (p. 59). But this memory haunts him and he returns to it when considering his Aunt Jeanne, who deceives her husband and who Bernard suspects of having loved his father.

This time the image is called up by a play on opposites:

> She *posed* as a woman with a *head* on her shoulders, with good
> sense, disillusioned with everything, especially with the illusory
> delights of *posing* on her *back*. (p. 64, my italics)

Thus it is this flow of plays on words and associations that
leads to the obscure passage quoted earlier.

Bernard's interior monologue is not only directed by the
"constraint" imposed by actual objects present, which, in
order to enter the "stream of consciousness," must sometimes
be mentioned in somewhat artificial comments, and by the
"flippancy" of the plays on words which sometimes stoop
rather low. There is also the entire past and its connections:
oddly enough, Claude Simon chooses, as in *Le Tricheur*, the
tense of written narration, the simple past, and not the tense
of oral narrative, the compound past, which would seem to
have been more appropriate to a monologue, even an "interior" one.

Another tense typical of Claude Simon's prose makes its appearance here, the present participle, whose effect is more or
less to freeze the action. But it is not yet clearly used to this
end, as it will be in the later novels. Here it crops up at particular moments, those concerning Edith, the sister of Bernard's pupil, the girl he is more or less unconsciously in love
with; and it would seem that in this context the present participle, instead of describing Edith's movements, expresses
the sort of paralysis that takes hold of Bernard when he is in
her presence:

> . . . both her eyes staring me in the face now with a sort of
> stupefied, insolent curiosity, her lips moving, saying, or rather
> shaping the words (I didn't have to hear to understand): "You're
> the one who's the step-son of . . ." but not finishing, the eyes
> almost immediately becoming indifferent again, expressionless.
> (p. 28)

The second chapter, which is in the third person, first shows
us a Bernard totally different from the grumbling, embar-
rassed boy of the interior monologue:

Despite the early hour, the ersatz daylight coming in through the curtainless window, he was already completely dressed, shoes and tie on, his hair parted on the side and carefully combed, his whole face, with its determined thoughtful expression, reflecting a sort of calmness, of diligent seriousness which contrasted with his youthful features, the mouth almost childish, the oval of the face where a conscientious and seemingly unnecessary razor had left a narrow nick. (p. 90)

This is the youthful knight, so well-armored, who will be put to flight and who, at the end of the chapter, will show himself inarticulate and ashamed in front of Edith.

In this "grayish uncertain light which almost at once ceased spreading, froze in an irremediable fashion" (p. 89), time does not seem to move. The city has a sad, stereotyped, repetitive air. The sign of the hotel Bernard goes to is "as dry, as unappealing as the other signs" (p. 94), the building across the street is "very nearly the exact replica" of the one he is in, the table is adorned with "the inevitable green plant" (p. 93), the stairways all have "the same dubious, shady look" (p. 94), the businessmen, in their offices "where electricity burns all day long," try to buy and sell again in perpetual motion "all that can be bought." Time seems to be punctuated only by the cigarettes Jacky keeps pulling out of his pockets and it is hard to believe "the watches, the clocks, the identical numbered disks with identical hands, slow, inexorable, repeating thousands of times on a thousand faces, like a tireless warning, a tireless reminder, the same hand signal watched for by thousands of anguished, impatient, or simply exhausted eyes" (pp. 101-102).

In this motionless climate, Bernard is constantly jolted by his own time, the time of his sensations and of his thoughts, which unfolds sometimes quickly, sometimes slowly. He rises to the surface in abrupt spells of awareness, bewildered, only to disappear again at once.

When he is asked to give the price of the ring he wants to sell, he has the sensation of time passing terribly quickly:

He was silent, stood there like a fool, staring in despair at the minuscule object, the minuscule sparkle held between fingertips,

> while at top speed a parade of figures superimposed as if in the slit of a car speedometer or a cash register danced by and he rejected them one after another as fast as he glimpsed them. (p. 103)

But there are also "holes" in the succession of events of which he is not even aware:

> "And even so," he thought again (outside now, walking in the cold gray half-light. . .) (p. 105)

and it is only after some effort that he is able to stick to the present even for a brief moment:

> Abruptly he stopped and looked her in the face, seemed, by concentrating, to remember her existence, her presence beside him (although the whole time they had been sitting there, he had nodded approval as long as she was speaking. . .). (p. 112)

These moments of lucidity also interrupt the narrative as "future memories":

> Later he remembered seeing himself there, at five o'clock in the afternoon. . .listening to a girl even younger than himself talk to him about movie stars and American films. (p. 108)

Occasionally, he is even conscious of his thoughts unrolling on two parallel tracks, in two rhythms, at two different tempos:

> He knew very well that he had something important to do. He was even perfectly capable of remembering (and for that matter he didn't need to remember since he had never ceased to be aware) what this something consisted of, and that he was there solely to do it. But now suddenly it appeared to him, if not unimportant, at least relegated to a dim background, whereas instead the present moment only counted, what could be immediately perceived, what was immediately apprehended, so that it was with a peaceful sense of detachment, a tranquillity without amazement, without emotion, that he heard her say, "You know I don't think he'll come now. It's too late." (p. 113)

The act of fixing his attention on one thing, letting the others remain, but blurred, in the background, is later expressed as a true "zoom shot":

> He could see nothing but her two shining eyes, fixed on
> him . . . and when she spoke . . . her teeth, also shining . . . the
> teeth he felt against his, an eye suddenly huge, completely filling
> his own field of vision, the brown pupil like a wheel, with its
> spokes fluttering under the wing of the eyelid, staring at him
> from the back of a warm soft humid hole. (p. 115)

This microscope that regulates itself to compensate for movement, this picture changing from blurred to clear, also produces a sensation of time that is microscopic.

And in this chapter a technique suddenly matures that will
be found in Claude Simon's later novels, where it will be particularly successful, namely, the use of the present participle:
"starting back, looking at her, dumbfounded, disconcerted,
hearing" (p. 114). And also, the discontinuous chain: "they
were outside" (p. 114), "and afterward" (p. 115), "a moment
later" (p. 118), and the future backward glances already
pointed out: "Later he would remember" (p. 125). We also
find "rectifications" of the sort, "he began to run then. Or
rather continued" (p. 123), and even times when haste and
feverishness force the text to skip the first link of the chain of
movements and say, "On the platform in one bound he continued searching his pockets" (p. 122), whereas it has never
been said that he was searching his pockets.

Oddly enough, this sudden acceleration is brought on by a
return to normal, universal time, the time of fate:

> "Yes. Because it [the earth] didn't stop turning for that,
> because it never stops . . . the whole time I was there in bed with
> her, and even asleep for a moment while everywhere else, asleep
> and she . . ." (p. 122)

It is under the pressure of this universal time, recovered in
the middle of a crowd, that he begins to suspect that he has
been robbed of the ring entrusted to him and the shock
becomes still greater. It foreshadows a much more concrete
shock, the fist which will stop Bernard a little farther on (pp.
125-26). But all this is nothing compared to the blow Edith
deals him when she confirms that she stole the ring, which he

has now lost, in order to get an abortion. Then time widens
and becomes immense:

> They faced each other for a time that seemed endless, both
> standing as they had the evening before in the incessant rain
> haloing them with its sparkling striations, their two faces con-
> fronting each other, the girl's, or rather the woman's, hardened
> now by that insolent contempt, the fundamental hostility of a sex
> both slave and despot for thousands of years, the boy's pleading,
> imploring, horrified, both of them prematurely aged, withered.
> [p. 136]

After the peak of intensity reached in this second chapter of
Le Sacre du printemps, what follows seems weak. The
chapter that takes place in 1936, a little too mysterious, is
reminiscent of the sometimes laborious plot of *Gulliver* and, if
the second chapter, told in the first person, seems intended to
add a sense of duration to the events first told in the third person, this sense of duration, more covert, is one that leads to
resignation, not one that leads to catastrophe. It is also
resignation the stepfather preaches in the last chapter where
the plot somehow or other reaches a denouement. The lesson
in wisdom seems a bit vapid and ends with the advice to accept the uniform flow of monotonous time.

But in the second chapter of this novel, Claude Simon has
discovered something he will develop in the following novels, a
more effective literary style than interior monologue, which he
had nevertheless tried out with some success in the first
chapter—but without the ease and lack of constraint found in
the first chapter of *Le Tricheur*. He realized that it was not
necessary to write in the first person for the text to unfold
within a character. This is largely because he has succeeded in
regulating time, in slowing and accelerating it, thanks to temporal dislocations, but also thanks to certain "zoom shots" in
both space and time, enlarging or reducing the field of view,
while adjusting the focus at the same time. He will no longer
need to try to introduce the temporal dimension by tricks of
composition—even though repetitions, recurrences, and
dédoublements will remain dear to him—for he now knows
how to make time well up from the text itself.

PARIS

9

Histoire or the Serial Novel*
Gérard Roubichou

> Nothing in this world is of a piece, it is all mosaic.
> Balzac

The reading of Claude Simon's novels—particularly since *The Wind*—may have given the impression of a fragmented, parceled-out universe at whose center a mind, a consciousness, or even a memory whose mechanisms seems unorthodox, was attempting to gather together and order the pieces. The studies devoted to Claude Simon's works have frequently resorted to this dialectic of order and disorder, placed in a psychological perspective, as a point of critical departure.

However, at the same time, Claude Simon laid stress on the problems proper to the textual universe of his books, to the novelistic constraints of writing—in short, on the pre-eminence he feels the production of the work (the dynamic process of composition, of revelation in and through writing, etc.) takes over its actual content.

To be sure, the fact that at least until *Histoire* the orientation of his novelistic universe has always been open to ambivalent interpretation did not permit us to perceive readily what was in the process of changing in these books. Indeed, a "novelistic" reading (focused on the "story," character, etc.) is still possible, perhaps even wanted—and it is certainly not our intention to reduce Aunt Marie's death struggle, Georges's "adventures," de Reixach's death, or Corinne and the pages on Spain to learned nonrepresentational combina-

---

* Translated by Jane Carson.

tions of words. But it is true that even in the most "*roman-esque*" of Claude Simon's novels, those which fascinate us most, it is impossible to ignore the *process of writing* and ultimately its fundamental importance to the reading. The reader is at the same time involved in what has also been called "the adventure of writing." [1]

One might therefore ask if what has been taken for a dialectic of order and disorder interpreted from a psychological point of view is not more simply the expression of a scriptorial tension between "representational" and "textual": the search for order in writing over that of order in fiction.

Perhaps more than any of the preceding works, *Histoire* reveals the faceting of the universe and of the book, and contrasts, by its very form (even at a typographical level) with the textual density of *The Grass*, *The Flanders Road*, or *The Palace*. Here, all at once, the page is, if one may use the expression, decomposed and broken up into fragments (indented sections),[2] while the reader, more or less accustomed to Simon's long and compact sentences, discovers a splintered narrative: paragraphs follow each other without necessarily being connected and the reader is constantly tossed about from one time and place to another, in a vast spatiotemporal collage, which carries him from a "present" to a multilayered past, from one scene in the past to another, from Spain to Greece, etc. As a consequence, this unusual book invites us to reconsider our reading habits.

The purpose of this essay is on the one hand to define some major characteristics of this novel, and particulary its textual layout, on the other hand to situate *Histoire* in the evolution of Simon's work from the point of view mentioned above.

Histoire is composed of basic elements, which we will call *series*, whose identification can be made on several levels (thematic, spatial, temporal, etc.) which do not exclude one another. We have found three:
— a series belonging to the "present" (*A*)
— a series belonging to the "past" *(P)*
— a series of images/imaginings (*I*)
Each one, in turn, contains *subseries* (basic units) which

form particular scenes. Thus, in the series of the present, which corresponds to the day of a narrator, we have various stages, various moments of this day, which could be reconstructed through analysis (since these basic units are scattered throughout the text). The series of the past consists of family and childhood scenes as well as episodes from the narrator's past (Spain, Greece). Finally, in the last series, we find the postcards. This series is in fact a privileged one, inasmuch as these postcards, which belong to the past, are actually evoked in the "present" of the narrator's day.

We should also note that the division into series/subseries is far from being as clear-cut as the analysis might make it appear. There are overlappings, superimpositions, and constant shifts since the series tend to contaminate one another and become intertwined, "the forms overlapping, intersecting, approaching each other or separating" (p. 231).

Lastly, in this textual mosaic, we must likewise emphasize the existence of "blocks" or "sets" containing serial combinations which seem to be chapters of a sort. It is difficult to define their content with respect to the series. Indeed, except for block 9 (pp. 229-39), which centers exclusively on the photograph of the uncle at the Dutch painter's, all the blocks include a varying number of combinations of series/subseries following what we believe to be definite criteria, as will be explained later.

The generalized sectioning of *Histoire* (blocks/series/ subseries) demands therefore a particularly active reading: the reader must be on the watch for a continuity that the actual text refuses to maintain. It is this dialectic of continuous/discontinuous that is undoubtedly one of the first and most obvious of the major characteristics of this book.

The series are positioned right at the beginning of the book in a textual space which we have elsewhere called "introductory microcosm."[3] We refer to block 1 (pp. 1-26). There are indeed in this block a certain number of subseries: the family, the mother's illness, the boarding school, the postcards, the father's journeys, Spain, etc. The basic units are arranged in what appears to be random fashion, so that by the end of this first block (p. 26) it would scarcely be easy to establish a coherent "story"; all we have is a text which has been set in motion revealing its components and internal dynamics. Let us not forget that the series of the present is not utilized in this first block; it will usher in block 2 (p. 27); this problem will also demand our attention.

Another role of the "introductory microcosm" is to reveal the transition techniques between the series/subseries. For the visible discontinuity of the text seems to be undermined by strong connectors such as the "as if's" on pages 2-3, or the scene-changing comparisons:

> the furtive passage of a tongue glimpsed, grayish, gritty, and seemingly adhesive like those of certain insectivores, greedy, impassive and precise, snapping up flies and ants
> A kind of prehensile organ . . .(p. 5)

It is the process of transition (ramifications of textual elements) that is emblematically represented by the tree (the tree in front of the house and the genealogical tree) of which both the branches and the network of family relationships are described.

But the continual transitions we have just observed and pointed out contrast at the same time with sharp breaks between elements in the text, and particularly in the form of crude and visible disjunction of syntagmatic structures, such as:

> . . . holding the key to a world endowed with the prestige of the inaccessible an assembly not actually of mummies . . .(p. 5)

The book is thus built on this constant tension between the continuous and discontinuous, each in turn untiringly sought out and then rejected.

This also happens between blocks 1 and 2: the abrupt transition which further emphasizes the movement from one page to the next, marks the beginning of a series which will be presented, as distinct from all the others, in "chronological order," since, strictly speaking, it deals with the successive moments of a day. In this way the absence of the series of the present in block 1 actually indicates that the function of this block is to codify some of the production procedures, after which the book can "begin."[4] The series will then be combined around the present and in contact with it—or in opposition to it.

No series—except the series of the present—is given to us in the chronological order of the fiction's constituent parts. In other words, we may single out two types of serial occurrences:

Type 1 (series of the present):

$(A) = A_1, A_2, A_3, A_4, A_n$

(A subseries appearing in the narrative corresponds to a chronological sequence in the fiction.)

Type 2 (series of the past and images)

$(S) = S_2, S_n, S_5, S_3, S_1, S_4,$ etc.

(In the second case, the series is only given as isolated fragments and not included in a continuous chronological flow, which in any case the series of images does not imply.)

The series of the present (A) is fragmented because it is separated into instants generally marked off by adverbs (then, now), by adverbial phrases (after a moment, and then), other terms (thinking, imagining), etc. In the series of the past we are concerned as well with temporal sequences (moments) either from the same time period or from different times:

Spain: "reminded of that sign to be seen almost everywhere on the walls . . ."

The Twenties: "and again that allegorical figure which in the twenties decorated the Memel stamps . . ."

Image: "the name (Memel) suggesting the French word *mamelle* . . ."

Youth: "Trades and bargains . . ."

Present: "The posters in pastel colors the length of the school wall . . ."

Youth: "on the landing . . ." (pp. 178-80)

Thus we see that within three pages the continuity of our reading has taken us through extensive spatial and temporal layers, not always close to one another, although they are successive and juxtaposed. The text of *Histoire* thus appears to be a generalized mosaic—or rather, to use a more dynamic metaphor, a generalized combinatory structure.

Before studying a few aspects of this combinatory structure we might notice that the quasisystematic cutting up of each series is a technique that may be called the *postcard* technique. Indeed, each subseries functions as a spatiotemporal unit in the same manner as the postcards. One might almost say that a functional connection is established between these varied fragments, all of them proving in the end to be parts of a whole never quite within our grasp: on one side of the postcards, fragments of a life which cannot be reconstructed (that of the narrator's father, his mother), on the other, the memories, fragments of a life just as impossible to grasp (that of the narrator himself). But the imbrication of these two "sides" of the work is marked on the one hand by the sliding from one series to another, on the other by the fact that it is from the present—presented as a stable factor—that each set we have been speaking about here is formed. This technique, to be sure, is not without significance; it indicates not only that the mental world of experience, that the past and all human life are fragmentary and cannot be restored, but also that, in the particular case of this novel, the "parallel lives" of the narrator and his family cannot be reconstructed as a whole, that basically any total grasp of a story, or of History, is illusory[5]: we merely stick the pieces back together as best we can.

Moreover, to limit our remarks to interpretation of the novel, it must not be forgotten that the serial structure of the book also furthers, to a certain extent, the search for simultaneity in a linear context. It is at this point that we realize most clearly how much psychological material remains in *Histoire*. Indeed, we notice many times that the serial combinatory structure is *also* intended to disclose what is passing through the narrator's mind at the very moment when he evokes a scene from the present. This may happen in at least two ways:

a. either by a simple juxtaposition of subseries; on pp. 72-74, for example, the unfolding of the text may be laid out in the following manner (the arrow indicates the trajectory of reading):

| *Series of the present* | *Other series* |

". . . all the same ended by ⟶ the lights the chandeliers doing it (. . .) it ends by . . .

"don't fool around ⟵ ⟶ violent obscene
"I won't even tell you ⟷ so pretty leaning forward . . ."

The linear sequence ot the reading and the textual layout allow us to experience a sort of simultaneity, the "real" data (from the present) interfering with the evocation of other moments which lack any particular link with this present.

b. or by contamination or linking through common elements: we here refer the reader to block 6 (pp. 141-70), where it may be observed that the ties between the moments in the restaurant (series of the present) and the recollection of Spain are more closely noted: (p. 151) by passing, through the depiction of light, from the Spain subseries to the present, then (p. 153) by the shift brought about by the weather's clouding over, or, throughout this block as well, by the reminder of the hunchback (pp. 164-65), the flashes of light (glasses/ring, p. 166), etc.

A "psychological" interpretation—and *Histoire* does not totally exclude the possibility (for we are after all in the presence of what might be called a consciousness—a narrator who says, "I," in the presence of his past, a past which is close to him) might emphasize the fact that this flagrant discontinuity is well suited to a search for simultaneity in a linear context and, in this regard, pages 83-111 would appear to be a remarkable technical achievement (see also block 6).

However, we have reason to wonder if this would not limit the richness and complexity of the book while at the same time reducing the entire work to simple data. In the novel a signifi-

cant textual work—also felt in the dialectic of the continuous
and discontinuous—is indeed going on, a dynamic effort to
construct, which goes beyond the framework of association
and simultaneity.

The technique to which we are now referring involves a progressive extension of elements which, moving from one to
another as a result of common factors, lead to an expansion of
the narrative. This is naturally what happens in the introductory microcosm where, as we pointed out, the delineation of
the tree branches has a special significance: the *ramification*
of the narrative takes place either by *association/juxtaposition*
(Baroness Cerise/cerise jacket, for example), or by *transfer-
ral/superimposition* (spots of blood/His blood), according to
the two poles defined by Jakobson (metonymic/metaphoric).

The transition from one subseries to another is also linked
to features of writing: these are "scriptorial" ties which in
many cases, as in the specific context of the novel, may pass
for psychological features.

Although the psychological may be introduced as a
justification for some serial transitions, it seems in any case
difficult to accept it in the case of the "blocks." It is difficult
to imagine a typographical parceling of this sort (for even if we
admit that these are not really "chapters," the break is
distinct), which could be explained exclusively as a
psychological device, since apparently no unity of a
psychological nature can be found in each block. In addition,
one notices, beginning with block 2, that no explanation at the
fictional level is satisfying: each block does not correspond to
any particular division of the day either. For example, several
blocks may cover the same spatiotemporal sequence (pp.
112-40; 141-70; 171-87); these deal with the restaurant between noon and 2:00 P.M. Block 2, on the other hand (pp.
27-52), involves several different places. Elsewhere, the
description of the other people at table (block 5, p. 129) does
not create a break, although this very reference does cause a
break at the beginning of block 6 (p. 141). In the same way
the narrator's going in to see the banker (block 4, p. 80) also
creates a major typographical break (block), although, when

he finds himself outdoors again, there is only a minor one (moving from one subseries to another).

One might, of course, find the divisions arbitrary—this possibility cannot be dismissed entirely, at least until *Conducting Bodies*. But we must go beyond this. In fact, one can say that each block constitutes a sort of "nucleus" of proliferation around a specific generating element, and that the material unity of the block (its length)[6] and its serial combinatory structure should be related to features of textual "coherence."

We have chosen to discuss—in a manner that necessarily remains very superficial—blocks 5, 6, 7 (that is, pp. 112-37).

We have on the one hand, in the context of the fiction (series of the present), a spatial unity (the restaurant) and on the other a relative length of time (noon to two o'clock). How can we explain:

—the division into three blocks of this seemingly compact whole;

—the multiplicity and the concentration of the different series around certain poles of attraction?

We observe that block 5 (pp. 112-40) is formed by a proliferating movement around religious data (Lambert's sacrileges, Corinne's communion, music) and privileged places (the school refectory). It is from this angle that Spain will be introduced (water colors of Barcelona) and then little by little will take over the text; the transition takes place with the words:

> How did you say it was?: you took your meal in that palatial hotel dining room, sitting on Louis XVI chairs hitherto accustomed to the buttocks of Anglo-Saxon or South American millionaires male and fema . . .
>
> And I: No: benches. The chairs . . . (p. 121)

On the other hand, most of the following block (6) is concerned with Spain, thereby becoming proof of its invasion of the text, while little by little other elements take their places (among them de Reixach, who finds himself enriched by the Spanish story, pp. 160-61). These new elements will in turn trigger others—the man with the sandwich, the hunchback, the banknote—to be developed in block 7, which will be more particularly oriented toward "pictorial representation" (statue, poster, stamp, banknote). We ascertain, then, that each block contains two leading functional elements:

—a major serial combination,

—a minor serial combination which is in fact the primer or the generator of the major combination in the following block.

In its proliferation the text thus lays out its own germinating elements, while at the same time amplifying the preceding ones. A more detailed study would be necessary to bring out these features more clearly. Here and now—while conceding a margin of error—we can define two characteristics of the serial combinations:

—some operate on the model of idea associations and imitate, in a way, a mental process (the psychological aspect of *Histoire*);

—the others operate on the basis of more scriptorial phenomena, in the sense that their combination is not necessarily justified by a referent. It is the act of writing (lining up words, metaphorical shifts, etc.) which is essential here.

The "newness" of *Histoire* originates above all from the fact that here the Simonian novel appears more completely than in the past as a site for textual production at every level. The serial form of the novel foreshadows, in its typographical (indented sections, blocks, etc.) and fictional (series of differing time periods) "clarity," the sequences of *Conducting Bodies* and *Triptych*, as well as the textual combinatory as has been noted. But the later novels will play on a combinatory in a generalized present as well as on a more strictly scriptorial link between series. *Histoire* still demonstrates the effects of an inheritance or tradition proper to Simon's novels: that is, the dialectic at work between the textual and the representative since *The Wind*.

However, *Histoire* takes Simon a step forward, although the work still must be emptied of its psychological content: it is up to *The Battle of Pharsalus* to constitute the last stage in this evolution, since the serial form with psychological tendencies, used once again in the first part, is then more or less erased to give way to the serial form with a scriptorial base in the third part (provocatively entitled "Chronology of Events"). *Histoire* thus makes possible the work to come.

FRENCH CULTURAL SERVICES, NEW YORK

Notes

1. Jean Ricardou, "La Littérature comme critique," in *Pour une théorie du nouveau roman* (Paris: Seuil, 1971), p. 32.

2. See our article "Continu et discontinu ou l'hérétique alinéa (Notes sur la lecture d'*Histoire*)" in the special issue on Claude Simon in *Etudes Littéraires* 9, no. 1 (April 1976): 125-36.

3. See Gérard Roubichou, *Lecture de L'Herbe de Claude Simon* (Lausanne: L'Age d'Homme, 1976), in particular pp. 294-95.

4. Recall that page 27 (beginning of block 2) starts with "Beginning . . . ," which, as it follows the departure of the father at the end of the introductory microcosm (p. 26), indicates both the beginning of the narrative (or writing) and of the events (or fiction), in short, the beginning of the double adventure—of writing and fiction.

5. See especially pages 85-86, where the parenthesis on historic events is simply a "long succession of images" placed one after another without forming an ordered whole, as we can see from the repetition of the word "and." Furthermore, at the end of this passage, by bringing together the basic units of writing, the relationship to be established is made sufficiently clear. It is further illustrated by the excerpts from Latin texts or from the book on the Russian revolution found throughout *Histoire*.

6. We have observed for instance that the determining factor is not a certain number of pages or of combinations of series.

10

The Generative Function of Translation in the Novels of Claude Simon

J. A. E. Loubère

Customarily, translation is considered as an attempt to effect an exchange with the minimum of robbery. The object of the exchange is to convey something "contained" by a language construct, with all its values of "signification," "syntax," and "rhetoric," from one system of communication to another. What is jettisoned in the process is, as Jacques Derrida points out, the actual "body" or physical being of the word. "The body of a word cannot be translated or transported into another language. It is the very thing that translation leaves out."[1]

Along with this body many other things may be lost: the links of sound with sense, the contributions of rhythm, the entire web of cultural association clinging to the language, and the imponderable action of words one upon another. Conscientious translators know only too well the anguish that can be occasioned by the desperate effort to cut losses to a minimum. To compensate they must endow the residue that is left after removal of the body—"l'esprit de la lettre"—with a new set of sounds and rhythms, inserted into a different network of connotations and reflections, subject to pressures and illuminations unknown in its previous incarnation. Occasionally, instead of being diminished, the spirit benefits from its reintroduction into a new physical form. Fortunate are those, such as Poe, who find a Baudelaire to reshape them. Such enrichment breeds suspicion, however. Do we really

have the "same" text? The feeling often is that we do not; that
what we have is an independent production, sometimes owing only its initial impetus to the "original." (An example
would be Fitzgerald's *Omar Khayyam*).

Such problems are well known. Less common is the device
of introducing the problems themselves into a text as
stimulators, not of discussion and contention, but of a narrative and the fictions it may embody. Readings of Claude
Simon's novels reveal considerable use of the foreign and
translated word and suggest that this particular technique, in
both its negative and positive aspects, plays an important role
in Simon's writing. As his text exposes the special nature of
these problems, it also demonstrates the fertility of various
solutions and uncovers further evidence concerning the
writer's approach to rhetoric and his relationship with
language.

Simon introduces into his work a number of other
languages besides French. In *The Flanders Road* there is a
curious translation from Italian. *The Palace*, *Histoire* and
Conducting Bodies contain a variety of Spanish phrases and
short texts, *Histoire* and *The Battle of Pharsalus* borrow from
Latin, and English appears in both *Histoire* and *Conducting
Bodies*. These various borrowings are used in the following
manner: (a) words and expressions are inserted into the text as
such and not translated into French; (b) texts from foreign
sources are presented in the French without the originals; (c)
texts are provided in both foreign and French versions.[2]

It is useful, before examining the role of longer pieces of
translation in Simon's work, to look briefly at the use made of
foreign words and phrases in the French text. They play a
very obvious primary part: that of communicating to the text
a flavor, generally exotic, implying *dépaysement*, distance,
difference from commonly known reality. The Spanish words
in newspapers, banners, posters, over storefronts, etc., in *The
Palace*, and on the postcards in *Histoire*, are affective rather
than informative. They provide a mood, a sense of
strangeness and incomprehension, a search for meaning that
is denied. Even if we do not understand the signification of

"VENCEREMOS" on the torn poster in *The Palace*, its tat-tered condition conveys the emotion that denies its sense. Even if we cannot read the postcards that the narrator's mother received from her Spanish friends, in *Histoire*, they tell us of some inclination in her toward the exotic and the violently alien, a taste for Spanish dress, bullfights and blood, and a dark, demanding religion, all confirmed by other elements in the novel. The postcards and the newspapers are signs from the outer world, intimating "other," "elsewhere," and a foreign code to be deciphered.

There are more complex implications than these in the ap-pearance of untranslated foreign words in Simon's text. Often in capitals, or detached from the regular print, they stand out, even more so if their script is not the Western one to which we are accustomed. Even within one system of writing a foreign word, particularly if emphasized by a change of type, italic or capitals for example, can appear as a physical obstacle to our immediate consumption of the text. Briefly, the word is of-fered in its "body," which we are forced to appreciate visually and also to try on our palates, to savor orally, as it were, before we are allowed to pass onward. As an object with form and flavor it draws attention to its real existence on the page, the more so if the script used is not our own. The Cyrillic Greek characters in *The Battle of Pharsalus* act like ideograms in their plastic suggestion, illuminating and sug-gesting in significant shapes themes embedded in the text —the erotic forms of the Greek Ψ and Δ, for example.

We may imagine that the untranslated word framed in the text signals a need and an absence in the writer's language, a gap that has to be filled at a given moment by a foreign body. If so, the need is not to be attributed to a failure in the writer's productive ability. It is the very richness of the bor-rowed term, not in the sense of any intrinsic "meaning," but in its wealth of suggestion, association, and potential forms of transcription that make it valuable in the particular spot assigned to it. The transparency of the text being momentarily obscured by the foreign obstacle that prevents the reader from making the habitual careless passage from sight to presumed

sense, we are forced into a realization of the loss generally in-
curred through heedless reading. The pause, therefore, draws
insistent attention to the work performed by a word, any
word, in constituting the text. If we assume that the writer is
not using such words through incompetence or snobbism, we
judge that he intends us to see what he has written in a special
manner. We dwell on the words, syllable by syllable, suspecting that, like the phrases read upside-down with difficulty in
Conducting Bodies, they carry some hidden message. "Since
the decipherment of the upside-down letters . . . requires more
time than a normal reading of them, it seems to confer on the
words spelled syllable by syllable that weighty significance
and odd solemnity of messages with a hidden meaning that
such words take on when laboriously read out by children or
near-illiterates" (p. 133). The words present a surface which
reflects back our thoughts and interpretations, as well as our
ignorance, misconceptions, and *idées fixes*. In them we see
ourselves briefly in relationship with language. The writer's
need must be to force this pause upon us long enough to make
us consider what our hesitation over the text may imply.

Distance, materiality, surface reflection: these contributions of the untranslated foreign term may throw some light
on the significance of the longer passages borrowed from
idioms other than French. Let us look at the short passage
translated from the Italian in *The Flanders Road*. The
page,"apparently transcribed from the Italian judging by the
translation of the words in the margin" (p. 55), found by the
narrator in a trunkful of old papers, is reproduced with old-
fashioned type and spelling, the illogical use of capitals, and a
final fading away in the last sentence from French into
Italian. Its subject matter is the description of an engraving of
a "femme-Centaure" holding a lyre and one of a pair of cymbals, the other being held by the young man who accompanies
her, in such a way that his arm slipped under her shoulder is
in a position to sound the instrument.

This short text offers a considerable amount of thematic
material, particularly centered around the techniques of
repetition, doubling, and ambiguity. The narrator-narrated of

the novel, Georges, is obsessed by Corinne, a woman he qualifies as a"woman-chestnut" whose lover he believes is her husband's jockey. Georges, who is sometimes "he" and sometimes "I," is also doubled by a partner in argument Blum. Further instances of doubling occur throughout the novel. The old-fashioned printing of the translated text, supposedly copied by an ancestor, recalls another predecessor whose violent death (suicide?) is paralleled by that of Corinne's husband, Georges's cousin and commander, de Reixach, in a World War II battle. The presumed unfaithfulness of his wife is repeated in the tale of the errant peasant's wife; and the dominant "horse" motif runs through the entire work. If we interpret the presence of the cymbals not only as a "symbol" of the doubling of themes, but also of clash and opposition (confirmed by the word *controversia* isolated and set by the side of the text), we may also find a link to the theme of war and clash of arms, the background of the novel.

Metaphorically, the fragment is interesting. Already prefiguring the beauty and the animal nature of Corinne, her connection with the jockey who "plays" her game and wears her colors, the passage goes much further in suggesting the nature not only of the material in the book, but also of its writing. Especially stressed are the skill and delicacy with which boundaries between one species and another are both suggested and disguised: "all deserves to be considered with an especial attention the node and juncture where the human part ends and the equine part begins is indeed admirable . . . one is then confused in attempting to determine the confines" (p. 56). In the same way, the limbs of the two figures are confused, the left hand of the young man "emerges from under [the] shoulder" of the woman centaur, forming apparently one instrument player. If we apply the metaphor of the subtle mingling of species and kinds to the novel itself, we see it first in the fragment where the French slides off in midsentence into Italian, via the word "*attenenza*," relationship, connection, further emphasized by the preceding words "bracelets" and "Colier," whose circular sense reflects the circling motifs and trefoil structure of *The Flanders Road*. In addition, the final reference in Italian is to Bacchus, whose animal connections are well known, and to Venus, whose power is omnipresent, and whose function certainly is to join. The little translation offers, then, a number of figures for the writing of the novel: not only the circular linkage, and the straddling or *chevauche-ment* of one part of the fiction by another, but also the *fondu* or shading off of elements one into another, so that, for example, the boundaries of time and space become more and more difficult to define, as in the gradual fusion of de Reixach's story with that of the ancestor.

Doubled also is the polysemic nature of language, when a text appears in two versions. In this fragment, the difficulties of accurate translation are suggested by the list of seven Italian words with their French equivalents printed by the side of the text; and also by the presence in the text itself of words crossed out and corrected. Several of these words have more than one possible translation, and the last two—*otremodo*, translated as "otherwise"[2] and *controversia*, "dispute"—do not appear to refer to anything in the French version, although they suggest further development, an "other" text, and the controversy at the heart of the text. *Controversia*, meaning in Latin "shock" or "clash," not only evokes the war, but by extension can easily suggest another "version" deriving from *contra* and *vertere*, "to turn against," or "*verser contre*," which can also mean "give in exchange for." Both clash and exchange are persistently present in *The Flanders Road* on all levels, thematic, metaphoric, linguistic.

This short passage at the outset of the novel, which could be taken for a piece of exotic memorabilia, is in fact an allegory of what is coming in the writing of the book, and its status as translation is no small part of that allegory. Similar comments might be made of the excerpts from Latin in *Histoire* and *The Battle of Pharsalus*. In the first book these fall into three categories: the distorted translation of the Mass, supposedly made by the narrator's boyhood companion, Lambert; the erotic extracts from Apuleius; the texts from Latin historians reluctantly translated by the narrator as a boy under the tutorial eye of his Uncle Charles. Each has a thematic relationship with the novel. The narrator's own attitude toward translation varies considerably with those themes. His

recollections of stumbling and unwilling efforts at rendering
history from Latin to French are sandwiched between
memories of death, revolution and disaster (*Histoire*, pp.
97-107), thoughts of his dead mother, his estranged wife, the
dead civilization of Greece, the Russian Revolution and its
massacres, the disastrous Spanish Civil War. "Massacre . . .
accumulation of the dying heaped up bloodless greyish in the
greyish twilight" (p. 97). Ironically, the brief Latin text
speaks twice of the *studio*, the ardor and enthusiasm with
which the soldiers fight (p. 97) and with which the commander claims he sought for peace before expediting his
troops into the fight (p. 106). Studious the student is not.
"Have you ever bothered to look it up in the dictionary?" (p.
106), asks Uncle Charles (p. 128). The student has indeed used
the dictionary, but not to look for words of destruction and
death; his ardent desire is to discover the living meanings in
the forbidden text, Apuleius's *Golden Ass*, and "with fiery
cheeks" (p. 108) he feverishly hunts down "the words like
those cups, those combs, those pins, those bracelets of bronze
or copper discolored, verdigrised, corroded slightly but with
precise, chiseled contours" (pp. 88-89). (What more solid
description of the material presence of the word!) The ancient
words are petrified forever in dictionaries, but they release a
stream of erotic imagery in the adolescent mind. Bearing the
everlasting themes of love and death, the classic language
stands physically on the page like the monuments in Greece,
crumbling little by little, a reminder of permanence and
decay, the permanence of desire, the inevitability of death,
and the sad spendor of man's attempts to communicate these
things in a lasting way through stone or language. Only the
dictionary with its "dusty insipid odor" (p. 108) preserves the
ambiguous life of a dying tongue, keeping it from becoming
absolutely illegible, victim of the "finger that cannot read
following the meaningless lines apotheosis and millenium
without end" (p. 99).

The physical presence of the Latin words, stirring the
physical reaction of the adolescent boys has a parodic twist in
the translation of the Mass in the early pages of the book.
Reminiscent of the first chapter of Joyce's *Ulysses*, the ir-

reverent "Arsenal of puns and spoonerisms supposed to free him by the magic of the Word from maternal superstitions and the lessons of the Catechism" (p. 31), reinforces the connection between the Latin and the eroticism of the novel, and at the same time points to the fragility of the link between sense and sound in the most solemn circumstances. A word is never sacred, says the pun, it can be subverted by the tripping tongue, and once we have ceased to give it credence, it can only reveal our preoccupation with ourselves. The word-monument, therefore, is not only destructible by time and ignorance, it is subject to humiliation and ridicule as soon as we lose faith in it. Yet, as the sexual nature of the puns emphasizes, the passage from the august Latin to the vulgar French is also a passage from a dead spiritual state to a vigorous, if crude, physical one, in which, through the inventiveness of procreation, the word becomes flesh and recreates the word.

The numerous passages from John Reed's *Ten Days That Shook the World* which also appear in *Histoire* do not fit so easily into the pattern of physical and metaphorical relationship with the text, although thematically they reinforce the references to revolution and struggle. English is not an ancient language and in this case, read in translation, it does not prompt reinvention in the French version. It is sufficient that this version contains the appropriate images, in a foreign setting (Russia during the revolution): death, war, women, conventional strife scenes, right versus wrong, the people versus the foreigners ("junkers"), and is embellished with exotic terms that emphasize its distance—"izvozchiks," "red guards," "Winter Palace," "Commissar for War," "comrade soldiers," etc. The only words given in the English tongue are Carlyle's "apotheosis and millenium without end" (p. 99), spoken of another revolution, and a bitterly ironic comment here on Reed's explosive, descriptive style, contrasting with the dusty memories of war in the narrator's mind. A strange tongue indeed. The sense of strangeness lies less, however, in the foreign expression than in the distance between the words themselves and all that they connote. The massacring warriors have eyes "innocent and clear like the eyes of children"; the

Commissar proclaims, "I have no need to tell you that I am a soldier I have no need to tell you that I want peace (p. 105), and his declaration is immediately doubled by that of the Roman general about to dispatch his troops into war: "He reminded them . . . that he could call his soldiers to witness . . . with what ardor . . . he had sought peace."

With its heroic *boursouflure* the Reed text in *Histoire* has the role of foil to the dreary truths of war and deflated idealism as the narrator remembers them. It contrasts the petty pretensions of Lambert and the disappointed heroisms of the narrator with the vast Russian experiment, and the "translation" is a staggering one, from the language of insignificant personal desires, to that of social upheaval. Yet the results may be the same. The words that attempt to cover that distance are filled with nothing but empty resonance. It is no accident that "apotheosis and millenium without end," in English, is preceded by "a finger that cannot read" (p. 99), searching blindly among the Greek ruins where the illiterate shepherds of Arcadia keep their flocks; nor that the same words are followed by these others: "the dead in heaps and the last crackling of the fires and here and there the last absurd incoherent detonations" (p. 99). Time, revolution, war, and the absurd, unreasonable expectations of men lead to no millenium but the final alienation of language.

In *The Battle of Pharsalus* we meet Plutarch, Lucan, and Caesar again, as well as Apuleius, sometimes but not always in the Latin text. The narrator remarks that if he is in Greece, searching for the site of the Battle of Pharsalus, "it's because of that assignment," (p. 18) in "Latin dead language" (p. 9), hammered out long ago with Uncle Charles. Since he had been such a *"cancre"* he had been unable to master the words satisfactorily and Charles had predicted that he would be unable to serve his future needs by anything but gestures and signs (p. 10). Charles admits, however, that "knowing everything never leads to anything but learning something more and words lead to other words," hence precision cannot be hoped for, and language can only have a practical purpose, such as obtaining shirts, pants, and jackets (pp. 9-10). Charles demands precision and rebukes his delinquent pupil, but diligent examination of the texts concerning Pharsalus only leads to impressions of action, fleeting figures of warriors and horses and a host of conflicting theories (p. 26). Even if exact measurements and locations had been given, they would in no way help to recreate the precise historical experience of the men and animals involved, now gone forever.[4]

However, Charles's conclusion that words lead only to other words, and can convey only abstract, worn-out ideas ("Work," "Duty") or practical orders ("You must at least be able to articulate more or less intelligibly the word shirt and the word trousers or else resign yourself to making your needs known by sign language [p. 10]), does not indicate for the narrator an abandonment of language. On the contrary, his course becomes clear. In the second and third parts of the novel he allows his *lexique* to proliferate in all directions, demonstrating his certainty that words producing other words, words set free from bondage to fact or utility, are in fact the writer's business. Now the unsuccessful translation becomes the prime mover of the text, setting in motion a whole process tending not toward precision and clarification, but toward a multiple interplay of images and themes. In *Histoire* the translations are linked with attempts to reconstitute the past. Released from the necessity of accuracy and precise historical sense, Plutarch and Apuleius can freely stimulate production of the text. The *impeditis ripis* which the student awkwardly translates as "obstacled shores" (p. 32), between one language and the other have been removed. "A cause de cette version" the principle of *sub*version is installed, the translation is no longer narrowly situated within the limits of meaning and historic reference, nor even within the specific bounds of the work in which it appears. Humor is one method of release, the (unconscious?) humor of the bad student who translates the Latin word for the wing of an army, *cornu*, as "horn," a word loaded with reference to the sexual misfortunes of the narrator-Charles. The teacher too slips into comic mistranslation: *quidam*, carrying the vagueness of the indefinite article in Latin, and predicting the gradual dissolution of the personality and the protagonist in *Pharsalus*, jokingly refers back to *The Flanders Road* as Charles says, "If

your teacher asks you to translate word for word you'll do fine
you'll tell him that the *quidam* fell into the river with the
obstacled shores it was probably a jockey don't you think?"
(p. 33).[5]

The *"mot à mot"* ("word for word") is indeed the principle
of writing for Simon but in a sense quite opposed to the traditional rendering of an established text. Here the word is
discharged into the lexicon with a force that explodes previous
notions of equivalence and value in semantic exchange. Not
that words are no longer considered as representing experience and reality, they are their own experience.
Meditating on the gap between his own apprehension of
meaning in that Latin text and the reality of war which he
tries in vain to grasp, the narrator says, "It was nothing but
words, images in books, *I didn't yet know, I didn't know,*" as
he goes on to attempt to describe what happened to him in the
rush of defeat, repeating, *"I didn't know . . . I don't know,"*
then *"I don't know how either,"* and finally, *"I don't know
any more"* (p. 54). Words cannot be exchanged for reality,
but they can fan out and communicate movement to the text,
like a battle command: "the movement coming closer and
closer as the order ran along the battle line so that it happened
like a fan opening then closing" (p. 57).

Exchange of words for exact counterparts can, if ritualized,
become an empty service to the dead. Between two long
passages from the Latin (pp. 161-62, 163) stands a paragraph
in which the anonymous O., replacing the Charles of
Histoire, is distributing pay (exchange for work), consisting of
bundles of paper money and coins, to the waiting workmen.
Into the paper money is woven the head of Julius Caesar and
a Roman soldier. In the fading light, soon replaced by artificial illumination, the workmen, who at first give off "a
strong smell of sweat and exhaustion," become "grayish
ghosts" and, unexpectedly, O. places the money in their
mouths, like tribute for the dead, "After which each ghost
leaves the office and O. makes an x opposite a name on a list"
(pp. 162-63). Instead of money for ghosts, exchange should
produce usable bodies, like the numerous coins and bank
notes in foreign currency which appear throughout the text.

An interesting counterproof of the *mot à mot* is to be found in *Conducting Bodies*. Here a text in a foreign language is offered, followed immediately by its exact translation into French. The listener-spectator at a congress of leftist writers is accompanied by an interpreter who faithfully renders the original Spanish into a version with no apparent deviation from the message: "Creo que el novelista contemporáneo (I believe that today's novelist, the interpreter says) es consciente a la vez (is simultaneously aware) de estas dos cosas (of the two following things): en primer lugar (firstly), la necesidad de expresar (the need to express) . . . de representar en la ficciones (of representing in works of fiction) su propio ser (his own nature), su propia realidad (his own reality), sus propios tormentos (his own anguish), sus propios demonios y (his own demons and) al mismo tiempo (at the same time) . . . (p. 41).

The listener explains that he can himself understand the gist of the speech, although with a small delay. Actually the texts are so alike, the vocabulary and syntax almost identical, that the efforts of the translator are unnecessary to the French reader. Although the writers' congress reflects important themes in the novel—the conquest and exploration of a new world, the overcoming of the inhabitants, the bringing of the Word (Spanish, religious, political), and metaphorically, the major motif of unending journeying and nonarrival—the verbal message it conveys is, by the time it reaches its destination, doubly useless. It is nevertheless repeated over and over again by the delegates, in an atmosphere of smoke and boredom, as if in a void. "The monotonous flow of voices speaking in a foreign language, . . . the return at regular intervals of the same words, groups of words, or their synonyms . . . further accentuate this sensation of being outside of time" (p. 149). In reality, the apparent precision of the translation betrays the weakness of the message: it is exact because there is nothing to translate. We are dealing with *signifiants* that have become almost entirely empty molds from which meaning has fled, whose relationship with other elements of language has become so slack as to be almost ineffective. That is why the delegation argues all night about formulas, but can come to no conclusion; each delegate pours into the mold his own personal meaning. "It would seem, however, that the speech deals mainly with considerations or declarations having a certain social and political import, in which nouns with a rather timeworn air about them, not unlike the faded colors of the posters, such as Liberty, Revolution, Solidarity, or Unity, reappear frequently" (p. 25). Like the "Work" and "Duty" of Uncle Charles, the words used ("Virtue," "Law," "Justice," "Labor" [p. 41]), have little by little been deprived of their content. If the translation is almost word for word exact, it is because zero equals zero, because each word carries with it a weaker and weaker conducting charge. The empty rhetoric demonstrates most tellingly that life and language are elsewhere. The writer, as distinct from the mechanical translator, profits from the *trop-plein* of meanings, from the burgeoning of images between the word and its "equivalent," from the gap or pause that generates. That such a comparison is erotic is no accident: it is implied in Simon's use of language, as Jean Ricardou points out in his study of *The Flanders Road*, which he does not hesitate to call "La Route des flancs."[6]

The translated text seems, then, to have particular generative functions in Simon's work that distinguish it from other "borrowed" words and passages, although Simon insists that as stimulators of the text all borrowings are of equal strength.[7] The introduction of a foreign code is an instant reminder of the existence of a number of codes, of the "elsewhere" and the "other," of the differentiation that is the basis of communication. Through the inclusion of a foreign text in the French we have a word for word demonstration of how the writer operates with words, and how the words operate on us. Besides serving as memory links with other selves and lives, they stir up connected groups of images and thoughts that release us in time and space. Behind the obvious utilization of the associative properties of language, there is unsettling comment: our notions of "meaning," "representation," and "exchange" are challenged. Dissociated from its body, says the translation, what is left of a word? Can there be anything there but stimulus toward another word? Why is one word "right," another "wrong"? Can we pour anything into the molds they offer except versions of our own experience, inducting them into an alien system? Is there any his-story but our own?

Most important is the desacralization of the original text, which is no longer immutable and inviolable if only because it can be rendered into another form. Routinely, the fact that a translation is in another language masks the importance of this transfer, but Simon's use of humor, error and satire brings it out into the open. The body has been violated. The original becomes only another text among many, and can become a number of other texts, none of which can lay claim to being close to the primary experience. We begin to suspect from this that the so-called original text is in its turn a transcript of something else which already "translates" or renders other texts and experiences. So the seeker after a definitive version discovers "nothing more than a few words a few signs without material consistency as though drawn on the air assembled preserved recopied traversing the colorless layers of time of centuries at a terrible speed rising from the depths and exploding on the surface like empty bubbles and nothing more Clear for those who do not try to verify it" (*The Battle of Pharsalus*, p. 61). However solid and admirable the word may seem to its user, it is no more durable than the monuments of Greece and Rome and must, eventually, resolve itself into what it is, evanescent shapes and thin air. Just as we recognize the present efficiency of the text upon the page, so we must acknowledge its perpetual tendency to decompose and become other than itself.

The function of the translated passage in Simon's work is above all a demonstrative one, allowing the writing to reflect on itself and to show us that reflection. A *version* is both a mirror and a *mise en abyme*: the "exact" translation mirrors itself in another system, producing the illusion of its own double; but the *mise en abyme* reproduces with distortion, including within itself that in which it is contained, leaving between the image it shows us and what it is an enigmatic space, a deceptive depth that questions the beholder. So the translated texts in Simon serve to show the text that contains them, and to cast its and their reflection upon one another in an increasing complexity of images, providing us with one more opportunity to see the activity of writing face to face with itself. The simple exchange value habitually associated with translation is thus enriched by a use value that far exceeds the supposed semantic content of the passages in question, and, far from being robbed in the process, we are made aware of receiving much more than we bargained for. In any catalogue of the procedures used by Simon to emphasize autoreflection in his work, to convert the text into active currency and the reader into its agent, the *version* must be included as one of the most wide-ranging, the least confined by the boundaries and obstacles of language.[8]

BUFFALO, N.Y.

Notes

1. *L'Ecriture et la différence* (Paris: Seuil, Collection "Tel Quel," 1967), p. 312. "Un corps verbal ne se laisse pas traduire ou transporter dans une autre langue. Il est cela même que la traduction laisse tomber." My translation.

2. All quotations are from the English translations by Richard Howard (New York: Braziller): *The Flanders Road*, 1961; *The Palace*, 1963; *Histoire*, 1967; *The Battle of Pharsalus*, 1971; and *Conducting Bodies*, translated by Helen R. Lane (New York Viking, 1974).

3. "*Otremodo*" is not a modern Italian word. Its nearest equivalent, "*oltremodo*," does not mean "otherwise" but "excessively."

4. It is entertaining to note that, in connection with Pharsalus, at least one commentator, Michel Rambaud, qualifies Caesar as a "*guide menteur*" and notes that "*le Bellum Civile* ne contient pas le nom de Pharsale." See "Le Soleil de Pharsale," in *Historia* 3 (1955): 346 and 350.

5. "La Fiction mot à mot" in *Nouveau roman: hier, aujourd'hui* II (Paris: U.G.E., Collection "10/18," 1972), pp. 73-97.

6. "Un ordre dans la débâcle," postface to *La Route des Flandres* in the Collection "10/18," 1963, specifically p. 293 and note, p. 301.

7. *Nouveau roman: hier, aujourd'hui* II, p. 113. All borrowed texts, says Simon, have "simplement une fonction de résonance." However, in the case of translation. the "resonator" is, as it were, made visible on the page.

8. This discussion may raise the interesting side-question of the translation of Simon's novels into other languages. The American translator, Richard Howard,

speaks of *"soumission"* to the text (see "Un mot d'un traducteur américain de Claude Simon," in *Entretiens: Claude Simon* (1972), pp. 163-66, but J. Ricardou observes: "On the contrary, we can imagine that, starting with the productive processes of any given book, the so-called translator will intervene as a producer, using the same mechanisms in another language. Modern literature requires its readers to be producers, and it requires the same thing of its translators." (*Nouveau roman: hier, aujourd'hui* II, p. 151) My translation.

11
Pictures for Writing:
Premises for a Graphopictology*
Claud DuVerlie

> Si je voulais décrire la structure aujourd'hui de
> toute expérience picturale, il me faudrait naturelle-
> ment préciser comment l'oeuvre d'art"elle-même"
> est le noyau . . . d'un ensemble de reproduction
> plus ou moins fidèle . . . et comment le halo verbal
> s'enracine d'abord à l'original, mais peut se
> multiplier, se diversifier autour des différentes
> reproductions.
>
> Michel Butor, *Les Mots dans la peinture*

Some time ago, I examined and compared briefly *Orion
aveugle* and *Conducting Bodies*, identifying the variants in
the reading of these two books and capitalizing on the rich interplay of pictures and text and the very original visual-textual
reading initiated by *Orion aveugle*.[1] I propose to develop more
fully here the problematics of the plastic referent and literary
discourse within the fictional text. Thus, my remarks will be
more directly concerned with *Conducting Bodies*.

It is necessary first to recall a few basic features about the
production of these two closely related works. Except for
minor modifications, the first eighty–six pages of *Conducting
Bodies* are the whole text of *Orion aveugle*: the main change
has been the addition of 140 pages to produce a new book.

---

* With appreciation to the N. E. H. Translated by Elizabeth Bails.

The lavishly illustrated text of *Orion aveugle* is the other main distinction between the two works. Simon indicated that *Orion aveugle* was a *bricolage* from a few paintings he likes and, in fact, there are various reproductions of paintings, etchings, maps, and photographs. A major part of the text appears composed of descriptions of these works of art or objects which are incorporated in the narration. *Orion aveugle* brings to the fore the frequently direct and close interrelations of the visual image and its description, since generally the latter finds a "guarantee" or at least a pendant in the illustration on the opposite or following page.

Since *The Wind* (1957), Simonian art is characterized by its descriptions, modeled apparently on paintings, photographs, etc., but more often mentally organized in painting or photographic forms. From that time on, Simonian descriptions have seemingly proposed a pictorial referent. Except for rare instances, however, the referent remained unknown to the reader. It belonged to the private world of the writer or, supposing it was a painting, it became concealed or masked by the text, or it would simply be invented. It would appear that the referent was kept at a deliberate distance so that the principal effect was to endow the narrative with (only) a certain degree of iconicity. Yet in recent works this procedure has been systematized and nearly inverted: now the movement is less that of directing a description toward the effort of literary image, or delivering the description to iconicity, than that of generating it somewhat more exclusively—and showily at times—from real art works and objects drawn from our common heritage and the everyday world. Attention has thus been shifted from the receiving end of the line to the point of its generation, and the reader, especially if he finds the provocation irresistible, will refer to the "origin" of Simon's texts.

Any study of the latest productions of Simon must be made through the following chain: pictorial referent—textuality—iconicity. This sets the text within a problematics to which we shall tentatively ascribe the neologism "graphopictology." Called for by this novel procedure extending beyond Simon's practice to new novelists in particular,[2] the term "graphopictology" allows multi-level and convergent readings. First, through its Latin construct, *graphopictus*, and its modern form, "graphopicty," it suggests an obvious inversion of "pictography." It implies a process which involves the (alphabetic) writing of pictures. It is only reminiscent of pictography, or the use of drawings as writing, in that it inverses this prewriting system: it does not translate thoughts or messages into drawings but uses pictures[3] to convert them into text and typography. In its first two components, *graphopictus*, which literally means "I write the painted" or that which is already represented, draws the attention to the *conversion* of a visual image into alphabetic writing, the change of one semiotic system into another, and to its status of metawriting. As a whole, graphopictology intends to be the systematization of the principles and rules of this conversion, i.e., a theorization of its various aspects so ultimately some form of "science" of the process may be contemplated. As such, the neologism also alludes to the act of writing a treatise on the use of pictures. Finally, this new *graphology* proposes a study of writing, a means of analyzing the character of the text.

Within the limits of this article, we will attempt only to delineate (1) the ways by which a picture can become a structural or architectural model for a long text, (2) the conversion of pictures into writing or, to remove the ambiguity concealed in the word "writing," *script-ure*,[4] (3) some characteristics of the Simonian fictional text. For we may well ask what modalities, if not method, enable words and a literary text to be sculptured and structured from visual images?

1. The Picture as a "Model"

> The canvas stands as an indication to the eye that the totality of that which is visible can be enclosed in a blank rectangle, and thus that the rectangle can represent the idea of world and cosmos.
>
> Max Loreau, *Premises for a Pictorial Logic*

1.1. *Generators. Orion aveugle* provides a list of twenty illustrations. We could wonder at length about what presided over the final selection of the illustrations accompanying the book; for our purpose, suffice it to notice that a small number retains a primarily decorative function, and some of the others constitute genuine generators for the text of *Conducting Bodies*. We could also wonder what prompted the writer to choose these material generators, the reproductions of which we have here. In brief, it appears that purely affective factors have come into play: a few paintings or objects in the more or less immediate field of consciousness of the writer triggered an impulsion to write. This is no doubt why Simon proposes to call them, very simply, pre-texts.[5] Finally, one can observe that the material generators are not all chosen at the outset of the work; the description in progress never fails to bring in additional ones.

We verify the generative role of certain reproductions through our personal identifications (some paintings, such as Poussin's *Orion*, are universally known), through information contained in the text and, to a lesser extent, corroborating outside information. Among the principal generators of the text of *Conducting Bodies*, we record: *Charlene* and *Canyon* by Robert Rauschenberg, an anatomical plate from the *Larousse classique illustré*, a photo of the Amazon river by Emil Schultness, the design on the inside of a cigar box lid, a lithograph by N. Maurin titled *Christophe Colomb bâtit une forteresse*, a woodcut of the signs of the Zodiac, an etching by Picasso, a woodcut of a dissected torso of a woman, *Orion aveugle* by Poussin, a photographic montage by Andy Warhol, a woodcut of a man's head.

These stimuli acquire in writing a presence which prevents us from perceiving them as simple points of departure and, through the insistence and recurrence with which they appear, raises them to "supports" for the text. The reader is indeed invited to make numerous observations and rapprochements between visual images and their intellection in a system of words and between the "writing" (*écriture*) of a painting and of a text.

1.2 *Charlene*. Simon makes a distinction between images "written" in the text and those which are not.[6] Among those he did not use, he includes *Charlene* and in fact there is no direct description of *Charlene* in *Conducting Bodies*. Rauschenberg's painting is, however, present: it plays a role of first importance, but on a very different plane than the generators previously mentioned. Charlene does not seem so much to generate words and themes as it organizes the fragments of the text: it is generative of forms and structures. It visibly constitutes an elaborate architectural model for the text. About *Orion aveugle*, which by its close complementarity shares its generators with *Conducting Bodies*, Simon states explicitly:

> Because of the title and because a detail of the painting appeared on the book jacket, many people thought that the point of departure for *Orion aveugle* was Poussin. In fact, the point of departure was not *Orion*, which occurred to me later, but Robert Rauschenberg's large construction, *Charlene*, which is in the Museum of Modern Art in Amsterdam. . . . *Orion aveugle* came out of my search for the "properties" (subjectively understood, of course) of *Charlene*. In simple terms, the process went something like this: *Charlene*—shops in ruins on the Bowery in New York, their windows boarded up with wood, bits of tar paper, rusty sheetmetal, strips of moulding with chipped paint, the walls smeared with dripping graffiti, etc., from there New York, from there the *Orion* in the Metropolitan Museum, from New York, the whole American continent, North and South, the Encuentro, etc., etc. (I, p. 14)

This passage reestablishes the primordial and multiplanar role played by *Charlene* and, implicitly in the background, by New York, prototype of a huge American metropolis.[7] The rapprochement is all the more well founded and productive if one recalls that *Charlene* belongs to Rauschenberg's red series and that, product of a collage, it is often appreciated as a "dynamic mosaic," a characterization that has also been applied to Simon's book.

Rauschenberg's painting divides and fills space with colorful rectangles: pieces of newspapers, fabric, and photos, etc., in a geometric composition with a dominant rectangular structure, covered with orange and red paint spots and drips. Simon exploits the meeting of *Charlene* and New York at the double level of the organization of forms within a delimited space (geometry) and of anthropology, where superimposed layers of readily known materials attest to presences and traces of a well-defined civilization.

The play of correspondence between a pictorial and geometrical composition and New York City which Simon reads into *Charlene* will enable the textual generation of *Conducting Bodies* by providing a basic machinery (*dispositif*) capable of production and expansion: New York, North and South American continents, the Encuentro, according to chain association. If, at the level of elements, the painting is a source of generators, it becomes in its wholeness a constant general model which orients the choices of the writer:

> The important thing, as I said, is for the chain to close back in upon itself, or, better still, to intersect itself continuously. I never know what the end result of a book will be, but I never lose sight of the initial design, no matter how vague it may be. (I, p. 10)

Such a procedure may evoke, making all due allowance, a printed circuitry as in electronics, where the metal in fusion follows the tracks of a prepared network. Similarly, the writer may appear to be pouring the freshly found words into the circuit of an already conceptualized model. The relationships between *Charlene* and *Conducting Bodies* reside in the multifarious activity of the quadrilateral model and are readily perceived through the text's persistent focusing on (*a*) the horizontal/vertical dimensions, (*b*) the geometric design of the ground plane (countryside and the city as checkerboards), or the textual plane (the book as a dense decoupage of rectangular fragments, juxtaposed and aligned on the page), (*c*) the invariable inscription of objects and scenes in a frame, be it that of a painting, a photography, or a door, a window, a newspaper, ad infinitum. This quadrilateral-shaped icon, susceptible to modifications and deformations, leads to a system of variable geometry. By addition and assemblage, basic rectangular planes are modified into three-dimensional constructions. The rectangle can impose itself as a geometrical matrix if one posits that it contains many other geometric forms. It suffices to let it undergo some deformations or to vary one's angle of vision in order to see a parallelogram, a trapezoid, a square, a diamond, which, divided, gives triangles. Thus, a complete system of variable geometry provides Simon with a basis for his book whose totality evokes a drawing with ever-changing forms ("le dessin qui se forme et se déforme au gré des mouvements," p. 133). We should note that this play with deformation is especially conspicuous in the second part of the book, with the sun spot, for example. The rectangular figure and its combinatorial geometric designs converge in the final breathtaking three-dimensional vision of an urban landscape:

> gazing out the [plane] windows at the bristling forest of prisms, of cubes, of towers, that stretches out below them as far as the eye can see, pitted with well shafts, canyons, narrow trenches, at the very bottom of which one can see the rosy glow of neon lights blinking on and off. (pp. 190-91)

Active at several levels, the quadrilaterial figure, through its piling up, saturates space by creating a geometric congestion. It is primarily organizing description by permitting an assemblage of elements as heterogeneous as a city, a building, a plane, a newspaper, etc., through their iconic isomorphism. In a strong warp and woof heterogeneous matters are reassembled and made to resemble one another. In so doing, *Charlene* is a powerful agent of organic coherence.[8]

2. Picture/Script-ure

> Les lois de l'image apparaissent sous une double condition: comme non spécifiques et dans la lecture de l'image.
>
> Jean-Louis Schefer, *L'Image: le sens investi*

Simon's poetics evoke a particularized case of "ecphrasis," which, to follow Jean H. Hagstrum's clear definition, is that "special quality of giving voice and language to the otherwise mute art object."[9] The plastic arts are not an end but a passage and a locus where the work and the book is being "plotted." In Butor's words, they can be "*un miroir germinateur*." Such a situation exemplifies the role of the visual image which is deemed to exist principally to be written and to be read.

A first foray into graphopictology, or the description of pictures constitutive of the writing of a text of fiction, can be made through its main components.

2.1. *Description*. The clearest and most obvious effect of the picture is to initiate and then guide an objective, precise, even meticulous description (see, in particular, the passages on Poussin's painting, the anatomical plates, the Picasso etching.) When compared to previous works, the *Conducting Bodies* text often appears to be less a free commentary on the picture than its analytical description. By so doing, Simon calls to mind a long iconic tradition which can be traced back as far as Homer and, in late Antiquity, Philostratus the Elder, Philostratus the Younger, and Callistratus. Hagstrum writes that "all three of these writers produced lengthy prose descriptions and celebrations of real and imaginary paintings in sufficient quantity to form collections" (H, p. 30), a goal still to be found in Balzac's portraits, for example, which purport to copy nature "textually";[10] but it is the status of this goal in its multifaceted aspects that deserves examination.

2.2 *Referent*. The status of the referent is the question, as fascinating as it is intractable, that underlies Simon's procedures. Opinions are, as we know, at the very least divided. Jean Ricardou's famous formulation on the constituent forces of the fictional event states quite well the components of the problem:

> Any fictive event is a paradoxical place, mobile resultant of two contradictory dimensions: the referential dimension, the literal dimension.[11]

The paradox resides in the fact that perception of one dimension can only be made at the expense of the other, by erasing it at least momentarily. Their coexistence, however, results in an "unthinking tension" about which Robbe-Grillet and other critics observe that "these tensions between the referent and the literal are not the same" among new novelists. Robbe-Grillet thus concludes:

> Claude Simon gives us the referents and . . . moreover, there is a fragmentary edition of *Conducting Bodies* where the referents are published as illustrations of the book. We must then believe that Simon concedes a greater importance to the referent than other novelists.[12]

For Simon, however, there is only a tenuous link between the product (the text) and the so-called initial document. Most often, he denounces the relation between the two since, for him, the operation is less to describe (*décrire*) them than to write (*écrire*) them (I, p. 14). The very processes of the intersemiotic transposition, as we have seen, clarify to a great extent the basic divergence between Simon and some of his critics.

On the one hand, writing distances us from the referent, and is very inadequate to present a painting or a picture. Literary pictorialism, on the other hand, has long been perceived as an attempt to get one step closer to the truth and reality of things, an attempt which is almost immediately thwarted by the metaphoric character of discourse. Through verbal analogue, an object devoid of any reality other than the one of print is elaborated. Further, from the standpoint of the doctrine that art imitates nature, iconic description is an imitation of the imitation since the first mimesis started with the picture.

2.3 *Deviation*. Attempts have continuously been made to correlate the visual content with its description in order to evaluate the difference and the distance between them. With regard to the three iconic writers of late antiquity, Hagstrum qualifies their descriptions with terms such as more or less

"rhetorical" or "rhapsodic," more or less "subjective,"
"detailed," or "particularized" from one another (H, p. 30).

Supposing for a moment that the writer adopts the most
rigorous standards of objectivity, the leap from picture to
script-ure can then be described as a balanced process of conversion characterized by a variation factor, since any picture
can be the source of an in(de)finite number of descriptions,
given that a description is inescapably a reading and an interpretation of the object, making a perfect description unattainable. And yet, this plurality of readings elicited by the
same referent points to a range of deviations, or *écarts*, which
it remains possible to gauge somewhat, if we only consider
that a threshold separates the identification of the picture
through the text from its nonidentification, and that a degree
of interpretation of the picture can be assessed in the descriptions. In other words, the phenomenon of iconicity suggests its
own limits. Probing the outer limits of the transformation will
circumscribe an area of interplay beyond which processes
more readily associated with fiction (invention) may be seen at
work.

The Simonian text builds its iconicity along three main
lines: (1) narration refers to an illustration (or organizes itself
as one); (2) inversely, that illustration is the origin and
becomes generative of the action; (3) numerous static descriptions, while close to being an inventory, seem to study the arrangement and properties of sets, and to explore specific
space. In reading the text any aporias of the description and
picture vanish. The complementarity of opposite techniques
erases any first role: the picture creates descriptions, the
description creates pictures in a perfect circularity of purpose.
Figure 1 will make explicit the strength vectors of iconicity.*

If, to a certain point, the painting is nothing but the reading
which is being made: narration, description, mise en scène, it
remains true that there still is (in theory) an optimal degree of

---

* All diagrams in this essay were drawn by Sheri Daniel.

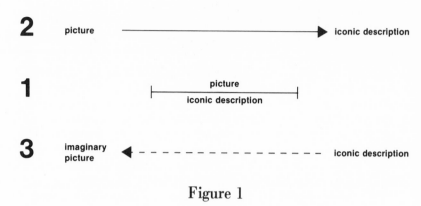

Figure 1

correspondence between the picture and the text (1). The subjective elements involved in any reading, however, make one
envisage this optimal degree of correspondence within a
system of plural and overlapping readings which, despite each
writer's idiosyncratic perception and interpretation, are all endowed with the highest degree of iconicity. A play of the
visible/legible could be said to delineate a series of closely
related descriptions forming a first nucleus. From there on
opens up a range of progressive *écarts* when the description is
made either to move away from the picture-referent (2), or, inversely, coming from afar focuses itself, more or less abruptly,
as a picture-referent (3). These two last instances are then
characterized more by a play of variable distances than by
mere intersemiotic translation. Now, if we appropriately
remember that the "visual" artist was originally in a similar
position vis-à-vis the object he appears to have reproduced,
this "signifying polyvalence," which we have seen generated
in the context of the reiteration of descriptions, becomes split
into a series of levels, since the reader, after the scriptor, reads

"the figures of his own desire in these that the painter's desire, representing, traces and displaces on the surface of the painting." [13] In sum, the reading of the text takes place within a system of at least three levels of plural readings.

Beneath the multiple superimpositions of readings which compose the process of reading/writing, we become aware of the variation factor that is authorized by the reading without affecting the basic "recognizability" of the picture. When this gap becomes too wide, however, the referent can be said to have been "released"—often a temporary gesture since at some point it will be surreptitiously reintroduced.

In short, the phenomenon of *écart* plays indeed a crucial function in that the total text can be generated from a principle of "elasticity" which allows writing to stretch considerably toward nonpictorial elements, namely, the narrative ones, such as the theme of the "sick man" in *Conducting Bodies*, which, by the very frequency of its resurgence, may seem like the guiding thread of this novel. These originally dissimilar elements are fully incorporated and integrated within an overall structure. On the whole, the text becomes inscribed in an internal movement of expansion and retraction to and from description and "pure" narration, giving it its pulse, or particular Barthian "fading" between the voices of extra- and intratextualities.

2.4 *Fragmentation.* In iconic prose writing, it is usual practice to describe the object in its totality, the idea being that this gives the fullest and best account of the artifact under consideration. Most frequently Simon's descriptions do not take into account the totality of the picture; some visual referents generate only a very partial description: witness Rauschenberg's *Canyon*, which seems to have interested the writer only for its graphic inscriptions and their deciphering rich in textual possibilities:

> No single word is completely legible. All that remains are a few enigmatic fragments, in some instances impossible to fit together and in other instances suggesting a possible interpretation (or reconstruction), or even several of them, such as, for example, ABOR (lABOR, or ABORto, or ABORecer?), SOCIA

(SOCIAlismo,   aSOCIAcion?),   and   CAN   (CANdidato,
CANibal, CANcer?). (p. 24)

The photography of the Amazon river would be, implies
Simon, a pseudo-generator since it was found after the fact (I,
p. 14). This is not just a happy coincidence, for the Amazon is
a prototype of a meandering river. The picture may also be
the source and convenient support of a description in progress. This is the main function of *Canyon* and the Maurin
lithograph, *Christophe Colomb*, among others, from which
some compositional details feed the rêveries, which at times
fill several pages. Moreover, a picture may suggest to the imagination several others with a comparable style or similar
themes and thus take retrospectively a quasisymbolic value.
In short, before the powerful stimulus and pictorial model,
the writer has at his disposal numerous options that he
generously taps and which can be summarized in Figure 2:

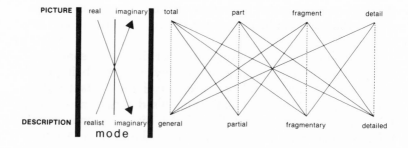

Figure 2

Figure 2 illustrates the extensive and complex interrelations
between image and text obtained by the combination of

dissimilar units of a picture with various stretches of description. An overseeing converter mechanism enabling a picture-like description of a mental content, i.e., projected in an imaginary picture, or vice versa an imaginary description of a real picture, further enlarge these combinatorial possibilities. To complete these observations we should mention the case of a long description ending on a parenthetical reference so as to authenticate it, "(Velin du Musée d'Histoire naturelle peint par de Vailly, vol. 80, no 54)" (p. 216). In this instance, the reader may not be able to determine whether the document is real or invented and, consequently, this precision will only be read as an iconic device.

Many *excursi* take place from these pictures as if they provided the writer with a supportive thread. Its creative unraveling will often take him outside of the frame but also brings him back into it in a judiciously choreographed dance whereby pictures in many ways appear as the stage of the narrative.

3. *Meaning-Effects*

On ne pénètre que dans une forêt de transpositions.

—Valéry, *Note et digression*

Where *Charlene* and *Conducting Bodies* do part radically is on the semantic plane. Determining significations and meaning in a so-called abstract painting devolves almost entirely upon the reader, whereas in the novel, semantism is inherent to the genre. At this level, the relationships between the two works are distant. By proposing a general architectural model and structure, the painting lends a guiding warp and woof to the production of meaning, which at the end of the process will have been completely covered by the text. The painting/picture plays an essentially catalytic role.

Consciously accomplished between boundaries, just as weaving can only take place within a frame, the movement of writing on smaller matrices produces a texture. For the most part, Simon sees writing as an activity that consists of pushing up and directing more or less wittingly a semantic nucleus to

surface textuality somewhat like the little bubbles in a fresh
glass of beer

> are rising from the bottom . . . and traveling up to the surface,
> where they burst or collect in clusters which float across the top
> in accordance with unpredictable laws. (p. 79)

In *Conducting Bodies* the network provided by *Charlene*
thus becomes in the truest sense a web, as if a plot were being
concocted around the materials, to surround them and hold
them firmly together, endowing them with organic cohe-
siveness. We may already have noticed the presence of
the metaphor of weaving throughout the text. Horizontal and
vertical lines cross, intersect, superimpose themselves, and
mix in a dense network which brings up the image of *damas-
quinage*, a technique which makes recto and verso completely
identical. It would be difficult to miss the insistent recurrence
of images such as *damier*, *quadrillage*, *mailles du filet*, *grille*,
carrelage, etc. and numerous "cross-sections." And as we
know, the last image of the book is the one of the *"trame mise
à nu."* *Charlene* and its "irregular checkerboard" await the
substance of the novel to shape it, give it its boundaries and
enclosure, its geometric surface. Thus the self-regulating
function of Rauschenberg's painting becomes apparent as it
organizes the space of the book, and structures its semantic in-
florescences.

If one recalls that in photoengraving the *trame* is the fine
pattern of squares interposed between the original and the
sensitive coating which is used in relief-production procedures, one could not define more appropriately the function
of *Charlene*, for it is what is interposed between the desire to
write and writing proper. *Charlene* is thus present while being
absent as it has been completely "digested" or transformed into the text.

To draw referents from the plastic arts is to choose them, on
one level at least, for their materiality and acute presence
which the very processes at work in fiction will then undermine
and deny. To take a painting or picture, to *write* it, to extract
fragmentary and not infrequently partial descriptions, to

amalgamate these fragments with those of other pictures into a verbal construct, constitutes as many techniques which can only deconstruct the most visible reference. While pictorial and iconic prose have traditionally purported to be one notch closer to truth and reality, Simon's brand has obviously taken the opposite direction. The exacerbated and irreconcilable tension between the referent and the textual may have been brought to its ultimate limit. We are in the midst of a system that succeeds in accommodating, conjugating, and playing on two opposite effects within the same element: the verisimilitude of the iconic fragment as an autonomous part and its "irreal" or fictional status when integrated into the overall structure of the text. In other words, the element has to establish its reality and representation to see it then negated. Simon's constructs seem to have realized the "impossible" equation of verisimilitude and fiction. This suggests not only a dialectic in the Simonian prose but also a didactic dimension which can be formulated as follows: in order to overthrow and dispose of the representation-expression dogma it is first necessary to establish it firmly so as to illustrate better its falsehood.

Equally interesting is the way that it attests to our difficulty in grasping two contradictory dimensions at the same time, just as in the case of the referential and the literal, which are nevertheless perceived at a subliminal level. The overall effect is an undecidable glistening at the heart of the text indicative of the transcoding of reality into a quasi-hallucinatory mode, since we perceive a constant flickering. Such a *dispositif*, whereby the referent is seemingly ambushed behind the iconic sign and always threatening to erupt on the scene of writing, is evocative of a dark mirror emitting brief glaring flashes, or endless questions and a fraction of time never to be filled.

Whether described in part or in toto, the picture or painting is absorbed, according to various modalities, into the text and exhibits a status of simultaneous presence and absence depending on the perspective adopted.

What the Simonian text achieves best is to bring the reader to indecision, indecisiveness, and to leave him off center, off balance. Vacillating stability is the modus vivendi here. Im-

mobile mobility. Frozen motion. Silent scream. Extremities
are made to meet, to ally, to cover one another over. Motion
will be faster as it is immobile, the scream louder if stopped
silent. Recto is verso. Conversely, recto and verso are co-
present, in full view, while retaining the possibility of
simultaneous and immediate reversals. A never-ending effect.
Orion blinded. The reader dazzled and blinded, with no
guiding ramp, no underpinnings to sustain him, understandably wishing there were a hint of a direction. Unceasing and
anamorphic snowflakes fall before the eyes with endless
displacements and replacements. Always the same,
procession-like. Continuity to be lived, density to be experienced by one's widening vision. Multiple, plural,
simultaneous contradictory visions.

The varied techniques composing Simon's graphopictology
cumulate to *dematerialize* and to *derealize* the visual image.
They are organized in an outward movement from reality, or
what has been traditionally perceived too easily as the world,
matter and realism, to the self-reflexivity inherent in writing,
and from the supposedly known to what is yet to be
discovered. The most consistent effect of the process is, to borrow a word from Fredric Jameson, "estrangement," which is
particularly tangible in the progressive deformations of the image as it is written.[14] Since Simon has used Francis Bacon's
paintings in his fiction, it would be difficult not to be sensi-
tized to a few intriguing similarities between the two artists, and
not only in their passion for (re)doing already existing works,
but at the very level of intentionality. About his conception of
art, for example, Bacon declares:

> What I want to do is distort the thing far beyond the appear-
> ance, but in that distortion to bring it back to a recording of the
> appearance.[15]

This capitalization on a work inscribed between the two poles
of distortion and appearance is particularly consonant with
Simon's art.

By the same token, the transformation of the image
amounts to its subversion by an insistence on undoing it while

rebuilding it, and thus proposing a subversion, i.e., a secondary version, another account which will necessarily be at odds with the original, without claiming to be truer, but simply an expectable appendage to the material object so as to counterbalance the long-standing fixity.

To write the image is to bring it back to life, opening it up to endless questioning. In entering the description, the visual image is not only being supplanted by the verbal, but it sheds successive layers of its massive wholeness, its affixed meanings, its presupposed reality. Finally, one could easily say that the plastic image performs the function it knows best: it *hangs*, in orbit, around the text. In condensing our indecision, our bewilderment, our anguish, it relentlessly signals that it is to be redone and rewritten again and again.

UNIVERSITY OF MARYLAND

Notes

1. "Sur deux oeuvres récentes de Claude Simon," *Die Neueren Sprachen* 9 (September 1972): 543-49. Cf. *Orion aveugle* (Geneva: Skira, Collection "Les Sentiers de la création," 1970) and *Les Corps conducteurs* (Paris: Minuit, 1971). All page numbers in parentheses without any other indication refer to *Les Corps conducteurs* or its translation by Helen R. Lane, *Conducting Bodies* (New York: Viking, 1974).

2. Numerous New Novelists painted at one point or another in their career, so the persistent and far-reaching relationships between painting and literature and, more specifically, between plastic referent and literary discourse should perhaps come as no surprise. Let us just mention, almost at random, Butor's interest in the words in paintings, or Robbe-Grillet's recent publications, *La Belle captive* (Paris and Lausanne: La Bibliothèque des Arts, 1975), a "novel" built systematically on seventy-five paintings by René Magritte, or *Topologie d'une cité fantôme* (Paris: Minuit, 1976), another novel composed of four texts, generated from (or with), respectively, Paul Delvaux, David Hamilton, Robert Rauschenberg, and René Magritte.

3. "Picture" is used here as a generic term to designate any kind of visual image.

4. script-ure: the "-" understood as a diacritical sign meant to deconstruct the theological connotation of the word and recall its first meaning: writing, especially as it pertains to a script. Recently, Northrop Frye introduced the expressions "secular scripture" in *The Secular Scripture: A Study of the Structures of Romance* (Cambridge: Harvard University Press, 1976). Although Frye's terminological choice has the immediate advantage of avoiding all artifices, the use of "secular scripture," by suggesting to our mind the here unwarranted opposition secular/clerical, inevitably

displaces the topic to a historical and diachronic terrain obstructing its synchronic perspective.

5. See DuVerlie, "Interview with Claude Simon, trans. J. and I. Rodgers, *Substance* 8 (Winter 1974): 8. Hereafter referred to as "I" followed by page number.

6. In the "Interview" in *Sub-stance*, Simon acknowledges the description of only three of the "documents": the aerial photograph of the Amazon, *Orion aveugle* by Poussin, and the erotic etching by Picasso.

7. The painting is thus: (1) a "structural" model, (2) a source of thematic generators: the page (boy), the checkerboard, newspaper clippings, etc., and (3) the point of departure of a chain association.

8. One could thus contract the use of the de Reixach portrait in *The Flanders Road* and the use of *Charlene* in *Conducting Bodies*. The portrait of the ancestor had a genesic role and a metonymic function by engendering a story while, on the other hand, *Charlene*'s primary function is more to organize and structure the book.

9. Jean H. Hagstrum, *The Sister Arts. The Tradition of Literary Pictorialism and English Poetry from Dryden to Gray* (Chicago: University of Chicago Press, 1958), p. 18. Hereafter cited in the text as H with page number.

10. See Bernard Vannier, *L'Inscription du Corps. Pour une sémiotique du portrait balzacien* (Paris: Klincksieck, 1972), especially chapter 2, "Striptural et pictural."

11. Jean Ricardou, *Nouveau roman: hier, aujourd'hui* I (Paris: U.G.E., Collection "10/18," 1972), p. 30. See also Ricardou, *Pour une théorie du nouveau roman* (Paris: Seuil, 1971), chapter 2.

12. Alain Robbe-Grillet in *Nouveau roman: hier, aujourd'hui* I, p. 33.

13. Louis Marin, "La Description de l'image: à propos d'un paysage de Poussin." *Communications* 15 (1970): 206.

14. Fredric Jameson, *The Prison-House of Language* (Princeton: Princeton University Press, 1972). See chapter 2, "The Formalist Projection."

15. David Sylvester, *Francis Bacon* (interviews) (New York: Pantheon Books, 1975), p. 40.

12
Aspects of Bisexuality in Claude Simon's Works
Christiane P. Makward

There is a disquieting aura of ambiguity surrounding the term "bisexuality" which needs to be dispelled. This study concerns itself with a particular, if complex, structure in Simon's writings and in no way constitutes a psychocritical approach to the writer himself. Rather, it is intended as a complement to the critical texts on sexuality in Simon's fiction to be found in *Entretiens* 31 and *Sub-stance* 8 particularly. Simon's eroticism has a different quality and perhaps is not on a level with what is traditionally considered "the best" in erotic literature. The missing dimension might well be the distance maintained between the agent and the erotic object, a distance essential to sadomasochistic relationships. Overall, Simon represents woman as an enigmatic *other*, an erotic partner and a subject.

Simon readily declares that he is neither sociologist nor philosopher[1] and his fundamental existential statement comes in the form of an obsessional question: "Comment savoir?" Both the desire to know and the impossibility of giving answers structure his approach of the real. This is why sexuality in his texts can only be represented in antithetical and reversible terms and only a critic's own blindspots make certain conclusions possible.[2] To a reader who measures Simon's erotic writings against "the masters" of the genre, it appears that his representation of sexuality is marred by "a powerlessness to feel pleasure," "a threat of frigidity or perhaps impotence," "rudimentary sexual behavior" and only "discreet allusions to *fellatio* and *cunnilingus*."³ Obviously Simon did not write *Justine*, *Histoire de l'Oeil*, or *Histoire d'O*, neither does he betray the *misérabilisme* of Sartre, Freud, and Bataille on the question of woman and sexuality.

A negative impression of Simon's representation of sexuality is bound to emerge from readings which simply rely on patent sexual behavior and selected fantasmatic processes. In Simon's texts the obvious is the "war of the sexes" and the traditional manicheistic pitching of male versus female. Femininity as embodied in a number of female characters does fit into the archetypal "images of women": the bitches and witches, the castrating mothers and saintly virgins. But a vast network of signs is ignored in such critical readings. There is a fluctuating fringe, a grey territory underneath sexual polarities. There is an intriguing semantic layer to explore which is the no(wo)man's land of bisexuality. What a non-phallocentric reading of Simon's texts can bring out positively is the writer's ability to relax, "To act woman in his manly text, the text of a man who tries to understand through all the pores of his body how a cosmic orgasm organizes: concentration. To act woman so he does not have to be heard, relentlessly and needlessly."⁴

The term "sex" implies separation and difference: a complementary opposition to the other sex. Like the analyst, the literary critic does not deal with sexuality but only with its symbolic representation through language. In analytical theory the term "bisexuality" encompasses a wide range of meanings, including manifest and latent homosexual behavior, dual sexual behavior, paradoxical psychosexual behavior and signs of identification with the opposite sex.⁵ This wealth of signification to "bisexuality" could lead to an entire book on this topic for there are thousands of notations to constitute the discourse of sexuality in Simon's texts. From the mass of data, three trends emerge more readily: the question of homosexuality; cases of psychological "transsexualism," where a character tends to "transgress" her/

his sexual role as defined by culture; and lastly, the "feminine" attention devoted to the body and the diffusion of eroticism throughout the text in recent works.

Homosexual behavior occurs explicitly in *The Battle of Pharsalus*, where an episode involves two young boys near a McCormick reaper (*Pharsalus*, pp. 143-44). It also occurs, but at the third remove, in the same text when a pornographic film is remembered: a gardener sodomizes his employer while the latter is in coitus with his wife. This situation is an interesting—if crude—reversal of the common use of woman as the mediating object for male homosexual relationships, as has been pointed out by Luce Irigaray.[6]

Nongenital homosexual contact occurs as well as numerous allusions and connotations to constitute the thematics of latent homosexuality. In *The Wind* Maurice is a problematic character who repeatedly makes advances to Montès and wants to secure his friendship. After the episode where Montès is severely beaten by Gyp, the gipsy, Maurice breaks into Montès's room, talks to him soothingly, like a man to a woman (*Wind*, p. 139). He nurses him and puts him to bed, expecting all the while some mark of emotional interest on the part of Montès. Maurice finally reaches a state of tension: "the stage, so to speak, of violation, of aggression, in that eager quest for the one thing Montès happened to be incapable of showing him, not that he would have refused it, at least in that way, a priori, if he had been in a position to grant it to him—would he have refused to pet a dog, even a mangy one?—but because he couldn't, couldn't for the good reason that although he probably knew the word . . . it was as alien to him . . . as what anyone, man or woman, might think of him" (*Wind*, pp. 144-45).

In a similar vein there are references to Proust's Charlus and to "decorative footmen" in *The Battle of Pharsalus* (*Pharsalus*, pp. 106, 108, 143). The same novel describes a young man wrapping his arm around the shoulders of a sleeping companion and waking him up with "maternal solicitude" (*Pharsalus*, p. 4). Similarly a sergeant addresses the grotesque Herculean soldier in a respectful military code that sounds

"like the kind lovers use" (*Pharsalus*, p. 98). With motherly
calm and patience he reminds the man under arrest to take
shoes and blankets before going down to the hole.

In *Triptych*, it is by the precise description of point of view
that a homosexual intimacy is suggested: two boys are watching a trout, the ephemeral image of erotic tension, which
disappears into a waterjug, at the bottom of the river: "the
zone defined by the parapet of the bridge and the outlines of
the two silhouettes . . . one of the boys stretches his arm out,
his fingers pointing to the trout and the reflection of his chest
grows closer to that of the other boy" (T., p. 15). In most sequences where they appear the boys are involved in
voyeuristic games or activities related to "feminized" water
such as touching the inside of a water tank lined with algae or
diving at the cascade, in surroundings that are described as
"gynomorphous" or evocative of female genitals.

Homosexual connotations in *Histoire* include the character
of Charles, the narrator's uncle. Charles is a poet who tends
to adopt embarrassing motherly attitudes toward his nephew
and Lambert, a teenage friend: he rubs the narrator's head,
insists on the boys snacking on pastries (*Histoire*, pp. 180-85).
Lambert, the leader of a peer group at a Catholic school, is a
master at dirty word-play and an expert at dubbing Mass
Latin with pornography. His comment on the uncle's exit:
"Who was that old fool?" (*Histoire*, p. 184).[7]

Georges embracing Corinne remembers observing Arab
prisoners in the concentration camp: their bodies smooth and
hairless like girls' bodies (*Flanders*, p. 264). He also evokes
cold nights in the camp, lying against Iglésia and "hoping to
preserve a little warmth wedged together head to foot[8] I was
thinking how he had held her like that my thighs under hers"[9]
(*Flanders*, p. 265). Elsewhere a cluster of phallic images
signals Iglésia's identification with de Reixach's desire to win
the race at the horse tracks. A victory would mean a confirma-
tion of de Reixach's mastery of Corinne. The chestnut mare
and Corinne are common female mounts between Iglésia
and de Reixach (*Flanders*, pp. 151, 154). This is perceived by
Corinne and enrages her. Implicitly Simon illustrates Lévi-
Strauss' fundamental thesis on the role of women in culture.

They are, as feminist philosophers formulate this thesis, objects of exchange between homosexual males. An awareness of this role is at the root of the great female wrath which punctuates Simon's novels.

In the triangle of the painter, his wife, and his model (*Histoire* and *Pharsalus*), the narrator suspects a "complicity" or "complacency" on the part of the painter's wife. Her apparent lack of jealousy could reflect a case of identification to "the desire of the other" (the painter's enjoyment of the model's favors) and sublimated—or actual—homosexual behavior: the model might be the wife's love object. The jealous narrator insists on the wife's unfeminine appearance and compares her to "a Russian nihilist," a "bomb-thrower," Joan of Arc, and even labels her "woman-man" (*Histoire*, p. 237, *Pharsalus*, pp. 88, 115).

In *Leçon de choses* an ammunition server discharges his spleen in a torrential delirium overloaded with homosexual, sadistic, and scatological elements. Shocked by a nearby explosion, he realizes that his companions and himself are "done like rats in a hole." Under the stress of imminent "erasing" —as Lacan puts it: "un rat, ça se rature"[10]—he reacts like Céline's Bardamu in *Voyage au bout de la nuit*: the discourse of universal defilement involves racism (antisemitic, anti-Arab, anti-German) and sexual slurs. The homosexual world of war is "manned" by two distinct species which are, as the text puts it, "rats" and "fags." The latter are those cavalry officers and caterers who are likely to survive (*Leçon*, pp. 65, 119, 121) because their retreat is protected by the entrenched "rats." A very particular onomastic series consists of pseudopatronyms invented by the soldier and referring to the officers' rear ends and genitals. These names punctuate the verbal flow where various violations of standard discourse can also be observed. Spelling, syntax, sentence structure are all forcibly raped in what must be the most Rabelaisian sequence in Simon's fiction. The "divertissements" have the same "terrible and pathetic grandeur" as the narrator had found in pornographic movies (*Pharsalus*, p. 109). On the transgressive mode, they reassert Simon's anti-heroic stand on war. His rejection of the myth of the war hero generates another crude

motif in *Leçon de choses*: the fecal stench of a dead rat
perceived by a woman thirty years later is also the stench of a
dying soldier wounded in the abdomen (*Leçon*, pp. 50 and
182).

Homosexual behavior appears in various modes in Simon's
texts. Patent in a few cases, it is mostly implied, suspected
and fantasized by frustrated teenagers or soldiers in the face of
death. In the context of war, homosexuality is conceived by
the characters as a perversion reserved to aristocratic officers
and their *protégés*. It has positive connotations in peacetime
contexts or in the mythical context of Antiquity (*Pharsalus*),
where fatal struggles allowed contact of the bodies and have
become the subject matter of creative art.

The second major aspect of bisexuality in Simon's works,
dual sexual behavior, consists of a departure from the expected or "normal" psychosexual identity which results in
paradoxical behavior. Such behavior can be described as "a
change of heart" in the case of Louise in *The Grass* and as a
case of identification to the opposite sex in the central
character of *The Wind*.

Louise's decision to stay rather than elope with her lover
can be viewed as a regression, an involution of the self in the
presence of death embodied in the old woman, Marie. Marie,
as fantasized by Simon, represents a "third gender" and a sexless creature. Without a wig, she is practically hairless and
resembles a man (*Grass*, pp. 51, 67, 69) and even her voice
sounds "unsexed" (*Grass*, p. 95). This sexlessness is equally
spurned and envied by Sabine: spurned because she is a negation of femininity, envied because time has no hold on her
(*Grass*, pp. 30, 43, 51). Before dying, Marie's most significant
act is to present her jewelry box and her account books to
Louise. The act is significant *because* it appears meaningless
and therefore creates a rupture in Louise's perception of life.
Reluctantly the young woman becomes fascinated by the
discovery, through trivial details, of an entire life devoted to
Pierre, his success and happiness. In the span of a few days,
Louise goes through a "modification" in the sense made
familiar by Butor's novel. She identifies with her dying aunt

"as though her own hands were the hands of the old woman" (*Grass*, p. 97), and constructs Marie's character as exempt from pleasure and pain, radically whole, isolated, and invulnerable (*Grass*, pp. 59, 179, 182).

The change initiated in Louise by the gift of Marie's account books and jewelry box is reinforced by elements surrounding the death of the old woman. Because of this death, "Nature" becomes "a temple" in Baudelaire's mode: rain and sunshine, smells and sounds, animals and objects all concur to signify Marie's death as a triumph of sisterly love and self-fulfillment through self-denial. The implications of such a model—that of the saint—can, of course, be defined as reactionary, conformist, and traditionally repressive. The restructuring of Louise's psychosexual identity consists in a shift of libidinal investment from the archaic—erotic gratification and "freedom" from the family—to the symbolic: Louise will appear to conform to patriarchal law when in fact she identifies with Marie's silent triumph over Time. Every character in the novel is engaged in the same struggle with Time: Sabine's answer is alcoholism and the typical feminine symptoms of anxiety: excessive concern with physical appearance and excessive talking. Pierre's manner of coping with the absurd takes the opposite direction: excessive eating, endless scribbling, and taciturnity. Similarly, Louise's husband, Georges, can hardly communicate with members of the family and spends his time wenching, gambling, and producing rotten pears. His character is a combination of two major archetypes: Sisyphus and Don Juan. To see Louise's metamorphosis—a "defemalization" and an identification with Marie's spirit of denegation of the body, with access to wholeness and autonomy—in the proper perspective it must be noted that Georges is also described as deviant from the norms of masculinity. He is viewed as "abnormal" by his mother (*Grass*, p. 45), muscular but frail and feminine in spite of his rough manners and dirty appearance (*Grass*, p. 124, 128).

Although Louise reintegrates the social order, the family structure she upholds for Marie's sake cannot clearly be defined as "partriarchal." Wealth and prestige have entered the family with Sabine, moral strength has been provided by

Marie, and Louise's mission is to continue providing support to the absurd trio: Pierre, Sabine, and Georges. For her to inherit Marie's strength, Louise must go through a double aggression, to which she reacts with anger. She feels dispossessed of her previous self by Marie's gift of the jewelry box and the account books (*Grass*, pp. 99, 138). The doctor's crude pass at her ("you must have lovely breasts," *Grass*, p. 85) enrages her equally. His suggestion that she could settle her husband's debt by sleeping with him causes Louise to break a vase and cut her finger. Like the modest box, the vase can be viewed as a symbol of female sexuality and a uterine image.[11] Louise cannot refuse the box: filled with petty objects without value, it really contains Marie's sublimated, unsexed power. The expensive vase, on the contrary, is linked with verbal rape and the suggestion of prostitution, an image of feminine powerlessness.

Cut or wounded fingers are a consistent motif in Simon's fiction. In the case of Louise, it signals her acceptance of castration. Because the site of Marie's death claims her own body and her presence, she must renounce erotic gratification. The same motif recurs in *The Battle of Pharsalus*: the jealous narrator breaks his finger on a door, in the pangs of the primal scene trauma. In *Triptych* a young boy cuts his fingers with a fragment of film he is retrieving from a used battery. The boys collect pornographic images to stimulate their voyeuristic and autoerotic games. Again, in *Leçon de choses* a construction worker hurts his finger with a tool and bleeds. He is the companion of the ammunition server of "Divertissement" I and II, the one who has indicated as particularly obnoxious Saint-Euverte's habit of "inserting his white little finger in the throat of the butt-end" (*Leçon*, p. 125) while inspecting firearms. The old worker has survived the experience of the war and of being a rat in a maze. Like Georges, he has come out of it symbolically emasculated. His penis, described as limp and blue-purple colored (*Leçon*, p. 111), can easily be contrasted with the powerful dark erect penis of the elegant young man (*Leçon*, pp. 163, 173), who emits "black" sperm and is afraid his costume might be soiled during a prolonged intercourse. Simon also links potency and power in the character of Estelle and the cut-finger motif. Before running into the woods to meet her suitor, the young woman goes through the kitchen of the house (she is not "one of the ladies," but a governess), where she breaks a glass and cuts her finger. The archetypal Sleeping Beauty motif of castration could not be clearer. Estelle's femaleness is eventually denied to her (her vagina ignored) when the man attempts sodomy on her. In counterpoint to the young fop's pleasures, Estelle's husband is away at war!

The second remarkable case of psychological "transsexualism" in Simon's works is that of Montès in *The Wind*. It differs from Louise's in two respects: Louise's goals change from "freedom" and erotic gratification to "sexless" spiritual fulfillment. Her modification is imposed from outside and successful in the sense that it is more than mere compliance with the new forces at work. On the contrary, Montès' modification is an attempted and aborted one. He is born "sexless," that is to say, non-masculine and non-virile even though his social identity is "male" as warranted by his name/his father's name, Montès, which has a phallic meaning ("mount"). If one arranges the characters of the novel on a gender-identity scale the distribution appears remarkably symmetrical:

Virile: Jep   MASCULINE
   Phallic: Attorney and Land-tenant
    "*Normal*": Narrator
     Homosexual: Maurice
      Bisexual or "sexless": Montès
     Androgynous: Cécile
    "*Normal*": Rose
  Female: Hélène
"*Sexy*": Land-tenant's daughter   FEMININE

The characters occupying the central zone between Masculine-"Normal" and Feminine-"Normal" are the major actors. It looks as though the fuller development of a "character" in the novel resulted in a less definable psychosexual identity, while the most peripheral are mere stereotypes. Those central characters are engaged in a Racinian situation, invariably choosing the wrong object of investment. But here the wrong object is the same for all: Maurice, Cécile, Rose and the narrator all love the neutral, Christ-like "idiot" Montès. Christian David has underlined the fact that it is often with a woman or man "without qualities" that one is infatuated. When this is not the case, when the subject actively seeks the "right qualities" in the other person, the relationship is motivated by narcissistic (anti-erotic) impulses rather than true "love."[12]

Montès is represented by Simon as a paradoxical "character" whose capacity to perplex and irritate as well as attract is unfathomable. Among the neutralizing (therefore "feminizing") traits noted by the narrator we find the following: Montès wears his hair "long" (the time is the mid-1950s); he is indifferent to money and passive (*Wind*, pp. 183, 192); he carries candies for children; he is frequently dizzy or nauseous; he wears a nightgown instead of pajamas; he is unable to drive[13] and completely blind to danger and intrigue. He generally does not listen carefully to others (except to Rose) but rather senses their emotional state behind the conversation. Montès is a "man" with a puzzling, undefinable psyche: every other character in the book labels him "idiot." The narrator, who really serves as his "masculine" double, describes his "fundamental inaptitude for being aware of life, things, events except by the intermediary of his senses, his heart . . . And there was also his continual use of the pronouns he or she without any antecedent" (*Wind*, pp. 153, 154). Constantly striving to classify and reduce humanity "to a series of myths, masculine and feminine subdividing vertically, first of all into childhood, maturity, and old age," Montès is obsessed with an impossible order and coherence because he embodies the very opposite of this need of order and stability (*Wind*, pp. 154, 156).

Montès' psychosexual structure could be described in psychoanalytical terms as a case of "faulty oedipal structuration," which implies a defect in the process of the twofold parental identification by the subject. It is interesting to note that Jesus is considered by some analysts as the prototype of such a faulty structure.[14] Indeed Montès is the one through whom scandal enters the city. The narrator tells us that Montès never knew his father and was raised by an admirable mother who had walked out on her faithless husband in the early stage of her pregnancy, and hardly ever mentioned the father to the child (*Wind*, p. 19). This situation, according to analytical theory, favors the development of a potentially "transsexual" individual, if the single parent is exceptionally good, and makes massive one-sided identification of the child to the other sex possible. Theory also holds that the love of the mother is the prototype of all loves and implies a total passivation of the subject toward her.[15] It is not after his mother's death that Montès comes to his father's town but after the latter's death, when summoned by the attorney.

Since the Law defines him as the owner of his father's estate, he tries to abide by this definition and cannot conceive of the property as exchange value. Various forces undertake his education in vain: he is unfit for any sort of possession. Unaware of his attraction to the most ineligible woman, from the good townspeople's point of view, he is first drawn to her because of her young daughters. His relationship with the girls is of the maternal type: providing company, candy, and rides to the children, he could not possibly protect them since he cannot protect himself physically. His love for the girls provides the only guiding thread out of the vacant daze created by Rose's death. Patriarchal Law, however, denies him the adoption of the girls: he cannot become the single parent his mother had been for him. In other words, he is an "impossible" character, a "distempered" subject like Georges. The narrator sympathetically views him as a misfit whose proper place might be a monastery (*Wind*, p. 248).

The following statement by Félix Guattari points to the link between creativity and the creator's relationship to matter generally and to his own body: "a man who loves his own body—without necessarily specializing in narcissism—is caught in the becoming-woman [*le devenir-femme*] . . . A man who breaks away for any reason—whether of a sexual or

creative order etc.—from phallic outbiddings that are inherent to any power structure, will pass through and beyond
this becoming-woman. It is only under this condition that he
can become, *on top of it*, animal, cosmos, letter, color,
music."[16]

Simon's (fictional) taste for human flesh is obvious. A
paraphrase to Robbe-Grillet's coy "women's flesh has always
occupied, no doubt, an important place in my dreams"[17]
could read under Simon's pen: "Human flesh has always occupied, no doubt, an important place in my books." No writer
had told the human body more minutely and amorously than
Simon until the new women writers came to be heard.[18]
Simon's modes of writing the body range from anatomy to
myth. The eye rests with equal intensity on the dissected
brain, eye or organ, the phantasmic phallus (gold in *Pharsalus*, black in *Leçon*), the erotic penis which is equally
foreign to man and woman (*Flanders*, p. 194, *Grass*, p. 110),
the pathetic exhausted *"p'tit tuyau"* (*Triptych*, p. 210, *Leçon*,
p. 111), the obsessing or objective curves and openings of the
female body, all the smells, tastes, colors and sounds of
human flesh. Its basic qualification, whether rotting or
glorious, bruised, cut, shriveled or juicy recurs as "incredibly
tender and vulnerable." Indeed, the ultimate as well as the
primary reality for Simon is that of being a body, like Lacan's
rat in the maze or Sartre's being-in-itself upon which consciousness tries in vain to construct its essence.

The word most aptly applied by Simon to the flesh reads
"libidinal," which is the basis of his nonsadistic vein of
eroticism. The meditation on the word "libidinous" in *The
Battle of Pharsalus* shows very clearly that the *emotion* aroused
by the sight of human flesh does not exclusively apply to
the erotic female: "the word libidinous with something pink to
its consonance, something soft, crumpled as it were by the
repetition of the same syllables and suggestive sounds."[19] The
same "pink and rubbery emotion" is called forth and inter-
relates various objects in this passage, which in turn relate to a
vast network of objects, "characters," and themes throughout
the body of Simon's works such as the paradigm of "pink."
Here "libidinous" links the body of the grotesque soldier

wielding his sword in the nude to the "unreal" body of a woman acrobat, that of a rubber doll, and finally to the bodies of a couple of male wrestlers in their "vaguely obscene embraces." This series of bodies and substitutes reflects Simon's representation of human sexuality in its basic variations: phantasmic/phallic, heterosexual, autoerotic, and homosexual.

The discourse of bisexuality in Simon's texts goes primarily through the representation of femininity in male "characters" and affects both the psychological and the physical traits. Next to Montès, a simple example is that of the Convention ancestor in *The Flanders Road* (*Flanders*, pp. 75, 82). Concomitant with the scission, multiplication, and disappearance of the narrator in the succession of his novels, Simon's earlier "characterization" disintegrates. The analysis of "characters" therefore becomes impossible but eventually the (psycho)analysis of the text itself could be considered.[20] A secondary trend in Simon's discourse of bisexuality includes the caricature of virility. This is achieved with phallic objects (weapons, tools), depiction of mechanical coitus, and evocation of monstrous creatures (centaur, woman-centaur, bearded old woman in *Flanders*). Even the most "normal" male, the red-bearded painter of *Histoire*, is perceived as a bisexual being made of two parts: "(one of which was green, mother-of-pearl, participating in the perfume, the night, the cyclamen—the other consisting of muscles and bones)" (*Histoire*, pp. 234-35).

Other levels of the texts could be explored in connection with bisexuality in Simon's texts. Physical abuse in peacetime contexts, for example, is often connected with female anger. A symptom of powerlessness to understand or an inability to act in men, violence in female characters is the language of frustrated femininity. Just as Corinne and Estelle hit their lovers because, through coitus, they have learned their "being-a-body" and only a body for men, so men learn through the war that they are bodies-for-death, and only that, for their superiors and Time generally. This demonstrates Simon's ability to fantasize gender-related frustrations on both sides. In *Leçon de choses* the "smiling cow" is substituted to the angry young woman after the quarrel. It is as though the text suggests that, as far as the element fop is concerned, a cow for a companion will do just as well as a "hysterical" woman. In Simon's recent texts, sexuality becomes truly polymorphous. Even though heterosexual coitus dominates the narrative, homosexuality acquires a new dimension with *The Battle of Pharsalus* and *Leçon de choses*, as I have shown in the discussion of the soldier's delirium. Phantasmically at least, in this character, it is an explanatory principle. More remarkable still is the general "erotization" of the environment in *Triptych* and *Leçon de choses*. Sensory perceptions, mostly pleasurable, diversify the inscription of *jouissance* and the libidinal. Objects are abundantly exploited as generators of pleasure: eating is particularly important as a substitute for erotic gratification and food is consistently associated with the "castrated of the earth," the workers and the little girl (*Leçon*, pp. 30, 40, 73).

Using objects as libidinal generators of the text is hardly a new device in Simon's writing. There was an ambiguous faucet with autoerotic connotations in *Histoire* (*Histoire*, pp. 31-32) and Sabine's flask of liquor to signify that alcoholism is often a problem of displaced sexuality (*Grass*, pp. 152, 154). Phallic paintbrushes and swords, spears with homosexual connotations (*Pharsalus*), various blades, sticks, and containers (*Triptych*), cigars (cigarettes for the workers), canes, flowers and fruits (*Leçon*)—all these objects have sexual overtones. There are even "bisexual" objects: the fieldglasses (*Flanders*, p. 151), the arumlily (also called "lords-and-ladies," *Histoire*, p. 6), and an umbrella (*Flanders*, p. 126). The privileged bisexual object is Estelle's attribute: a sunshade. It is treated by Simon as a veritable cornucopia of erotic as well as geometrical metonymies (*Leçon*, pp. 143 et passim), the major single source of dissemination and an image of Simon's style itself.[21]

To claim that psychological bisexuality—and, therefore, femininity—pervades Simon's writing amounts to taking a nonmechanistic, nonmanicheistic look at a truly *human* artist. A psychoanalytical approach to the text may appear devious to the formalist critic or reader. The risk taken is that, more than in the sociological or the structuralist perspectives, the reader may become the "analyzed" of the text rather than the analyst of it. While delineating aspects of bisexuality in Simon's fiction, I have investigated themes and situations where the text conjoins opposites involving sexuality. At the level of linguistic structures, of stylistics primarily, any theoretical guidelines that might be used are only just emerging and cannot be relied upon.[22] It would take an army of readers, computers, and linguists to establish with any certainty whether and how sexuality is inscribed in linguistic structures, and what the objective differences are between feminine and masculine modes of expression. Should the difference be established, one would still have to deal with the question: Are these differences natural or cultural, or—as I surmise—inextricably symbiotic?

A psychoanalytical approach to texts should at the very least entail considering every sign and signal of the text as meaningful. One cannot conclude that Simon's representation of woman is that of the domineering *other* if careful attention is paid to the narrative structure (who says what and when). The entire content of *The Flanders Road*, particularly the relationships between the sexes, are designated as *fabulation* spun by sexually frustrated narrators (*Flanders*, pp. 294-95). While the women appear excessively female (Sabine, Corinne) or reluctantly female (Louise, Cécile, Rose), the men are often represented as less than "normally" masculine. They are physically impotent (Pierre), absurd nonachievers (Montès, Georges in *The Grass*), antiheroes trapped by war or their own obsessions (Georges in *The Flanders Road*, narrator in *The Battle of Pharsalus*), they can even be sexually inadequate (de Reixach). This paradigm—the somewhat deviant woman paired with the less than masculine man—points to a conception of sexual identity as problematic for Simon, and not merely a question of genitals.

There are striking similarities between Simon's portrayal of male and female erotic pleasure. In both cases it is described as "cosmic," a dissolution of the body into the earth. For Louise (*Grass*, p. 209) or Georges (*Flanders*, p. 263) a climax is a return to the womb of the earth. This could signify Simon's understandable failure to fantasize the originality—if any—of female pleasure. Beyond the fact that few writers would even dare describe female pleasure "from the inside" unless they were women themselves, this similarity in the poetic rendering of sexual pleasure could reflect an intuition that the "difference" is a cultural myth. Freud's contradiction on the matter is significant: he holds as impenetrable the mystery of "the dark continent" of femininity and postulates on the other hand that bisexuality is the substratum of psychosexual identity.

The imagery of sexual pleasure in Simon's texts does not differ substantially from Colette's scheme of fusion with the vegetal and the mineral when she reiterates her quest and phantasmic union with the archaic mother through the mediation of Sido. In the last lines of *The Break of Day* she notes that the man she might have loved failed to join her because he did not take the time, "touching the ground, to abdicate his form. But let me help him and he will be brushwood and sea-foam and meteors." It is even more revelatory to find that, when modern feminist writers think they inscribe the female body in its radical difference, the very same imagery recurs: "I too am a foetus around you, we can stay like this for centuries in touch with each other, your skin against mine and the skin of the earth; the sun and the rain and the grasses and lichens and insects will visit us, the sea will visit us."[23]

Could it be that the subconscious really ignores *the* difference?

PENNSYLVANIA STATE UNIVERSITY

Notes

1. Jean Ricardou et al., eds., *Claude Simon: Analyse, Théorie* (Paris: U.G.E., Collection "10/18," 1975), p. 405.

2. Claud DuVerlie refers to "rape" for a situation where a character, Cécile, decides *to do away with her virginity (The Wind)* in "Eroticism in the Works of Claude Simon," *Sub-stance* 8 (Winter 1974): 26.

3. Ibid., p. 26.

4. Nicole Brossard, "*E* muet mutant," *La Barre du Jour* 50 (Winter 1975): 12.

5. Cf. R. Stoller, *The Transsexual Experiment*, quoted by Christian David in "La Bisexualité psychique, éléments d'une réévaluation," *Revue Française de Psychanalyse* 5-6 (September-December 1975): 746.

6. Luce Irigaray, "Des marchandises entre elles," *Quinzaine Littéraire* 215 (August 1975).

7. The French text also means: "Who's the old ass-hole?"

8. The expression "*en chien de fusil*" is regrettably lost in translation. "Dog" and "gun" are two powerful generators of images in *Flanders* and *Leçon* particularly.

9. Again in the French text "*les siennes*" allows for a stronger ambiguity of the referent. Applying both to Iglésia's and Corinne's thighs, it serves as a shifter.

10. Jacques Lacan, *Le Séminaire de—Livre 20; Encore, 1972-3 (Paris Seuil, 1975),* p. 125.

11. This is also used in fiction by women with the same symbolic meaning. See Ellen Moers, *Literary Women* (New York: Doubleday, 1976), pp. 253-54.

12. C. David. *L'Etat amoureux, essais psychanalytiques* (Paris: Payot, 1971), p.192.

13. The remarks on women's poor driving (*Wind*, p. 66) as well as most stereotypical statements on women are made by the narrator and not by Montès.

14. See Denise Braunschweig and Michel Fain, *Eros et Antéros, réflexions psychanalytiques sur la sexualité* (Paris: Payot, 1971), p. 38.

15. See André Green. "La Sexualisation et son économie" in *Revue Française de Psychanalyse*. pp. 913-14.

16. "Une sexualisation en rupture" in *Quinzaine Littéraire* 215 (August 1975): 14.

17. A. Robbe-Grillet, *La Maison de rendez-vous* (Paris: Minuit, 1965), p. 11.

18. Among them Chantal Chawaf's *Retable* (Paris: Femmes, 1974) seems to be the true counterpart of Simon's erotic writing.

19. My translation in this case, since Richard Howard's discards the *word* "pink" (*Pharsalus*, p. 95).

20. The 1977 Cerisy Colloquium on "La Psychanalyse du texte" should start defining a new approach to which R. Barthes also contributes when he reiterates that the detours of the subconscious cannot be transcended, no matter how carefully disseminated and controlled the production of the text may be. See *Barthes* by himself (Paris: Seuil, 1975), p. 99.

21. J. Derrida equates *style* and the *umbrella* in "La Question du style" (which is also "*la question de la femme*") in *Nietzsche aujourd'hui?* (Paris: U.G.E., Collection "10/18," 1973), 1: 238.

22. Essentially pioneered by Anglo-Saxon feminist critics. On the "Feminization of Literature" consult Lisa Appignanese, *Femininity and the Creative Imagination, A Study of Henry James, Robert Musil and Marcel Proust* (London: Vision Press, 1973): on stylistic/speech differences see Annette Kolodny's "Some Notes Towards Defining a Feminist Literary Criticism" in *Critical Inquiry* 2, no. 1 (Autumn 1975); also for book reviews on the subject see *Women and Language News* (Linguistics Department, Stanford University), which is a very helpful newsletter for research on language and sex differences.

23. Blanche: untitled spiral-calligram in *Sorcières* 4 (1976): 43.

III Toward a World View

13

Faulkner, *Gulliver*, and the Problem of Evil

John Fletcher

Evil consists, according to Sartre, in the irreducibility of the world to human thought: this is well illustrated by William Faulkner's novel of 1931, *Sanctuary*, which exerted such a profound influence on the French novelists of Claude Simon's generation, and which ends on the assertion that the sky lay "prone and vanquished in the embrace of the season of rain and death." The temple, or sanctuary, of womanly virtues—the puns on the name of the heroine and on the book's title are, of course, deliberate—is drawn to evil and yet terrified by it; the sanctuary can be defiled, and is: Temple the flirt, and Ruby the whore, are left as damaged survivors of the invasion of that refuge of innocence and peace. Men are especially hypocritical about this famous sanctuary, as evidenced by the cynicism of the taxi driver who says of Goodwin's burning, "Served him right. We got to protect our girls. Might need them ourselves."[1] *Sanctuary* is thus a powerful depiction of the sheer strength of evil, which is described, as seen through Horace's eyes, in these terms: "Perhaps it is upon the instant that we realize, admit, that there is a logical pattern to evil, that we die, he thought, thinking of the expression he had once seen in the eyes of a dead child, and of other dead: the cooling indignation, the shocked despair fading, leaving two empty globes in which the motionless world lurked

profoundly in miniature."[2] But although this evil is depicted with Dostoyevskian intensity, to combat it Faulkner
sets up a weak and in many ways inadequate individual.
When Horace weeps in the car in which his sister is
driving him away from the courtroom, he reveals his
feebleness. He thinks that what he lacks is courage, but this is
not in fact true: his behavior later when threatened by the
lynch mob shows that he is fearless. What he does lack,
perhaps, is a touch of the corruption he is combating: he
himself is too naïve and thus too ineffectual and vulnerable in
the struggle against the overpowering forces he is up against;
he is at once feeble and rash in his fight with it.

Almost every form of imaginable human corruption is
depicted in *Sanctuary*. There is first of all sexual perversity, in
the person of Popeye and the inhabitants of the Memphis
brothel. Next there is political chicanery in the person of
Snopes. Then there is hypocrisy exemplified by Narcissa, or
by the district attorney who openly invites the mob to execute
Goodwin with gasoline and who cynically invokes "that most
sacred thing in life: womanhood."[3] The courtroom itself ex-
udes "that musty odour of spent lusts and greeds and bicker-
ings and bitterness"[4] which an assize court, like all sumps of
human misery, inevitably drains into itself. God himself does
not pass muster either: he is called a "gentleman" at one
point, but Temple's boyfriend described himself as "a
Virginia gentleman," and this quality was of no service in her
protection. Even disinterested goodness such as Horace Ben-
bow's is suspected by Ruby, who assumes that he will demand
as his payment the "fee" which she has been accustomed since
girlhood to render to the lusts of men.

Sanctuary is therefore a bitterly angry book about tragedy
and despair, about fake sanctity and false sanctuaries, about
corruption and evil of every kind. It is a fatalistic work, for its
moral is that it is impossible to haggle with putrefaction. It is
thus a novel almost entirely without hope, a much more sombre work than its successor, *Light in August*, in which the
forces of predestined doom engulfing Joe Christmas, Joanna
Burden, and Gail Hightower are contained within the life-

giving nature of young Lena Grove's fecund—and fecundating—role.

But it is, I believe, the brooding concern with squalor and evil in *Sanctuary* which accounts for the impact it made on Simon's contemporaries (as most dramatically exemplified by André Malraux's historic preface to the French translation, in which he suggested that the work represented "the intrusion of Greek tragedy into the detective story"). It has long been evident that in his early work Claude Simon owes a considerable debt to Faulkner, but this is usually seen in stylistic terms. Thematically also, however, there are interesting connections between the two novelists. In particular, their attitude to human tragedy, wickedness, and corruption is very similar: both perceive the "logical pattern to evil" and explore its ramifications in their books.

It is especially the case with Simon's second published novel, *Gulliver* (1952). The atmosphere in this work is sombre, with a brooding sense of the end of things, as of existence on a cold, long-dead planet "continuing its aimless journey through the immensities of the constellations, a mineral lump on which matter solidified by temperatures making any form of life impossible rang hard and resonant like metal."[5] In such a world man is made of "soft and perishable stuff,"[6] violence and misery and insanity are of banal, even daily occurrence, and tragedy can be read in the hard, closed faces of men and women just as easily as it may be seen in the empty vastness of the sky. *Gulliver* projects a harsh picture of the world: people die uselessly, illusions are lost and hopes are destroyed; and a harmless, gentle and well-meaning person like the Jew-Herzog is subjected not only to atrocious suffering through the loss of his wife and daughter (the latter in all likelihood to an army brothel) during the German retreat from occupied France, but also to the humiliating insults of those who are exasperated rather than touched by his weakness and need. Unlike some other tragic novelists, including Malraux, Simon is not detached; his refusal to accept the state of affairs he exposes in *Gulliver* and other early works is akin to Faulkner's: anger and resistance shine through his prose. Just like Faulkner in

Sanctuary, Claude Simon broods over justice, or rather the
lack of it, in human affairs: it is significant that the title he
gave provisionally to *Gulliver* during its preparation was "The
Judges." His resentment against man's fate is motivated by
the respect he feels for mankind in spite of everything—in
spite of cowardice, cruelty, and rapaciousness, all of which
are seen in good measure in *Gulliver*. Thinking of the human
skull, capable of containing so much wickedness, he calls it
nonetheless "a fragile sphere of bone, a crumbly shell in which
divinities are born and live and die."[7]

Nevertheless, there are some important differences between
Faulkner and Simon even over the matter of evil, where they
are so close. For one thing, Faulkner often gives the impression of believing in a sort of "original sin." His
characters—not only the obviously tainted Joe Christmas or
Popeye, but apparently moral citizens such as Snopes and Narcissa—are more or less "predestined" to commit or condone
evil. One does not get quite this feeling from Simon's people:
they range from the despicable (the *crapules*, in the French
text) to the bunglers, such as Bert in *Gulliver* or *Montès* in
The Wind, who despite the best of intentions often involve
other people in tragedy; but in no case can one say that a particularly wicked individual is directly instrumental in bringing
matters to a head. The nearest we come to a Joe Christmas or
a Popeye in Simon's fiction is Rose's gipsy lover in *The Wind*,
but he is distinctly peripheral, a creature of the simplest in-
stinct, almost a cipher in the plot.

Simon, in other words, appears to have a definitely less
"religious" attitude than Faulkner, for reasons that are readily attributable to their different cultural backgrounds. It is
significant, I think, that in translating the word *"mal,"* which
usually means "evil" in English, Richard Howard preferred
the term "pain."[8] This difference of perspective perhaps helps
account for the greater amount of humor in Simon, even of
burlesque. One might almost say that, whereas Faulkner's
mode par excellence is the tragic stance, for Simon the
characteristic manner is tragicomedy. This is strongly in
evidence in *Le Sacre du printemps* and *The Wind*, but is seen

at its most exemplary in *Gulliver.* The novel is relatively little known, and has been—rather unjustly in my view— repudiated by its author. But it *is* part of the canon, whether Simon likes it or not; and it is a perfectly typical early novel of his, neither worse nor better than others published before *The Grass.* However, because it is not much read, it might be as well if I were briefly to summarize this most "Faulknerian" of all his books.

It consists—like Beckett's *Murphy,* curiously enough—of thirteen chapters in achronological order. The first is set on a Monday evening in winter in a French provincial town, and tells of a characteristic piece of vengeance, such as was common during the *épuration* phase of the liberation of France in 1944-45. Typically of Simon's world, however, this act of terrorism misdirects and the wrong man is executed. The background to the murder only gradually emerges in the chapters which follow: the reader, as in Faulkner's novels, is expected to piece the story together from clues let drop as the book proceeds. The second chapter takes us back in time to the previous Sunday afternoon and a rugby match attended by a girl and her brother—it is only later that the reader is able to attach the names of Eliane and Jo respectively to them. What is clear is that the girl is in love with a rather older man called Max, who in turn seems to be obsessed by a youth, later to be referred to as Bobby. We are also told in this chapter that Jo, an airman who fought with the Free French in England, has a brother who joined the notorious French auxiliary force, called the *"milice,"* which assisted the German occupation troops in anti-*maquis* operations and thus earned the undying hatred of the resistance fighters. The reader guesses at this point that the man the murder squad was after in the first chapter was the renegade brother of Jo and Eliane, a man known as Loulou.

Chapter 3 brings a further complication into play: we learn that a political columnist and bookstore proprietor called Bert is in love with Eliane, and therefore jealous of Max, who has, however, given him encouragement and financial assistance. By chapter 4 Sunday afternoon has turned into night, and the

Jew named Herzog (whom we have already met talking to
Bert in the previous chapter) visits Loulou, who is extorting
money from him in return for the illusory promise of news of
his wife and daughter in a German concentration camp. The
next chapter brings to the fore Thomas Serres, of whom Jo appears to be afraid because of some blemish on his resistance
record which Thomas suspects. Chapters 6 and 7 are set in a
restaurant   in   the   country   and   recount   a   terrible
Walpurgisnacht in which Bobby is shot dead by Loulou, who
in the next chapter escapes by jumping a train. In the same
chapter Eliane reveals to Bert, who is naturally devastated by
the news, that she has been Max's mistress and has borne him
a child. Chapters 9 and 10 consist of an extended flashback into Max's past life, especially his increasing homosexuality in
spite of his affair with Eliane, who in the next chapter finds
happiness with Thomas at the very moment when Max, in
despair at Bobby's death, commits suicide.

After romance, after tragedy, the atmosphere changes to
farce: in chapter 12 Bert makes a complete fool of himself by
acting throughout Monday on the false assumption that it was
Max who murdered Bobby the previous night. Chapter 13
(Tuesday morning) reveals that the execution squad the night
before has killed not Loulou as they had intended but only his
servant, who had in his possession the large sum of money ex-
torted from Herzog. This is the only chapter to take us in time
beyond the first, which recounts the servant's death on Monday night, and the middle chapters, which culminate in the
small hours of Monday morning with the murder of Bobby
and Max's consequent suicide; but this last chapter ties up the
ends not only chronologically but also in other ways, for instance, by revealing that the cleaning woman who looks after
Herzog is Bobby's mother. Linking up characters who at first
sight would not appear to have anything in common is, of
course, like the rather confusing treatment of chronology, a
device which Simon learned from Faulkner. So, too, is his
habit of leaving "holes" in the narrative by omitting vital
details which are supplied only later, or his tendency to prefer
pronouns to proper names, leaving the reader to guess who is
referred to.

What is less characteristic of Faulkner is the irony which Simon employs at the expense of some of his characters—especially those, one suspects, with whom he identifies most closely himself. Bert and the resistance fighters, in their different spheres, put up a pitiful showing, both jumping to false conclusions and making serious errors of judgment; and yet, to be biographical for a moment, Claude Simon is, like Bert, a writer and intellectual, and fought in the *maquis* during the last war. In this respect Simon is closer to Flaubert (who subjected the romantic illusions of his youth to scornful scrutiny in *Madame Bovary* and *Sentimental Education*) than he is to Faulkner. There is certainly something distinctly Flaubertian about the bitter kind of malentendu through which Bert is shown to be made a fool of by fate; one is reminded of the way other author surrogates are treated in the canon, Louis in *Le Tricheur*, for instance, or Bernard in *Le Sacre du printemps*. This comic, ironic, self-criticizing dimension is profoundly characteristic of Simon but not, I think, of William Faulkner.

It is counterbalanced by something equally untypical of Faulkner, a rather romantic love story, that of Thomas and Eliane. As I have argued elsewhere, Eliane is representative of a distinct type of woman in Simon's world, the vulnerable, gauche, and mercilessly honest young girl[9]. Usually her fate is not happy: Cécile in *The Wind*, for instance, gives herself bleakly to her fiancé out of enraged disappointment over her unrequited love for Montès. In this respect Eliane is luckier: although her relationship with Max fails because of his developing homosexuality, and if for a time it would seem that the only alternative is the pompous, self-opinionated Bert, she does at last find love with a "real man," Thomas Serres. The description of their first night together—symbolically, Max's last on this earth—is one of the most tender and least insistently erotic treatments of the sexual act in all Simon's novels. This romantic episode, admittedly, is as uncharacteristic of Simon as it would be of Faulkner.

With the story of Herzog we are, as I have already implied, much more in Faulkner country. He is a kind of persecuted saint, clumsy but lovable, whom others either shun in embar-

rassment (such as Eliane's grandmother), or cynically exploit
(such as Loulou), or despise even for his acts of generosity (the
cleaning woman, for instance, who utters the last words of the
novel—"filthy Jewish pig"—in spite of, or rather because of
his kindness in giving her money and time off to allow her to
bury her son decently). Characteristically, it is Eliane and not
Bert (who nags him about his unreasonable faith in human
progress) who sympathizes most deeply with him, weeping
bitterly for him after trying in vain to dissuade him from giving in to her brother's blackmail. Herzog does not, of course,
represent suffering Jewry alone, but all mankind: his cries of
pain, a crucial passage informs us, are "made to pierce the
heavenly layers of indifference and force the Judges to lower
their eyes and see on the forgotten and tragic face of the earth
the sites—temples, slaughter houses, and prisons—from
which rises up a chorus of lamentation."[10]

The overwhelming feeling the novel conveys, as exemplified
in this passage, is of the pitiless cruelty of fate and of the indifference of the universe to our sufferings. Herzog's grief has
more justification than most,but there is a kind of pathetic
grandeur in the destiny even of a weak character such as Max,
whose wealth attracts unfeeling spongers and hangers-on,
foremost among whom are not only the utterly despicable
Bobby, but also the ungrateful Bert. Max's suicide is not
without its dignity, but it is preceded by cries that are barely
human, so much so that workers on a nearby construction site
imagine they emanate from an animal in pain. If, indeed—as
Sartre argues—evil consists in the irreducibility of the world to
human thought, *Gulliver*, like *Sanctuary*, is redolent with it.
We die like dumb beasts, for no better purpose and often with
less dignity; the good are usually destroyed and the wicked
triumph (both Faulkner's Snopes and Simon's Loulou get off
scot free); and the imperturbable Judges prefer to cast their
gaze elsewhere. This, then, is the bitter message which in his
fierce indignation against cruelty, stupidity, and ignorance
Claude Simon puts across passionately in the novel most clearly indebted to Faulkner's style, method, and thought:
Gulliver.

UNIVERSITY OF EAST ANGLIA

Notes

1. William Faulkner, *Sanctuary* (Harmondsworth, 1970), p. 237.

2. Ibid., p. 176.

3. Ibid., p. 226.

4. Ibid., p. 224.

5. Claude Simon, *Gulliver* (Paris: Calmann-Lévy, 1952), p. 168: "qui continuent à errer sans but dans l'immensité des constellations, masse minérale où sous des températures interdisant toute espèce de vie les matières solidifiées prennent la résonance et la dureté du métal" (translation here and elsewhere my own).

6. *Gulliver*, p. 306: "molle et périssable substance."

7. Ibid., p. 114: "la fragile boule d'os, la friable coquille où naissent, habitent et meurent les divinités."

8. Claude Simon, *The Wind*, trans. Richard Howard (New York: Braziller, 1959), p. 248.

9. *Claude Simon and Fiction Now* (London: Calder and Boyars, 1975), pp. 181-83.

10. *Gulliver*, p. 69: "fait pour percer les couches célestes d'indifférence, forcer les Juges à abaisser leurs yeux et découvrir, sur la surface de la terre oubliée et tragique, les lieux—temples, abattoirs ou prisons—d'où montent les lamentations."

14

Claude Simon and Latin American Fiction: Some Common Grounds

Salvador Jiménez-Fajardo

The intellectual tradition and relative sociopolitical stability of France have preserved and often encouraged formal experimentation in literature as well as the other arts. Such has not been the case in Latin America, where the writer had to seek or create his own ancestry, and where the immediacy of human suffering seemed to overtake his possible involvement with critical theory. It is interesting that we should find aspects of this very concern at the heart of a narrative sequence from Simon's *Conducting Bodies*—certainly one of his most experimental novels: in an unspecified Spanish American capital political concerns impede the progress of a writers' conference; delegates disrupt the proceedings, asserting that the debates evade urgent problems of repression and poverty. This apparent gap between humane and esthetic values is reflected in the novel's text: the French prose is parceled by frequent incursions of Spanish, its formal continuity constantly threatened. In more general terms, each of the six sequences in the novel begins with a basic disjunction whose elements become increasingly distant. Yet, this inner pressure toward dispersion is ultimately encompassed by the narrative's total structure as one of its principal cohesive forces. Thus the dilemma of "engagement" emerges as not only a theme, but an important support of the novel's composition.

One need but recall the broad lines of Simon's novels to realize the range and importance of his social and ideological concerns. The issues, vigorously stated, invite reflection in historical, political, or cultural terms; but always these same issues play their further role in the work as a creative experiment. A comparable attention both to esthetic and human problems characterizes the writing of several contemporary Spanish American novelists. This generation of writers— Cortázar, Fuentes, Donoso, Vargas Llosa, to name a few— by asserting formal prerogatives, achieved a necessary integration of purpose which the temptation of regionalism or political conviction denied to many of their predecessors.

Although the impact of these writers on recent literature has amounted to a revelation, they look back for the most part to the prior efforts of two of their elders in particular, Borges and Carpentier, whose writing anticipated their own in many ways and accompanies it still. As we shall see, both writers, early in their careers, chose to express personal ideologies and particular backgrounds as functioning elements in an esthetic framework. More specifically, and here their preoccupations converge with those of Simon, their reservations about the assumptions of realism led them also to realize the distance that persists between fragmented reality and the linearity of prose. As we know, Simon himself situates the point of departure of his fiction subsequent to *The Wind* in his awareness of the incompatibility "between the discontinuity of the perceived world and continuity of writing."[1] Besides Carpentier and Borges, and among the "new" Spanish American novelists, Cortázar also stands out as one who has explored the problem with particular acumen. While on the surface the fiction of these writers presents striking differences, such differences actually illuminate one another as expressions of similar fundamental perceptions.

In all of Simon's fiction previous to his "objective" period history was very much a matter of memory. The documents, literary or otherwise, that entered the picture were immediately transformed by uncertain remembrance—the Convention-

nel's portrait in *The Flanders Road* acquires the significance
of myth, becoming "poetic" material; the postcards and other
family relics in *Histoire* are likewise altered by memory and
speculation—in an endlessly retold and reshaped past,
language is the spur of memory as well as its vehicle; it is finally
the very material of that past. A rewriting of history, of
recorded history in particular, also interests Borges; this and
an effective manipulation of narrative techniques have always
been distinctive to his tales. His art is one of compression and
allusion: like Simon's, his universe is one of words where
history—individual or cultural—is a series of variations on
limited themes and the writer's creations are recreations.

Almost all of Borges's characters discover themselves to be
incarnations of other existences whose reality was also
literary: their lives are born of words and return to them.
Thus in "The Immortal" the epigraph, a quotation from
Francis Bacon, already suggests a multiple interior duplica-
tion. Bacon cites both Solomon's maxim—There is no new
thing upon the earth—and Plato's own version of it. Borges's
use of the epigraph constitutes a restatement of the thought.
In the narrative the same concept is further illustrated by
the various personifications through which the original character, Marcus Flaminius Rufus, passes, to become Homer,
who antedated him, and Joseph Cartaphilus, who follows
him and who concludes: "There no longer remain any
remembered images, only words remain."[2] The story, a tale of
voyages and misadventures on the way to a homeland, is a version of the *Odyssey* and also a manifestation of the epigraph.
Just as the Homeric poems are thought to be the result of a
many-voiced tradition, so is the fiction presented as a com-
posite by many writers, over many centuries; Borges seems
but the final transcriber.

As is commonly the case with Borges's stories, we have the
clear but somewhat schematic expression of an idea. The
reader is led to deduce a concept of history and of language.
In Simon, on the other hand, language *elaborates* the cyclical
pattern of events, but seems to acquire an independent impetus. Thus in *The Palace* the student sees the effort to
reorganize his past turned against him; the death-related im-

agery that his memory, the language of his past, gathers to itself and carries into his present condition transforms vague uneasiness into unbearable guilt.

We need go no further than "The Immortal" still—the tale actually contains facets of several Borgesian themes—to discover another important use of history and language that will lead us once more to Simon. The postscript to the short story (it is, of course, part of the "fiction") refers to a commentary on its contents by a later writer; in this commentary the tale is described as a patchwork of interpolations from many authors ranging from Pliny to Shaw. In effect, it is possible to detect these various "thefts" as well as many thinly veiled allusions to still other writers. By extending even wider the referential technique of his fiction, Borges suggests that all literature is as our racial memory, of which this very tale merely participates. Through our reading and criticism our personal pasts and futures extend indefinitely, though they remain inextricable from literary words. Ultimately then, only what was once narrated can be narrated once more.

Simon also links his fiction with those of the past through the frequent use of literary allusion or straightforward transcriptions: passages from *The Golden Ass*, from Caesar's *Civil Wars*, from Proust, from schoolbooks, and so on. These fragments are recalled by the narrative when needed and provide it with a precise written past. They also become part of its lexicon, contributing thereafter to the ongoing "invention." So that, whereas allusion in Borges reflects a desire to situate his writing within a compact body of preexistent prose, the same technique in Simon is a result of the text's progress in cementing, as it were, the fissures of represented reality.

The myth of the Eternal Return which Borges's story reenacted emerges in Simon as a preference for cyclical action. Within individual novels his characters seem destined to suffer a fate anticipated for them by the fiction's formal requirements. In *The Palace*, the correspondence of Chapter 2 to Chapter 4, reinforced by textual parallelisms, turns the death of the American into a probability. In *Histoire* the narrator's daily actions and his thoughts must bear the burden of his past and of family tradition. Each time the inner logic of verbal connotations and of metaphor controls characters and events. In both writers the technique of repetition is also aimed at either destroying or containing the structures of time, which they see as among the contributing forces to the discontinuity of events. Borges has always questioned, in his fiction, the actuality of "Western" or "Christian" time, that is to say, of a past to future, Creation to Judgment succession, wherein each action and each individual are unique. He feels that, by accepting this scheme, man, forgetful of his past, condemns himself to lose the present for the sake of an uncertain, or at least unascertainable, future. His fondness for the mirror image and cyclical action, by turning the present into eternity, manifests his desire to deny time its forward movement. As for Simon, the narrative voices of his earlier novels already reformulated temporality through an inquiry that took them endlessly over the same ground (cf. *The Grass, The Flanders Road, The Palace, Histoire*), abolishing any possibility of progression. In later works, from *The Battle of Pharsalus* to *Leçon de choses*, we encounter a pure *récit*; appeals to traditional concepts of time, space, and so on, would introduce an external framework where only fiction-producing values obtain.

A point of view akin to those of Borges and Simon with respect to traditional realism moved the Cuban writer Alejo Carpentier early in his work. Nothing could be further from Borges's spare prose than the rich, baroque texture of Carpentier's style. His careful attention to detail, nuances of lighting, the lines of a scenery, to ornamentation and architecture, approximate him much more to Simon. Both writers, Carpentier perhaps to a lesser extent, want to explore the potential of description as a source of invention, rather than its customary supportive role.

It is, however, in his manipulation of time structure that Carpentier most resembles Simon. This attention comes into play with peculiar clarity in the short story "Journey Back to the Source." Already at that time (the story was first published in 1944)[3], Carpentier made use of the reordering capacity of writing as an element of composition.

From the outset language has a decisive effect on duration: an incantation uttered by an old Negro reverses time's flow and the life of the protagonist unravels itself backwards. His palace reverts to its materials, to earth, as he himself moves beyond birth to nothingness. Closer reading reveals that the inverse flow of time polarizes the logic of the text so that anticipatory details, which in accustomed narration are graduated forward toward a climax, function here in reverse: for instance, the crucial event of the hero's adult life (his wife's drowning) is followed by the sequence of suggestion and metaphor which would normally have prepared it. In this fiction language undoes an unsatisfactory, incoherent picture of reality, while replacing it with a more continuous one.

With Simon, words acquire constellated associations as he proceeds, so that they may bear an entire complex of imagery, or have events and even whole sequences linked to them. Gestures, situations may be interpolated into the ongoing narrative flow. In *Histoire* this technique results in the concerted advance of several blocks of narrative, juxtaposed to one another and moving at different speeds. The text is segmented according to the crossovers from one "block" to another which connotations, parallelisms, or echoes elicit. As a consequence, the usual progression of action is negated. The advance, or rather the movement of the fiction underlies that of its segments and results from their interplay.

In the short novel *Manhunt (El acoso)*[4], published in 1954, Carpentier manipulates time in a manner designed to stress the subservience of memory to the pressures of narration. There, too, we recognize the concept of memory characteristic of Simon's early work up to and including *Histoire*: the past is not uncovered, it is created by the text. In this respect Carpentier's novel is reminiscent most particularly of *The Palace*. In *Manhunt* a funnel-like penetration of remembrance initially set off in long parentheses, gathers memories whose recovery depends less on their intrinsic importance than on a double imperative: 1) the hero's present situation as a hunted man; his mind imposes a heuristic role on past events; 2) the inner order of the text whereby a set of motifs is introduced, allowed to accumulate emotive content, and developed thereafter in a series of interlocking variations. The characters brought in at the outset are initially connected by anecdotal coincidence. Soon the women in the tale, embodiments of a love-death polarity, create actual and metaphorical centers of turbulence that permeate the entire narrative. They come close to representing *sources* of invention, as they so clearly do in Simon—e.g., old Marie in *The Grass*, Corinne in all her appearances, the women in *Histoire*.

Necessities of imagery and the associations of motifs guide the inner course of Carpentier's short novel, so that the particular moments that the fugitive remembers are likened to certain concepts and their connotations—such as verticality, silence, exposure—or other demands of the structure. The idea of order offers a particularly good instance of the ramifications of such motifs: order, or elaborated form, is linked to Catholic ritual, to Estrella, a prostitute (she likes to repeat to the fugitive, "I am an orderly person"), to the "Very Important Person" (presumably the leader of the revolutionaries), and to churches. The individuals in this series partake both of order and disorder: the V.I.P. disappears and his home is demolished (disintegrated architectural form). Estrella embodies the love-death duality in all its fascination: love offers temporary serenity, coherence; venality, spurious conformity make of her an informer and an agent of death. When danger increases, all these motifs reappear in a chaotic state. Previous symbols of restraint and succor, now metaphors for death, accumulate near the end to negate all possibilities of escape and make death inevitable.

The student of *The Palace* also allows his memory to elaborate a web of deadly connotations, which at the end threatens figuratively to suffocate him: the inner course of a text has superseded and reshaped events, and the protagonist is denied his liberation from the past. Further aspects of *Manhunt* are reminiscent of *The Palace* in particular but also of other works by Simon. For instance, the return to "the beginning," to an inescapable situation rendered more so by the intervening text (cf. *Histoire*) is also present in Carpentier.

The novel opens as the fugitive tries to hide in a concert hall—his flashbacks, which form the bulk of the narrative, actually originate from the temporary security afforded by the crowded auditorium—and he is shot there at the end of the performance.

These analogies of technique imply not only a similar understanding in Simon and Carpentier of what fiction really does, but also an awareness that the value of their research is ultimately linked to social and political circumstance. Simon's rejection of certain traditional novelistic axioms is a manifestation of that generalized attack on petrified custom which runs through most of his fiction. In *The Wind* Montès embodies a threat to immemorial modes of living which are inured to adultery, dissipation, greed, but are scandalized by the young man's lack of conformity to custom. In *The Flanders Road* the creaky social and military traditions to which de Reixach adhered incapacitated him for modern warfare and lost him his wife: Corinne uses him to further her own ends but flaunts her infidelities and becomes the very antithesis of those traditions. A dying past exerts the same debilitating effect on the protagonists of *Histoire* and *The Battle of Pharsalus*.

Carpentier has known how to explore in his writing both ideological and artistic concerns. *Manhunt* demonstrates this, and so do his later novels, where he continues to deal with constant human problems such as revolution, the dehumanizing effect of power, cultural traditions, and so on, as well as with purely literary problems. With respect to his latest fiction, where human issues seem to have diminished in importance, Simon has felt the need, on occasion, to anticipate the objections of some who might look upon these works as "word games" by pointing out their ultimately epistemological nature. Words are not merely words: "If . . . we must never forget that the word fire is not fire, that the word blood is not blood, we must also not forget either that the words fire and blood refer us to the images and concepts of fire and blood."[5]

In Latin America there has been much criticism of the experimental bent in some recent writers. Oscar Collazos, for instance, a critic of some repute, speaks of "the forgetting of reality, the disregard of all concrete references from which is initiated the gestation of the literary product."[6] (We may raise here a first objection as to whether the "literary product" originates exclusively from concrete reference. It seems as often as not to start simply with language). Julio Cortázar answered this charge with the care and seriousness which it duly deserves in the context of Latin American letters: "Forgetting of reality? Not at all; my tales not only do not forget it but attack it on all possible flanks, seeking its most secret and richest veins. Disregard for all concrete reference? No disregard whatever, but a selection, that is the choice of grounds where narrating is like making love so that enjoyment may create life, and also invention from a 'sociocultural' context, invention born, as were born fabulous animals, of the faculty of creating new relationships among elements disconnected in the daily-ness of the 'context.'"[7] These words, which might well have been uttered by Simon himself, confirm views on the possibilities of narration.

Characteristic of both Simon and Cortázar is a constant renovation of their technical means in the art of narrative. Few readers unacquainted with the various stages of transformation in Simon's writing would recognize in *Leçon de choses* the author of *The Wind*. In fact, these striking contrasts are among the features whereby his writing remains unique, ever fascinating. No less striking is the decision to experiment that inspires Cortázar's itinerary from *The Winners* to *62. A Model Kit*. He finds the motive force of this evolution in "the search for ultimate possibilities that literature can give . . . translated into forms ever more experimental, more 'open,' farthest away from the preceding work."[8]

His best-known novel, *Hopscotch* (1963), seems to answer within its very design such tenets on forward-seeking experimentation. The axis around which revolve its many levels is the quest, incessantly contested, for the unifying principle of the fictive reality. As soon as we examine the conditions of this quest it breaks up into a basic duality: the protagonist Horacio Oliveira's pursuit of a coherent view of the world, and the fiction's own. The disposition of the text itself underlines the duality as allowances are made for two modes of reading: the passive reader may proceed from chapter 1 to chapter 56 in succession: the active reader should begin with chapter 73 and follow the author's suggested sequence (which includes, of course, 1 to 56) to chapter 131.

The grounds on which the novel's ultimate versatility rests are the interpenetration of the reader's "work" and the novel's evolving structure. This development is reflected by one of the characters' statements concerning the "birth of the book": "First there is a confused situation, which can only be defined by words; I start out from this half-shadow and if what I mean (what is *meant*) has sufficient strength, the *swing* begins at once, a rhythmic swaying that draws me to the surface, lights everything up, conjugates this confused material and the one who suffers it into a clear third somehow fateful level: sentence, paragraph, page, chapter, book."[9]

An approach to self-generating composition is also developed in Borges's "The Approach to Almotasim" and may shed further light on the mechanism of *Hopscotch*. In this story, presented as the review of a suspense novel, a man seeks a great spirit through the traces it leaves in other, lesser souls. At the end of his search, the implication is that he will find a mirror. The seeker has created himself through his search. Such relations between writing and reality, or writing and its reflection of reality, are also those which sustain the quest of *Conducting Bodies*; Simon saw it in the preface to *Orion Aveugle* as "the singular adventure of the narrator who does not cease to search, discovering groping the world in and through writing."[10]

Cortázar's next novel, *62. A Model Kit*, grew out of "the intentions sketched in the final paragraphs of chapter 62 of *Hopscotch*, which explain the title of this book and perhaps are realized in its course."[11] Critical commentaries in that chapter dealt with recent theories on the chemical origins of thinking and pictured a group of individuals interacting unawares and thinking "it reacts psychologically in the classic sense of that tired old word, but which merely represents an instance in that flow of animated matter, in the infinite interactions of what we formerly called desires, sympathies, will, convictions, and which appear here as . . . foreign occupying forces."[12] Thus, in *62. A Model Kit* as in *Hopscotch*, the world discovered by writing tends to be a supra- or infra-reality, truer perhaps than is our daily one. As we know, Simon also wants words to relate normally disparate aspects of the real, although these aspects remain perfectly straightforward. The relationships established between them by writing, while they belong exclusively to the printed page, are intended to renew the reader's acquaintance with a familiar, if imperfectly recognized, world.

In *62. A Model Kit*, as well as in *Hopscotch*, Cortázar tries to develop among quotidian aspects of existence relationships which define what he calls "figures." As he has expressed it to Luis Harss[13] he feels that we inadvertently form part of larger figures, beyond our personal lots—that we are interconnected by links that defy reason, unrelated to ordinary human bonds. This intuition is also a facet of the autocritical element in his fiction, whereby the use of language becomes an instrument of discovery. In *62. A Model Kit* the concept functions in such a way that not only generally disparate aspects of reality but also otherwise remote parts of the fiction are brought into conjunction. We think here of Simon's "ensembles" interlinked according to "common qualities."[14]

Ultimately necessary to the final composition of these novels is the reader's effort of construction itself, to reveal the "mandala" unattainable to Horacio and his friends through Paris and Buenos Aires in *Hopscotch*; to draw the "figure" that choreographs the lives of the various characters through London, Paris, Vienna in *62. A Model Kit*. Simon too wishes the reader to find the perspective encompassing the hamlet, the resort and the industrial city in *Triptych*, a perspective from which the pieces of the total puzzle may uncover a recognizable design. Also in *Leçon de choses*, the reader must discover the proper spatial and temporal focus that will relate the construction-destruction components of the war scenes, the workers' progress, and the erotic episodes.

This necessary involvement of the reader in what is, essentially, a reelaboration of reality, a renewal of our perception of the world, does not shun human concerns but incorporates them, broadening their scope. When uncertainty undercuts our most secure perceptions, ideological factionalism appears in its proper perspective as merely an aspect of more fundamental fragmentations. Recent Hispanic writers who address themselves to similar concepts see in the transformation of narrative form a necessary inquiry into basic premises of fiction. In this, their work and Simon's coincide.

ILLINOIS WESLEYAN UNIVERSITY

Notes

1. "Réponses de Claude Simon à quelques questions écrites de Ludovic Janvier," *Entretiens: Claude Simon*, ed. Marcel Séguier (Toulouse: Subervie, 1971), p. 18. My translation.
2. J. L. Borges, "The Immortal," in *Labyrinths* (New York: New Directions, 1964), p. 118.
3. Alejo Carpentier, *War of Time*, trans. Frances Partridge (New York: Knopf, 1970).
4. English translation by Harriet de Onis in *Noonday* 2 (1958).
5. Claude Simon, "Réponses de Claude Simon . . . ," *Entretiens*, p. 29. My translation.
6. Oscar Collazos, "La Encrucijada del lenguaje," *Literatura en la revolución, y revolución en la literatura* (Mexico: Siglo XX, 1970), p. 4. My translation.
7. Julio Cortázar, "Literatura en la revolución y revolución en la literatura: Algunos malentendidos que liquidar," in *Literatura en la revolución*, p. 55. My translation.
8. Ibid., p. 59.
9. Julio Cortázar, *Hopscotch* (New York: Signet, 1967), pp. 331-32.
10. Claude Simon, *Orion aveugle* (Geneva: Skira, Collection "Les Sentiers de la création," 1970), end of preface. My translation.
11. Julio Cortázar, *62. Modelo para armar* (Buenos Aires: Sudamericana, 1972), prefatory page.
12. Cortázar, *Hopscotch*, p. 305.
13. Luis Harss and Barbara Dohmann, *Into the Mainstream: Conversations with Latin American Writers* (New York: Harper and Row, 1967), p. 227.
14. See Claude Simon, "La Fiction mot à mot," *Nouveau roman: hier, aujourd'hui* II (Paris: U.G.E., Collection "10/18," 1971), pp. 73-97.

15

Modernist Survivor: The Later Fiction of Claude Simon

Morton P. Levitt

I

There was a time, less than a decade ago, when Claude Simon seemed the ultimate Modernist novelist, acknowledged heir of Proust, Faulkner, and Joyce, a survivor—in an age given over to a new, post-Modernist dialectic—who continued to believe in and practice the fictional and human values of the old. Critics might reasonably complain that Simon's work had become anachronistic, but it was difficult not to be drawn by the rhythms of his prose, by our own intense involvement in the lives of his characters, by his gradually expanding personal universe, built, so we felt, of the bricks and blood of his own experience. Even those raised in the New Criticism and scornful of the biographical approach were attracted to his Proustian "reconstitutions" of this experience, the magma (another of his favorite words) of an inchoate world, which afforded to the creator almost endless possibilities of giving life. But his was more than a private vision. It was Simon who helped us to see—in that remarkable series of novels beginning with *The Wind* in 1957 and continuing through to *Histoire* in 1967—that the Modernists had not repudiated the legacy of humanism, as early readers had felt, but had placed it at the core of their work: hidden by irony perhaps, diminished because the world had diminished, but somehow raised precisely because creative potential seemed less certain in their time than it had in Homer's or Milton's or even in Tennyson's. From Joyce's Bloom to Simon's (the Blum of *The Flanders Road*), the Modernists saw heroic potential in the man who merely survived, who continued to act on the humane values at a time in history when all value had seemed to vanish.[1]

Critics today speak of a new Simon. His style has changed: "No longer do we have in his later novels long, intricate sentences, replete with parentheses, dominated by present participles. Instead . . . we read rather short statements, minimally qualified, impersonal"[2]; there has been a shift in reader involvement from his characters to his text: "By challenging the reader to examine carefully what is signified by a text, these last works lead him further and further down a path along which it is difficult for him to retrace his steps. He may indeed, if he follows the arguments scrupulously, be led from a study of the text "the one personage who is undeniably true and present and verifiable" to a reconsideration of his relationship with the world"[3]; his universe has expanded geographically (the action of *Conducting Bodies* takes place entirely in the New World) but has contracted in all other respects. Simon appears in his latest books to have abandoned the Modernists and their basically humanistic concerns and to have followed Robbe-Grillet and Butor into the post-Modern era, with its radically different critical interests.

The turning point is *The Battle of Pharsalus* (1969). Themes, images, even characters and narrative patterns are familiar here, but there is a new dynamic operating as well: the author's own self-conscious involvement with the process of writing as process, with the literary text as a manifestation of a reality ostensibly more basic than that of love or politics or betrayal, with the reconstitution of a text as if it were life. The obvious analogies are to Robbe-Grillet's denial of metaphor and his repudiation of humanism and to Butor's abandonment of narratives based on myth and psychological motivation and his adoption in their stead of open-ended, experimental constructions ordered only by internal structural demands. In each case, the movement is away from man-centered celebrations of inner life, as in the best Modernist novels, and toward a fiction that plays on the technical advances made by the Modernists and abjures their human concerns: a fiction made to order for that new school of critics who write as if fiction were no more than anthropology.

The Battle of Pharsalus is, in a sense, Simon's *Mobile*, the book which marked a major change in direction long before its readers could detect that change. As Butor's prior novels had dealt with the psychological disintegration of their protagonists, this transitional work was itself disintegrative, destructive of the very form on which those earlier works had been built. It was logical, when *Mobile* first appeared in 1962, to trace its connections to *Passing Time, A Change of Heart* and *Degrees*.[4] Today we can see that, connections aside, Butor had already progressed into the new sensibility: he is perhaps the best single example of a Modernist writer moving willfully and articulately into the post-Modern age. Simon appears now to be making a similar transition. The parallel with Butor seems instructive.

We may be even more struck, however, by the specific comparisons between Simon's present work and that of Robbe-Grillet, who once seemed his opposite pole among the writers of the so-called Nouveau Roman. Most evident is the stylistic change from the richly expansive, Faulknerian diction of Simon's major novels to a prose that is very nearly as reductionist as Robbe-Grillet's. But there are other parallels as well: images that seem to be drawn from Robbe-Grillet, for example, the torn series of circus and movie posters in *Triptych* (an image that can also be found in Butor), palimpsests of experience which come alive for their beholders; here, too, are images that promise to grow into metaphors but may never quite do so; some of the acts of love in *Triptych* are described in geometrical terms, as if they were being perceived by the (dis)ordering consciousness of an early novel by Robbe-Grillet; the obsessive jealousy of the protagonist of *The Battle of Pharsalus* seems worthy of the hero of *Jealousy*; scenes are suddenly frozen, and we may suspect the presence of the same camera eye that orders *Last Year at Marienbad* and *The Voyeur*; external objects obtrude into the perceiving consciousness and threaten to usurp it, as if they all along had been the source of the vision, as in *Project for a Revolution in New York*; even the sad, old, cuckolded Picasso king of *Orion aveugle* and *Conducting Bodies* may have his origin in the mad, old king Boris of *La Maison de rendez-vous*. The evidence, at first glance, seems highly persuasive. It may also be highly misleading. For Simon is no Robbe-Grillet, nor even a Butor. His artistry has certainly altered in these last books—the discontinuity grown greater, the point of view more diffuse, the self-concern still more obsessive. But the continuity with his major works is equally undeniable; the humanist Simon continues to function even as he seems to become a post-Modern artist. The opening image of *Orion aveugle*—a drawing by Simon himself—is of the workplace of the writer: his desk, the postcard lying on his dictionary, his cigarettes and matches; some extra pens; his manuscript being revised by his hand. It is the same image as at the end of *The Battle of Pharsalus*: the artist observing himself, the man of feeling using his own experience, his own emotions, as the basis of his art, both subject and object of a narrative trick done with multiple mirrors: the reflexive Modernist artist whose obsession with his own task provides technique and theme for one of the central post-Modern subjects. But there is more. In both novel and drawing, the window in the room opens outward, away from the desk and the self-involved writer, into the world.

II

Part 3 of *The Battle of Pharsalus*, "Chronology of Events," begins with an epigraph from Heidegger announcing a change of technique and intention. The change of technique is immediately apparent in the jarring new prose style that marks this section: simple declarative sentences, conventional punctuation and syntax, an almost total avoidance of the lush rhythms which characterize Simon's previous prose. The old tool spoken of by Heidegger is presumably no longer usable,

and so the author endeavors to forge here a new piece of
equipment, a new language and consciousness through which
to approach a new-forming world. As a result, the viewer in
The Battle of Pharsalus is more self-consciously concerned
with his role as viewer, as creator, than are any of his
predecessors. This much is clear. The change of intention,
however, is less easily perceived, for the major theme—the
relationship between technique and theme—is unchanged:
these events are no more chronological, no less subjective in
presentation and effect than comparable events in earlier
novels.

Simon's object, again, is history, more specifically the inter-
connection of past and present, the Proustian lesson that we
are beings constantly in process, autonomous products both of
our youth and our maturity, responsible for our lives even
when we do not quite comprehend them. The narrator of *The
Battle of Pharsalus* is as tied to his past—it is virtually the
same past—as are Montès or Georges or the student of *The
Palace* or the unnamed narrator of *Histoire*. Their creator too,
despite this newly fashioned equipment of his, is himself tied
to the past. Thus throughout the novel, even in part 3, we
hear echoes of earlier works: familiar patterns of imagery and
metaphor, the same literary sources and analogues, even
aspects of narrative technique that we have long been accustomed to. Simon fills his novel with revealing signs of the
continuity which in his work must accompany change.

And so *The Battle of Pharsalus* begins with the open window and the wings of a bird: the same bird seen through the
window in Barcelona at the start of *The Palace* and heard
through the window in the provincial French town, perhaps
Simon's own Perpignan, in the first scene of *Histoire*. It closes
with the narrator-author as he sits at his desk, watching
through his window as "a pigeon passes in front of the sun,"
writing the first sentence of the novel that would eventually
become *The Battle of Pharsalus*. "O. feels the pigeon's
shadow pass rapidly over his face, like a sudden touch. He remains a moment in the same position. Then he lowers his
head. Now only the upper corner of the page is in shadow. O.
writes: Yellow and then black in the wink of an eye then

yellow again" (p. 187). Having built on the presumed facts of his life as a man, Simon gives us now, through his persona, his life as an artist. The two are inextricably linked, even congenital: in the final scene of *Histoire*, sifting through the pile of postcards which constitutes so much of his past, the author imagines his mother as she writes the card, surrounded by palm trees around a tropical bay, bearing in her womb her child, himself. He is his own past, even his future: the first image of *Triptych*, written six years later, is a postcard picturing palm trees and a tropical bay.

The growth is organic, emerging naturally from within the life and the art. But it is also conscious, intentional, derived in part by analogy to other Modernist works. The novel's reflexive concern with its own creation, for instance, finds contemporary parallels in Beckett, Borges, and Barth, among others, all of them rooted ultimately in *Ulysses*. (For we know that Stephen Dedalus at the end of *Ulysses*, having found his subject in Bloom, will soon write the novel that we know as *Ulysses*.) The remaining parallels serve similarly to reflect the variable reality which confronts each Modernist hero. Chronology is jumbled and scenes reproduced in new and differing contexts, as in Cortázar's *Hopscotch*, so that one version of the past overlaps with and contradicts another, so that past becomes present and threatens to become future action as well. The possibilities of chronology seem almost limitless in such a narrative system, the possibilities of certainty virtually nil. An unread book on a train journey through Italy somehow provides the source of subsequent events, as in Butor's *A Change of Heart*; to the would-be readers these imagined events are as real and convincing as are those that take place outside the text. For them there is no single, objective reality, only a series of realities with their separate, overlapping demands. Peering down through the window at the world outside, like the protagonist-author of Claude Mauriac's *The Marquise Went Out at Five*, O. becomes one of the world outside, looking upward now to the window and imagining the occupants within. As Mauriac's watcher identifies with those whom he sees and imagines—makes them part of his projected fiction—so this obsessed viewer becomes not just jealous lover but the woman who is the cause of his jealousy, also called O., and even her new lover, his friend and betrayer. At this point even identity grows ambiguous. What little stability there is comes, ironically, from that paragon of uncertainty, the jealous lover who knows in his heart that he has been betrayed but who remains unsure to the end if his jealousy is justified, Proust's Marcel.

Simon uses Proust much as Eliot once claimed that Joyce had used Homer: as an established pattern designed to give order and form to uncertain events in a chaotic time. Proust functions, then, as a kind of myth for Simon, a universally accepted norm of technique and behavior. For O., as for other Simon protagonists—for the community of men which they represent—Marcel provides a sense of continuity within the community, the certain knowledge that events in the present are allied to and evolve from the deeds of the past, deeds that may now seem exemplary indeed. Marcel serves as well to foster the moral judgment drawn from such a historical perspective; here, as with Bloom, that judgment is largely ironic. Bloom seems diminished in contrast with Ulysses; O. learns from Marcel only to follow in the path of betrayal, to intensify his master's example. For Proust speaks, finally, as all myth does, to our deepest fears and desires. And for O. that is the fear, and perhaps in a strange way the desire, of betrayal.

Leopold Bloom, the modern Ulysses, does not read Homer. O. appears almost never to be without his Proust. The names of Marcel, Oriane, Albertine, and Odette ring with surprise throughout his narration; his childhood memories—arriving, for example, with his mother and grandmother at a hotel in Lourdes (p. 83)—recall those of Marcel at Combray and Balbec; we can almost trace his jealousy to its roots in Swann and Marcel. The name "Marcel" is "scratched in pencil" alongside the door at which the narrator listens for the sounds of his lover's betrayal (p. 11), his "Seeing ear" (p. 13) creating what he cannot experience at first hand; her full first name, we discover eventually, is Odette (p. 132). Most of his narration, like Marcel's, proceeds from heightened sentence to heightened sentence, charged with meanings that he can only partially grasp, "(like those magic-lantern images sliding from right to left then from left to right, one driving out the last . . .)" (p. 44). Part of his narration comes directly from Proust. O. remembers his uncle, also apparently a victim, "Saying that jealousy is like . . . like . . .

"Remembering the place: somewhere at the top of a right-hand page. Could recite reams of verse that way once I managed to visualize the page and where on the page" (p. 10). Skimming through the several volumes of *A la recherche du temps perdu*, he searches continually for that half-remembered phrase—"jealousy where was it right-hand page near the top" (p. 60)—but he can never quite find it. Swann's jealousy serves him explicitly as metaphor of his own; reading about Swann's distorted love for Odette intensifies his love. Proust even appears himself in a photo which recalls Charlus (p. 108).[5]

Marcel, let us remember, does not write of the events of his life until some time after he has lived them. At this late point, the act of writing itself becomes an implicit event in his account. The sole exception to this is the action of "Swann in Love," events occurring before his birth, which he reconstitutes many years afterwards from the several sources available to him and from his own conjecture. Swann's affair with Odette surely helps shape Marcel's own relationship with Albertine. But since he does not begin to write of Swann and Odette until long after he has known and lost Albertine, we might reason that in a circular manner it is his own affair which influences the earlier account: life imitating art; art, in this reflexive account, infiltrating life. O. similarly finds analogues to his state in the characters of Proust. And perhaps, too, he models his state after those of Marcel and Swann. Perhaps he needs Proust even to name his state, as if the mythic source alone can give stability to his life and to his art.

We can follow this process further in the lovemaking scenes which O. recreates behind the locked door and window. For the images that he envisions—images so intense that he appears to be acting not merely as voyeur but as each individual participant as well—are drawn only in part from his own experience and his knowledge of the participants; they come

largely from imagination and from external, almost scholarly
sources. The opening image of the passing bird, barely
registered on the retina, brings with it "a recollection (warning?) a recall of the shadows . . . the air rustling or perhaps
not heard perceived merely imagined bird arrow . . . like the
one in that painting (where was it?) some naval battle between
Venetians and Genoese . . . the feathered arch humming in
the dim sky one of them piercing his open mouth just as he
rushed forward sword raised leading his men transfixing him
stabbing the shout in his throat" (p. 3). The uncertain "he"
merges with the passage from Caesar's *Gallic Wars*,
translated with his uncle many years earlier, in which
Crastinus, who casts the first lance at Pharsalus, is killed in
the battle. "Plutarch, Caes., LXIV, gives the details: 'He
received in the mouth a thrust of the sword so violent that the
point emerged at the back of his neck'" (p. 163). The red
spear becomes the man's thrusting penis, the mouth and vulva
an open wound, sex and warfare united.

The process is compounded as the image blends with other
paintings and pieces of sculpture whose subject is warfare or
love (Polidoro da Caravaggio, Cranach, Poussin, the elder
Brueghel, Piero della Francesca, and Uccello, among others),
with a series of photographs, some of them quite old, part of
the inheritance of *Histoire*, and with other strange and surprising sources: a catechism illustration, an ad for farm
machinery; a comic strip, postage stamp, matchbook cover,
and Gauloises wrapper; a box of paper clips, some coins, a
five-mark note and a one-thousand-lire bill. Each separate
picture becomes a work of art to be judged critically; each provides analogues to "his" fate. O.'s betrayal, in the process,
merges with the imagined one, in an earlier generation, of his
Uncle Charles. Betrayal, too, seems an inevitable part of his
inheritance.

Do the imagined lovers reflect the paintings he has seen, or
are they themselves some sort of Ur-painting, source of all these
other illustrations on warfare and lovemaking? He is clearly of
two minds about them. On the one hand, each is viewed from
the perspective of the art critic as historian, as if it were part of

an essay that he is constructing; on the other hand, each feeds his obsession. From the old photo of Charles in an artist's studio, he recreates his uncle's presumed betrayal by his friend, the artist; upon this scene—like Marcel with Swann—he erects the elaborate structure of his own betrayal by his artist friend, the Dutchman Van Velden, whose model, Odette, has become his mistress. He becomes himself a participant in the act of betrayal, perhaps even its inventor (like Swann, like Marcel, like Bloom), reacting with passion and yet with a cool objectivity, as if this scene too were part of his essay. Like each of his predecessors, he is unable to express or confront his emotions except indirectly (one of the functions of his art criticism); as in each of Simon's previous novels, the reader is forced to fill in and deal with the emotional details.

O. goes to Pharsalus for the same reason that the narrator of *The Palace* returns to Spain: to uncover past history, to find his own past as well. The history of the race, for Simon, is individual history, each one a reflection and source of the other. This is why his fiction is so intensely personal and at the same time so closely tied to historical events. In the lesson of past civilizations, conned long before with his uncle in that old Latin text but never learned truly, O. seeks to discover the source of his own betrayal. But he finds no Jungian truths about himself or mankind; he cannot even locate the site of the battlefield with certainty: only a soccer game at modern Pharsala, a folk memory of a medieval battle against the Turks on a nearby hill, his own memories of World War II. In the process, however, he may teach us something about the state of humanity.

"I didn't yet know" . . . "I was suffering like"—these refrains sound throughout O.'s narration. What he comes to know is riding to war and betrayal; he suffers like a man, justified perhaps by his suffering. Inexpressive he may be, yet as art historian and critic he easily finds metaphors to communicate his feelings. Thus, the dead horse alongside the Flanders Road becomes in this narrative the grim shell of a McCormick reaper, Heidegger's equipment made manifest, "rusty lying on its side a tangle of plates wheels and gears bristling with broken rods like some wreck cast up by the sea stranded after a flood" (p. 22). A symbol of natural decay, remnant of "antediluvian" times, the reaper is linked somehow to the imagined, yoked lovers (a modern variant of the beast with two backs) and to his own childhood memories—a brief masturbatory scene with an older boy, a voyeuristic scene as they spy on lovers in a barn—played out near a similar shell. O.'s memories of the war constitute a reprise of the battle scenes of *Histoire*, where we learn for the first time some of the details of the terrible cavalry battle fought at the start of World War II; the lovers in the barn look ahead to *Triptych*. One battle scene, one pair of lovers, overlays another, the thrashing legs of horses in battle mix with those of soccer players and lovers; imagination, memory, and physical perception are indissolubly joined; all times merge into one time; all metaphors coalesce. In front of the House of Parliament in Belgrade—seen on his trip to Greece—stand two bronze statues, "each representing a man supporting the legs of a rearing horse over his arms." Even to an ex-cavalryman, he admits, "the meaning of this allegory is obscure. The naked, muscular men seem to belong to that race of creatures doomed to superhuman and endless tasks, ceaselessly repeating the same gestures . . . combating an invisible enemy ceaselessly vanquished and ceaselessly reviving" (p. 167). We suspect that he knows all too well what the allegory means and how it applies to his life.

Pharsalus, in northern Greece, is no different for Simon's hero from the palace in Spain or the prisoner of war camp or his native town: "not a country: a place, something apparently unknown to geographers" (p. 93), a place, that is, where the blind man can seek for himself through space and through time. The ultimate metaphor for Simon's questing hero is another work of art, "the extraordinary *Blind Orion Searching for the Sun* precipitating the spectator precipitating himself" (p. 111). For his search, in the end, is our search as well, and the sun endlessly recedes from the blinded seeker of light.

III

Conducting Bodies (1971) consists in large part of that work of art criticism researched and written by O. in *The Battle of Pharsalus* and published separately in a Skira edition (part of the series *"Les Sentiers de la création"*) under the title *Orion aveugle*. Combining the texts shows us for the first time the actual images—drawn from painting, engraving, collage, and photomontage; symbols of contemporary culture, an old map of the heavens, several charts of the human body—which serve as source of the narrator's imaginative life and become finally the metaphors by which he implicitly defines himself. Poussin's "extraordinary" *Blind Orion Searching for the Sun* is at the center of his quest. Pictures of the conquistadors and of modern political violence point up its moral. The charts of the body encapsulate his physical disease. The temptation is great to read *Orion aveugle* not merely as sourcebook for and gloss upon *Conducting Bodies* but virtually as the identical work, less complete perhaps (if any of Simon's open-ended books can be called complete) but even richer because of its illustrations and the presence of the author's revealing preface. Simon the art critic speaks in his preface of Simon the novelist, providing the evidence for the next text-laden approaches to his latest books: the revealing physical presence of the artist at work at his desk, writing in his own hand and speaking directly to his readers of the artistic process, what in the old New Criticism would have been discussed in terms of point of view ("omniscient" on the one hand, "reflexive" on the other), or in the language of art criticism would be called "painterly."

Surely the preface encourages such a post-Modern, text-oriented approach. Seen through the eyes of the art critic and historian Simon, the novelist Simon seems almost a passive participant in the artistic process, creator of a text that exists apart from its creator and his intentions. From his starting point—"un magma informe de sensations . . . de souvenirs plus ou moins pièces accumulés;" to his basic equipment, the

incantory power of words, which are separate from the objects
and acts they are meant to represent—"aucune goutte de sang
n'est jamais tombée de la déchirure d'une page où est décrit le
corps d'un personnage;" to his ultimate, unreachable
goal—"l'aventure singulière du narrateur qui ne cesse de
chercher, découvrant à tâtons le monde *dans et par
l'écriture*" italics added—Simon speaks as if preparing a text
were a reflexive act that virtually produces itself, as if art
criticism and fiction were one, as if, implicitly, the reading of
Conducting Bodies were really no different from that of *Orion
aveugle*: the perfect post-Modern statement. And yet, at the
same time, he speaks of these acts as some sort of Odyssean initiation rite—"l'épuisement du voyageur explorant ce paysage
inépuisable"—as if protagonist, writer and reader alike were
engaged still in a traditional Modernist quest. How are we to
reconcile this evident dichotomy?

The point is, of course, that however much we can learn
from *Orion aveugle*, and particularly from its preface, this is a
very different work from *Conducting Bodies*, and its lessons
are only partially applicable to the later text. A new process
may well be at work here, but so is the old; the preface implies
both a new start and continuity with the old.

For the novel exercises that conscious and articulate control
(even over what might loosely be termed "biographical" data)
which the art-book preface appears to deny, and it does so
without sacrificing that intensity of commitment which
characterizes Simon's previous novels. Moreover, this tor-
tured portrait of the artist who turns his own body and blood
into universal history—an image derived from *Finnegans
Wake*—is as appropriate to Simon as to Joyce, both voyagers
exploring inexhaustible landscapes.

The immediate landscape of *Conducting Bodies* is that
place "unknown to geographers" which is spoken of by O.
This is not quite the same as saying that it is purely imaginative, however. In none of Simon's fiction, it is true, is
there a Lawrentian spirit of place. Yet we can extrapolate
from the few given facts of *The Palace*, for instance, as well as
from the attendant historical events (the civil war within the
Civil War), and conclude with some assurance that the setting

is Barcelona and not, say, Madrid. Similarly, we can use the name "Perpignan" to identify the locale of *The Wind* and *Histoire* not because we know for certain that this is the geographical town that is involved, or even that a single, identifiable town is involved, but simply because such a name will serve as well as any other to represent that southern French town where the wind blows fiercely during certain months of the year and the force of heritage and memory is always fierce. Pharsalus is one of the rare places that Simon identifies specifically, and yet we discover with O. that it is not even a recognizable site, that its reality is a matter of time (of history and memory) rather than of space: it is the metaphoric Pharsalus that we seek for so blindly. The confusion is compounded in *Conducting Bodies.*

Geography is important in *Conducting Bodies* if only because Simon's hero journeys for the first time to the New World. Certain scenes are set unmistakably in New York City, most likely on the Upper West Side of Manhattan. (No subway system in the world can be mistaken for the West Side IRT.) But these are most likely remembered scenes from an earlier trip (made perhaps to study Poussin's *Orion* at the Metropolitan Museum of Art).[6] Present action takes place in Latin America—at least this is probably the present—and there are many clues to the specific site. The clues, unfortunately, are all contradictory: the murals in the assembly hall seem to allude to Mexico, the jungles seen from the plane to Central America in general, the carnival to Brazil; there are even hints of Cuba or Chile or Argentina, differing points on a political spectrum. It is not impossible that Simon is confusing us willfully, playing an ironic post-Modern game of misleading detective stories and atlases (a game that begins with Robbe-Grillet's *Erasers*). Or perhaps he is merely attesting to the ascendancy in our day of fiction from Latin America. But there is a more likely thematic justification for this geographic amalgam. For *Conducting Bodies* is part of a long European tradition of metaphoric books about the New World (often by writers who have never been to the Americas). We think readily of Kafka's *Amerika*, Yves Berger's *The Garden*, Butor's *Mobile* and *Niagara*. Simon's may be the first to be set in Latin America, but the metaphor for all is the same: "Our world hath of late discovered another (and who can warrant us whether it be the last of his brethren. . .)." The quote is from Montaigne's essay "On Coaches" as it is made manifest in Butor's *Degrees*.[7] It speaks, obviously, of the interconnections between continents of geography and of mind, of the effect on the Old World of the conquest of the New, of the myths of renewed hope and of the disappointed hope implicit in America. It represents, finally, a new manifestation of that blind search for political and artistic truth and for personal awareness that is at the core of *Conducting Bodies*—and, indeed, of every other work by Simon.

The most evident failure chronicled in *Conducting Bodies* is the political. But this loss achieves none of the dignity or stature of those earlier betrayals of ideals (the assassination of General Santiago and the murder of the cynical American in Barcelona, the death of Blum the Jew in the prisoner of war camp, the shock of riding to battle on horseback against tanks and machine-gun emplacements). The issue here, by contrast, seems trivial, almost parodic: the precise wording of a resolution to be passed by a conference of writers: "The translator leans over and whispers: The writer defines himself politically by his active participation in the revolutionary struggle, whether by way of his spoken words, his writings, or his acts" (pp. 105-106). For the individual writer the issue is real and significant; we see this throughout Simon's canon. What makes it suspect here is its official status, as if the passage of such a resolution would be binding on every writer. In those earlier novels, we feel the narrator's loss directly through his heightened language and intense emotional reactions. Here we are presented solely with words, heard in part in translation from the Spanish without authorial comment or reaction by the narrator: simply the meaningless verbiage of irrelevant resolutions (there are several variants), the interminable droning on of arguments heard in a foreign tongue in a foreign city, the petty intellectualizing of writers who have never themselves been in battle.

Yet the ultimate failing chronicled in *Conducting Bodies* is neither political nor artistic, but personal: not sexual, but physiological. The narrator's attempt to construct another lover's betrayal (reading into the Picasso engraving of the aged king spying on his young wife and her lover) is one more mask for his own pain and decay. He merges with the faltering members of the jungle expedition (drawn from the magazine read on the plane and from the murals in the conference hall), identifies with the cuckolded old king in his grief and his pain ("the round, highly magnified eye contemplates with an expression of calm desolation the tangled jumble of intertwined limbs"—p. 110), becomes one in his fruitless, blind search with Orion: "With one of his arms stretched out in front of him, fumbling about in the void, Orion is still advancing in the direction of the rising sun. . . There is every indication, however, that he will never reach his goal" (p. 187). The various charts of the body point, finally, to his own diseased organ; the gray mass which covers the floor of the doctor's examining room, which spreads to the conference hall and follows him back to his hotel room, is his own decomposing substance: "forms of the animate and the inanimate world that are indistinguishable from each other," as he thinks of Poussin's great landscape (p. 63).

Perception blurs as a result of his illness; normal separations of time and space disappear; unrelated scenes are juxtaposed without evident order or logic. We appear to have before us another Robbe-Grillet, a perfect technical exercise in the limited consciousness of a mind made feverish by illness, a further denial of the possibilities of human emotion in favor of the (distorted) physical perception of unfeeling, unsignifying "things"—in short, another *Voyeur* or *In the Labyrinth*. We should not be surprised, however, that this is not in fact the case.

The narrative of *Conducting Bodies* is not an aimless recording of (and reacting to) arbitrarily given images, as if the eye of the viewer were a malformed camera eye with no substance behind it but the physical. It is, instead, the most thoroughly sustained example of the pure stream of consciousness since the major works of Faulkner, a meticulously structured progression of images and scenes which are subjected to a most rigorous logic,[8] a work that reveals with great force the disabling potential of unexpressed emotion. There is no conscious attempt to mystify (and perhaps to delight), as in Robbe-Grillet, no sense that the images being observed exert mastery over their observer. The close observation of detail, an effort to mask the narrator's pain, makes us aware of that pain. Human emotion is implicit throughout, lying extremely close to the surface level of observed detail. (Even when he collapses at the end of his narrative, he can record only the view from the floor and not what he feels. But we have some sense of the feeling involved.) As the narrator's diseased body merges in his perception with the doctor's abstracted chart of the body, the result is increased, not lessened humanity. Unlike Robbe-Grillet, who will dehumanize even human objects, Simon finds human potential even in the inorganic, as if all those bodies represented by the chart were capable of such individualized suffering.

IV

As its title announces, *Triptych* (1973) represents a further expansion by Simon of the working metaphor of art and art criticism, an opening outward from his typically artful scene into three separate yet interrelated tableaux, a narrative altarpiece in effect. The novel provides in the process additional evidence for the new text-oriented approaches to the fiction of Simon. And so critics speak now not only of the effect of the text on the act of reading: "If *The Battle of Pharsalus* deals with the action of the text upon itself and *Conducting Bodies* with the variety of interrelated structures it can accumulate, *Triptych* can be considered as an examination of 'text-ure,' that is, the use of the 'weave' of a text to influence the reading of a novel."[9] They speak as well of a text that is virtually autonomous—self-involved, self-generating, even self-critical: "As the momentum of the text grows, so will its capacity to invent . . . The novel's plot is, on one level, the composition of its representational mosaic. On another, it is the very *activity* of creating this structure. In previous novels the composition was the real plot. Here the effort to discover this composition creates it and is the ultimate coordinating force of the fiction."[10]

It is difficult to deny that *Triptych* does indeed make increased demands on the reader and that the process of reading may need to be rethought as a result. But the issue is not quite as shiny and new as some of the text- and reader-oriented practitioners appear to believe. For this is a historical demand, made first in the implied contract which Henry James formed with his readers almost a century ago and manifested in the generations that followed by the responsibility which the Modernists placed on their readers to become active participants in the creation of a continuously evolving, if often ambiguous fiction. What is new here is the emphasis on reading as an art in itself. But even this does not necessarily mandate an entirely new critical vocabulary. The familiar Modernist discussions of narrative technique—and, in particular, of the reflexive workings of a fiction whose central subject is its own creation—might provide at least a starting point for this current discussion and lead us to those other writers who have for many years been engaged in a similar pursuit. The new vocabulary may have the virtue of providing new emphasis to the critical colloquy; its danger is that it seems to deny at least part of the continuity which is vital to an understanding both of Simon's own evolving canon and of the entire fictional context from which he evolves and within which he continues to create. Even in the stylized and often artificial *Triptych*, the familiar human concerns do somehow emerge.

In this spirit, then, the really significant change of *Triptych* is in point of view. The familiar limited consciousness of the previous novels, which reaches its peak in the stream of consciousness of *Conducting Bodies*, becomes here almost no consciousness at all. There is no recognizable person or consistent group of persons to mediate the events of *Triptych*, accepted body of facts or impressions, however ambiguous, to serve as their source, no unified community to provide them with background. Instead, there are several prisms—partial, inconsistent, sometimes overlapping, often contradictory—through which the events are revealed. Loubère is certainly correct when she speaks of Simon's challenge in *Triptych* to "our weakness as readers for story telling," our urge (to extend Simon's own metaphor) to join together the pieces of a narrative puzzle as if we were detectives and the deciphering of the plot were our primary mission. Yet the pieces of this puzzle, however cleverly we extrapolate, will simply not fit together. For there may be more than one puzzle here—or perhaps less; more than a single focus of character, setting, and time—or no focus at all; more than one metaphor through which to approach technique and theme in this novel. The narrative lacks not merely a beginning and end but a realizable center as well. But it does have a history of sorts, and it may be within this context that we can discover the author's full goals and our complete function as readers.

Reading *Triptych*, we are reminded less of other novels[11] than of certain aspects of film technique, as in the fictions of Robbe-Grillet: several of the narrative sources are literally films or filmstrips or advertisements for films; there are even scenes of films being produced, sequences which form in their turn an additional source for the narrative. Such scenes are viewed through what seems a true camera eye, distant, impartial, unselective in what it chooses to shoot and to screen, and operating before an equally undiscriminating audience. And so characters in one film may suddenly appear in another or emerge in new guises outside the film or enter again as figures in a novel or in an engraving, aspects of the mise en scène of still some other film. Some drunken projectionist is surely at work here, mixing reels from different films, projecting images from one onto another. Or perhaps some deranged editor has simply spliced together passages from different but related films to be shown by the unwatching, unthinking projectionist. But we know as readers that this cannot be the case, that no controlling intelligence operates here—not even a drunkard or madman or one of Robbe-Grillet's psychotic seers. For this is, finally, the fiction promised in the preface to *Orion aveugle*—unplanned, unstructured, almost accidental, growing by some narrative parthenogenesis, starting from nothing "sauf un magma informe de sensations," to be mediated by no one: chastisement perhaps for Modernist

Index

305

end, can be more basic than life. Through the window of his art, as a continuing function of the Modernist endeavor, he looks outward still to the world.

TEMPLE UNIVERSITY

Notes

1. Something of this emphasis can be seen in my earlier essays "Disillusionment and Epiphany: The novels of Claude Simon," *Critique* 12 (1970): 43-71, and "The Burden of History: Claude Simon's *Histoire,*" *The Kenyon Review* 21 (1969): 128-34.

2. Salvador Jiménez-Fajardo, *Claude Simon* (Boston: Twayne, 1975), p. 191.

3. J. A. E. Loubère, *The Novels of Claude Simon* (Ithaca: Cornell University Press, 1975), pp. 227-28.

4. See, for example, my essay "Michel Butor: Polyphony, or the Voyage of Discovery," *Critique* 14 (1972): 27-48.

5. See Randi Birn's essay on "Proust, Claude Simon, and the Art of the Novel," *Papers on Language and Literature* 13, no. 2 (Spring 1977).

6. It is unfortunate that he could not have delayed the visit for a time since the Poussin has only recently been cleaned, and by a technique whose name and character would surely appeal to Simon. Called "reforming," it is designed to reconstitute a surface whose pigments have broken down over the years into separate particles. As a result of the process, "The microscopic particles coalesce. Poussin's wonderful, philosophic landscape is largely recovered. . . . The annihilation of space by dominating intelligence has never found a better metaphysics." Thomas B. Hess, "Unvarnished Truths," *New York* 10 (January 17, 1977): 61.

7. Trans. Richard Howard (New York, 1961), p. 286.

8. In one brief sequence (pp. 53-56), as the narrator leans against a fireplug on the sidewalk in an effort to recover from a (kidney? liver? gall bladder?) attack, he watches an old woman through a hotel window as she reaches over to pick up her boa, sees a young mother in Bermuda shorts reach to the sidewalk to lift her child's fallen toy (a wheeled rabbit on a string), envisions the limbs of lovers, recalls a model of the human body, moves finally to Orion in perpetual motion just as the old woman begins to move forward. The associations are free but under strict, logical control: connected by images of motion and of the body, by hints of organic (especially sexual) capacity (and incapacity), even by the sudden sun in his eyes, which connects to an earlier moment on the plane when, with the sun "striking his eyes and his burning eyelids with such force as to be actually painful" (p. 54), he first imagines the lovers. He has, after all, flown over great distances and several time zones, and he has experienced much pain. He is entitled to a few shortcuts and thus to expect us to provide the links that are missing. But it is obvious that there is nothing accidental or

haphazard about his creation. The intensity of this organization of the stream of consciousness is akin to that of the classical Modernist efforts of Faulkner and Joyce.

9. Loubère, p. 221. More specifically, she writes, "In *Triptyque* Simon demonstrates our weakness for story telling by getting the process going in the reader and then leaving him to carry on by himself . . . To such a reader, Simon proposes that he revise his reading habits, his opinion concerning the function of the text, and the function of the reader himself" (p. 218).

10. Jiménez-Fajardo, pp. 176, 190.

11. But see Claude Mauriac's *L'Agrandissement*, which reverses the narrative procedures of *Triptych* by limiting the focus of *The Marquise Went Out at Five* but "blowing up" the images being perceived there. Mauriac's purpose, of course, is to make us more, not less, aware of the perceiver.

16

Simon on Simon: An Interview with the Artist*

Randi Birn and Karen Gould

Question: Much has been said about pessimism in your work. In the interview you gave Madeleine Chapsal after the publication of *The Flanders Road*, you expressed, on the contrary, an almost hedonistic love of life. Do you still feel this love of life today?

Simon: Unlike Anaïs Nin who declared (I am quoting from memory): "Daily life and nature don't interest me," these things have never ceased to fascinate me. Compared to the simplest object (a leaf, a shell, a bird's feather) or the most banal human action (a walk, a conversation overheard in a café), the thing we customarily call, in art or literature, "the marvelous" has always appeared to me to be laborious and childishly deficient.

Far from fading with age, this grateful wonder I feel before things and life grows ever greater. I noticed this same phenomenon when I was in prison or seriously ill: it seems that everything limiting our freedom sharpens our faculties for apprehending the world as a result. The smallest detail stands out. In the same way the blind have far better-developed

*Translated by Jane Carson.

senses of touch, hearing, and smell than normal men. Peeling an apple for dessert distresses me now (the chef-d'oeuvre I am about to destroy!. . .) and I spend a long time turning it and contemplating it regretfully before I can bring myself to pick up my knife . . .

As an argument against Anaïs Nin and her like, this saying of Picasso's comes to mind (again I quote from memory): "It is not with princesses that kings produce their most beautiful children; it is with shepherdesses."

Question: According to you, what role could the artist play in modern society?
Simon: The role (the function) of the artist seems to me to be to participate in and partake of History (in other words, to be *in* and *of* this incessant transformation of the world) by producing new forms.

This does not mean that all that is new is art. As they say in mathematics, newness is a *necessary* but not a *sufficient* condition for art. In addition, these new forms must be produced in accordance with the profound logic which presided at the elaboration of the language and its functioning.

Question: Do you ever reread your books? If so, in what spirit?
Simon: Occasionally, for papers or studies on my work. Otherwise never. Just as Bonnard went to museums to touch up his canvases when the guards weren't looking, I would constantly want to make corrections. Since it's impossible (and perhaps even stupid) I prefer to abstain.

Question: Have your own literary tastes changed? What kind of reading interests you today? Do you spend much time reading the works of your contemporaries in France and abroad?
Simon: (a) Yes.
(b) When I was thirty, it seemed to me the greatest writer was Joyce. Now it appears to me that the most revolutionary writer of the twentieth century is Marcel Proust.
(c) I read very few contemporary authors.

Question: There are critics who think that your work, like
Proust's, forms a whole. It is said, for example, that one cannot read *Triptych* of even *Histoire* without being familiar with
the preceding novels. What do you think? Does the problem
of the reader preoccupy you at all? As for the *active* reader so
much talked about these days, does he exist outside of
university and professional groups?
Simon: (a) It seems to me (at least this is what I have
strived for) that each of my works constitutes a whole. But of
course each of them has its place in the movement of my
research and evolution and for this reason belongs to a whole.
But they can be separated from it. I mean, for example, that
one can easily read *Triptych* without having read *The Grass*
or *Histoire*, and vice versa.
(b) The problem of the reader preoccupies me insofar as
I want (like any writer) to have as many readers as possible.
Having said that, I don't see how one can bear this problem in
mind while writing. To write with a hypothetical reader in
mind would mean trying to guess his tastes and desires, or, in
other words, to do what is called a "market survey." In this
sense there are recipes for writing "best sellers." They are simple. The tastes of the general public are known. They tend
toward tireless repetition of the same forms. In music, painting, or literature, the general public only experiences pleasure when it encounters something resembling what it has
already heard, seen, or read. Any new form disturbing
(disarranging) this reassuring state of comfort is ill-received.
The general public pronounced successively that Flaubert,
Proust, Joyce were bad writers—confusing, incomprehensible, and boring, that the Impressionists were daubers, the
Cubists jokers, that what Beethoven, Wagner, and Debussy
were writing was "not music," etc.
(c) Certainly. One need only look at the conformity of
taste and the mental laziness of most university people and
most "professionals" (critics) who cultivate a spirit of repetition. It sometimes happens that unbiased readers who have
not been spoiled by false traditional culture are more receptive to
an innovative work. (There is a great deal to be said concerning this on the pernicious and anticultural role in the mass
media of what is called "culture.")

Question: Do the ideas about "word by word" fiction (*"la fiction mot à mot"*) and the craftsman's aspect of writing still seem valid to you?
Simon: More than ever.

Question: What direction does your current work seem to be taking? Are you going through another evolution since *Leçon de choses* or do you ever envisage the possibility that to advance it is necessary to retreat?
Simon: I don't know what direction my work will take. Especially since, as my work progresses, it changes me. Each novel demands particular forms and methods of working. The one I have undertaken is creating itself (and me) in a very different fashion from *Leçon de choses*. Moreover, I don't quite see how one can *advance* by *retreating*. It seems to me that the two actions are incompatible.

PARIS, 1977

Postface

Simon's evolution as a novelist has been relatively clear-cut. Gradually and painfully the artist liberated himself from an obsession with the problems of human existence, those questions of time, space, nature, war, and love. The passion to know was replaced by a need to investigate the possibilities of language. Even in his most experimental works, however, Simon is never abstract or abstruse. His novels are far from being linguistic puzzles or intellectual exercises. On the contrary, Simon's novels are firmly rooted in a pulsating, physical world. As a matter of fact, moving away from archetypal images of the human condition, the novels have come closer and closer to the immediate experiences of the author's daily life. A trip to a writers' congress in Latin America is the source of the airplane perspective that dominates *Conducting Bodies*, memories of his childhood village provide the unity of *Triptych*, the demolition of a Paris apartment offers a focus in *Leçon de choses*. Increasingly, Simon's works bear witness to an exceptional appreciation of nature and the ordinary objects of our lives, grass, wild flowers in the field, the ripples of streamwater, the delicate shades of color on a piece of fabric. While the emphasis on visual perception dominating Simon's later works suggests photographic objectivity, the descriptions remain the product of a personal vision rather than images recorded on a camera lens.

"Vision," of course, must be defined literally as "ability to see" the objects of the physical world surrounding the individual. Above all, it must not be confused with "visionary," or a supernatural ability to see *beyond* or *behind* apparent reality. When Simon compares himself to a "blinded Orion," he admits that he is an artist without visionary powers. Like Poussin's *Blind Orion Moving Towards the Rising Sun*,

Simon the artist moves in fumbling fashion toward the direction where the source of light appears to be located. Since the artist has no special insights into the future of the world or the novel, his only recourse is to advance and learn through exploration and experimentation. Simon likes to look upon himself not as an artist with a God-given talent, but as a craftsman whose creations are the result of hard, conscious work, an uncompromising demand for quality, and a passion to mold any material at hand into new forms. Thus, paradoxically, as Simon relinquished claims to "visionary" powers, he gained the craftsman's appreciation of the possibilities of his immediate environment.

While Simon's latest works undeniably earn him a place among France's New Novelists, his artistic evolution has been autonomous, built upon internal necessity and personal quest rather than influenced by any contemporary, external stimulus. Each successive novel contains elements of self-questioning and self-destruction as well as the seeds of a new beginning. Simon admits that the works of his own contemporaries hold relatively little interest for him, and that the most significant influences upon his own writing have been Joyce and Proust. Simon's relationship to Proust is particularly intriguing. It can best be compared to a stormy love affair or the relationship of a child to an overly admired and respected father. Simon deals most directly with this problem in *The Battle of Pharsalus*, which may be read as a "battle" against the influence of Proust. Interestingly enough, once the struggle is won and Simon the novelist considers himself independent of the master, he resumes the relationship, though on a more harmonious basis. In a conversation in March 1977, the novelist told me that he had "rediscovered" Proust after the composition of *Triptych*, and that his only recent serious reading had been *Remembrance of Things Past*. Rather than regarding himself as a New Novelist associated with the Robbe-Grillet school, Simon perhaps would prefer to think of himself as a Joycean or Proustian disciple exploring in their wake the possibilities of the novel.

According to Simon's own definition, the significance of a novelist must be measured in proportion to the degree by which he has transformed the genre. It is therefore comprehensible that he should attach more importance to the experimental works written since *Histoire* than to the previous and more traditional novels. In his latest works Simon has dispensed with the questing narrator and diminished pathos in favor of pure, self-generating description. The novels are constructed according to the principle of analogy, and the novelist explores whatever mental associations come to mind, however farfetched they appear. More fully than any other novelist, Simon has explored the relationship between literature and painting. His contribution in this area compares to Proust's in the realm of literature and music.

Nevertheless, while recognizing the significance of Simon's latest work and sharing his enthusiasm for exploring new territory, it would be unfortunate if we were to underestimate the importance of his earlier novels. The books written prior to *The Wind* are the very foundation upon which Simon's later aesthetic philosophy was built. These novels are the products of an artist searching for appropriate themes and a personal style, and they bear witness to Simon's disillusionment with the novel of political involvement and his rejection of any faith in progress. *Le Tricheur*, *Gulliver*, and *Le Sacre du printemps* are the only Simonian novels that can be characterized as genuinely pessimistic. While these books are not in themselves significant works of art, they are essential to the reader who wishes to gain a fuller understanding of Simon's artistic evolution.

In the works from *The Wind* through *Histoire* there is a sudden upsurge of creativity which was essentially lacking in the first three novels. While the human condition remains Simon's central theme, an extraordinarily subtle use of imagery and metaphor provides the reader with a sense of recurring adventure and pleasure. The novels written during this period, especially *The Grass*, *The Flanders Road*, and *Histoire*, contain a spontaneous element which is profoundly satisfying to the reader. Question of innovation aside, this ability to transmit pleasure, which simultaneously lends itself to and defies critical analysis, is surely also a mark of great literature.

RANDI BIRN

Note on the Author

Claude Simon was born October 10, 1913, at Tananarive, Madagascar, of French parents. The family returned to France when the child was nine months old. The father, an officer, was killed in the 1914-1918 war. The boy spent his early childhood at Perpignan in the eastern Pyrenees. Between the ages of seven and sixteen he attended the Collège Stanislas in Paris. He dropped his plans to attend the Ecole Navale, deciding instead to study painting with André Lhôte. Painting has always been Simon's greatest love. During the 1930's, he traveled extensively in Spain, Germany, Russia, Italy, and Greece. He participated on the Republican side in the Spanish Civil War. In 1939, at the outbreak of World War II, he was drafted into the cavalry. In May 1940 he became a prisoner of war in Germany, but escaped from the camp in November of the same year. He lived in Perpignan until 1944, when he returned to Paris. Since then he has lived alternately in Salses, a small village near Perpignan, where he was a wine grower, and in Paris.

Simon finished his first novel, *Le Tricheur*, in 1941, but the book was not published until after the end of the German occupation. "Since then, he says, my life, like that of all writers, has mingled with my books, most of which (notably *L'Herbe*, *La Route des Flandres*, and *Le Palace*) are autobiographical."[1]

In 1963, *La Séparation*, a play based on *L'Herbe*, was produced in Paris without much success. Simon won the Prix de

[1]*World Authors 1950-1970*, ed. John Wakefield (New York: The H. W. Wilson Company, 1975) p. 1307.

L'Express in 1960 for *La Route des Flandres* and the Prix Médicis in 1967 for *Histoire.*He became a Doctor of Letters honoris causa at the University of East Anglia, Norwich, Norfolk, in 1973. Since 1967, Simon has been invited to lecture at universities in many parts of the world. He has traveled all over Europe (except the Soviet Union and Spain), as well as in the United States, Chile, Japan, and India.

Notes on the Editors and Contributors

RANDI BIRN, coeditor of the anthology, received her Ph.D. from the University of Illinois; she teaches at the University of Oregon. Professor Birn has written a book-length study, *Johan Borgen*, and articles on Proust, Simon, Claudel, Genet, and Borgen.

C. G. BJURSTRÖM, literary critic and friend of Claude Simon, resides in France and has published a number of articles on Claude Simon and a critical study on Camus. He has translated into Swedish all of Simon's novels since *The Wind* and has recently been awarded the title of *Doctor honoris causa* from the University of Uppsala.

SERGE DOUBROVSKY, novelist, and well known as a literary critic, has contributed many articles on French literature to a variety of periodicals and is the author of *Corneille et la dialectique du héros*, *Pourquoi la nouvelle critique*, *L'Enseignement de la littérature*, as well as the novels *La Dispersion* and *Fils*. Professor Doubrovsky teaches at New York University.

CLAUD DUVERLIE has published several articles on Claude Simon and a number of interviews. He earned his Ph.D. at the University of Chicago and now teaches at the University of Maryland (Baltimore County).

JOHN FLETCHER is the author of *Claude Simon and Fiction Now* and author or editor of a number of books on contemporary literary figures, including *New Directions in Literature* and several critical studies of Samuel Beckett. He is professor of Comparative Literature at the University of East Anglia in Norwich, England.

KAREN GOULD, coeditor of this volume, is the author of an article on Simon and a book-length study, *Claude Simon's Mythic Muse*.

She holds a Ph.D. from the University of Oregon and teaches at Virginia Polytechnic Institute and State University.

KARIN HOLTER, who is a professor of French at the University of Oslo, has published a critical study on Camus and several articles on the French New Novel.

SALVADOR JIMÉNEZ-FAJARDO earned his Ph.D. from the University of Chicago and currently teaches at Illinois Wesleyan University. His publications include essays on Pachero, Unamuno, Pinget, Simon, and the contemporary Latin American novel, as well as two critical studies, *Claude Simon* and *Luis Cernuda*.

TOBIN JONES has published essays on Ricardou, Claudel, and the French New Novel, and has recently completed a book-length study, *Form and Formulation in the Nouveau Roman*, which is now awaiting publication. Professor Jones did his Ph.D. work at the University of Minnesota; at present he is teaching at Colorado State University (Fort Collins).

MORTON P. LEVITT completed his graduate work at the Pennsylvania State University and is a professor of English at Temple University. He is the author of *Bloomsday: An Interpretation of James Joyce's "Ulysses"* and has also written articles on modern writers including Simon, Butor, Durrell, Pynchon, and Barth.

J. A. E. LOUBÉRE has written a full-length critical study, *The Novels of Claude Simon*, and has also published articles on Valéry, Balzac, Simon, and Borges. Ms. Loubère was formerly a professor at S.U.N.Y. (Buffalo), where she received her Ph.D.

CHRISTIANE MAKWARD, who received her D. Lit. from the Sorbonne, is a professor of French at the Pennsylvania State University (University Park). She has published articles on Simon and women's studies and is the editor of *Bulletin de Recherches et d'Etudes Féministes Francophones*.

GERARD J. ROUBICHOU, author of *Lecture de l'Herbe de Claude Simon*, and a number of articles on Simon, received his D. ès L. from the University of Lausanne. He has taught at the University of California (Berkeley), the University of Virginia, and the University of Moscow. At present, Mr. Roubichou is the French Embassy's cultural attaché in New York City.

PHILIP H. SOLOMON earned his Ph.D. at the University of Wisconsin and currently teaches at Southern Methodist University. Professor Solomon has written the critical study *The Life after Birth: Imagery in Samuel Beckett's Trilogy*, is coeditor of *Choix d'essais du vingtième siècle*, and has published articles on Beckett, Simon, and Céline.

ELIZABETH WEED has taught at Wheaton College and now holds an administrative position at Brown University, where she received her Ph.D.

Selected Bibliography

Works by Claude Simon

Le Tricheur. Paris: Editions du Sagittaire, 1945.

La Corde raide. Paris: Editions du Sagittaire, 1947.

Gulliver. Paris: Calmann-Lévy, 1952.

La Sacre du printemps. Paris: Calmann-Lévy, 1954.

Le Vent. Paris: Editions de Minuit, 1957.

L'Herbe. Paris: Editions de Minuit, 1958.

The Wind. Translated by Richard Howard. New York: George Braziller, 1959.

The Grass. Translated by Richard Howard. New York: George Braziller; London: Jonathan Cape, 1960.

La Route des Flandres. Paris: Editions de Minuit, 1960. Reprinted in Collection 10/18, 1970.

The Flanders Road. Translated by Richard Howard. New York: George Braziller; London: Jonathan Cape, 1961.

Le Palace. Paris: Editions de Minuit, 1962. Reprinted in Collection 10/18, 1970.

The Palace. Translated by Richard Howard. New York: George Braziller; London: Jonathan Cape, 1963.

Femmes (sur vingt-trois peintures de Joan Miró). Paris: Editions Maeght, 1966.

Histoire. Paris: Editions de Minuit, 1967. Reprinted in Editions "Folio," 1973.

Histoire. Translated by Richard Howard. New York: George Braziller; London: Jonathan Cape, 1967.

La Bataille de Pharsale. Paris: Editions de Minuit, 1969.

Orion aveugle. Geneva: Editions Albert Skira, 1970.

The Battle of Pharsalus. Translated by Richard Howard. New York: George Braziller; London: Jonathan Cape, 1971.

Les Corps conducteurs. Paris: Editions de Minuit, 1971.

Triptyque. Paris: Editions de Minuit, 1973.

Conducting Bodies. Translated by Helen R. Lane. New York: Viking Press; London: Calder & Boyars; Canada: The Macmillan Company of Canada, 1974.

Triptych. Translated by Helen R. Lane. New York: Viking Press, 1976.

Leçon de choses. Paris: Editions de Minuit, 1975.

Selected Articles and Interviews

"Avec *La Route des Flandres* Claude Simon affirme sa manière." Interview with Claude Sarraute. *Le Monde*, October 8, 1960.

"Le jeune roman." Interview with Madeleine Chapsal. *L'Express*, January 12, 1961.

"Entretien: Claude Simon parle." Interview with Madeleine Chapsal. *L'Express*, April 5, 1962.

"Je ne peux parler que de moi." *Les Nouvelles Littéraires*, May 3, 1962. "Débat: le romancier et la politique. Et si les écrivains jouaient le rôle de la presse du coeur? demande Claude Simon." *L'Express*, July 25, 1963.

"Pour qui écrit Sartre?" *L'Express*, May 28, 1964. Translated into English: "Whom does Sartre write for?" *London Magazine 4, no. 5 (August 1964)*. "Le roman se fait, je le fais, et il se [sic] fait." Interview with Josane Duranteau. *Les Lettres Françaises*, April 13-19, 1967.

"Claude Simon, franc-tireur de la révolution romanesque." Interview with Thérèse de Saint-Phalle. *La Figaro Littéraire*, April 6, 1967.

"Littérature: tradition et révolution." *La Quinzaine Littéraire*, May 1-15, 1967.

"Il n'y a pas d'art réaliste." Interview with Madeleine Chapsal. *La Quinzaine Littéraire*, December 15-31, 1967.

"Interview avec Claude Simon." Interview with Bettina Knapp. *Kentucky Romance Quarterly* 16, no. 2 (1970).

"La Fiction mot à mot." *Nouveau Roman: hier, aujourd'hui*, vol. 2. Publications du Centre culturel de Cerisy-la-Salle (50). Collection 10/18. Paris: Union Générale d'Editions, 1972, pp. 73-97.

"Interview with Claude Simon." Interview with Claud DuVerlie. *Sub-stance* 8 (February-March 1974).

"Dialogue avec Claude Simon: le poids des mots." Interview with Monique Joquet. *Figaro Littéraire*, April 3, 1976.

"Interview—Claude Simon: The Crossing of the Image." Interview with Claud DuVerlie. *Diacritics* (Winter, 1977).

"Un Homme traversé parle travail: Entretien avec Claude Simon." *La Nouvelle Critique, Revue du Marxisme Militant* 105 (1977).

Critical Studies

Alphant, Marianne. "Claude Simon: *Leçon de choses.*" *Cahiers du Chemin* 26 (January 15, 1976): 137-44.

Anex, Georges. "Les feuilles de l'acacia . . ." In *Les Critiques de notre temps et le Nouveau Roman*. Ed. Réal Ouellet. Paris: Garnier, 1972, pp. 82-85.

Berger, Yves. "L'Enfer, le Temps." *La Nouvelle Revue Française* 97 (January 1961): 95-109.

Birn, Randi. "Proust, Claude Simon, and the Art of the Novel." *Papers on Language and Literature* 13, No. 2 (Spring 1977): 168-86.

Bishop, Thomas. "L'Image de la création chez Claude Simon." In *Nouveau Roman: hier, aujourd'hui*, vol. 2. Paris: Collection 10/18, 1972, pp. 61-71.

Bjurström, C.-G. "Dimensions du temps chez Claude Simon." *Entretiens* 31 (1972): 141-58.

Bourdet, Denise. *Brèves rencontres*. Paris: Grasset, 1963, pp. 215-24.

Bourque, Ghislan. "Le Parabole." *Etudes Littéraires* 9, no. 7 (April 1976): 161-87.

Brosman, Catharine Savage. "Man's Animal Condition in Claude Simon's *La Route des Flandres.*" *Symposium* 29 (Spring-Summer 1975): 57-68.

Chapsal, Madeleine. *Quinze Ecrivains*. Paris: René Julliard, 1963, pp. 163-71.

Deguy, Michel. "Claude Simon et la représentation." *Critique* 187 (December 1962): 1009-32.

Doubrovsky, Serge. "Notes sur la genèse d'une écriture." *Entretiens* 31 (1972): 51-64.

Duncan, Alastair B. "Claude Simon and William Faulkner." *Forum for Modern Language Studies* 9 (1973): 235-52.

DuVerlie, Claud. "Pour un *Comment j'ai écrit certains de mes livres* de Claude Simon." *Romance Notes* 14 (1972): 217-22.

———. "Amor interruptus. The Question of Eroticism or Eroticism in Question in the Works of Claude Simon." *Sub-stance* 8 (February-March 1974): 21-33.

Fitch, Brian. "Participe présent et procédés narratifs chez Claude Simon." *Revue des Lettres Modernes* 94-99 (1964): 199-216.

Fletcher, John. "Claude Simon and the Memory Enigma." In *New Directions in Literature*. Ed. John Fletcher. London: Calder & Boyars, 1968, pp. 116-28.

———. "Erotisme et création ou la mort en sursis." *Entretiens* 31 (1972): 131-40.

———. *Claude Simon and Fiction Now*. London: Calder & Boyars, 1975.

Gould Karen. *Claude Simon's Mythic Muse*. Columbia, S.C.: French Literature Publications, 1979.

———. "Mythologizing in the *nouveau roman*: Claude Simon's Archetypal City." *French Literature Series: Mythology in French Literature* 3 (1976): 118-28.

Guicharnaud, Jacques. "Remembrance of Things Passing." *Yale French Studies* 24 (Summer 1959): 101-108.

Heath, Stephen. *The Nouveau Roman: A Study in the Practice of Writing*. Philadelphia: Temple University Press, 1972, pp. 153-78.

Janvier, Ludovic. *Une Parole exigeante: le Nouveau Roman*. Paris: Editions de Minuit, 1964.

———. "Sur le trajet de ces corps." *Entretiens* 31 (1972): 69-80.

Jiménez-Fajardo, Salvador. *Claude Simon*. Boston: Twayne, 1975.

Jost, François. "Claude Simon: topographies de la description et du texte." *Critique* no. 330 (1974): 1031-40.

———. "Les aventures du lecteur." *Poétique* 29 (February 1977): 77-89.

Lancereaux, Dominique. "Modalités de la narration dans *La Route des Flandres*." *Poétique* 14 (1973): 235-49.

———. "Modalités de la narration dans *Le Palace* de Claude Simon." *Littérature* 4, no. 16 (December 1974): 3-18.

Lesage, Laurent. "Claude Simon et l'Ecclésiaste." *Revue des Lettres Modernes* 94-99 (1964): 217-23.

Levitt, Morton P. "The Burden of History." *Kenyon Review* 31 (1969): 128-34.

――――. "Disillusionment and Epiphany: The Novels of Claude Simon." *Critique: Studies in Modern Fiction* 12 (1970): 43-70.

Loubère, J. A. E. *The Novels of Claude Simon.* Ithaca and London: Cornell University Press, 1975.

Makward, Christiane. "Claude Simon: Earth, Death and Eros." *Sub-stance* 8 (Winter 1974): 35-43.

Mauriac, Claude. *L'Allitérature contemporaine.* Paris: Albin Michel, 1969, pp. 292-305.

Mercier, Vivian. "Claude Simon: Order and Disorder." *Shenandoah* 17, no. 4 (Summer 1966): 79-92.

――――. "James Joyce and the French New Novel." *TriQuarterly* 8 (1967): 205-219.

――――. *The New Novel. From Queneau to Pinget.* New York: Farrar, Straus and Giroux, 1971, pp. 266-314.

Merleau-Ponty, Maurice. "Cinq Notes sur Claude Simon." *Médiations* 4 (Winter 1961-1962): 5-9. Reprinted in *Entretiens* 31 (1972): 41-46.

Mortier, Roland. "Discontinu et rupture dans *La Bataille de Pharsale.*" *Degrés* 1, no. 2 (April 1973): c/1-c/6.

Nykrog, Per. "Om Claude Simon: *Histoire.*" *Prépublications* (Aarhus) 1 (1973), 19-31.

O'Donnell, Thomas D. "Claude Simon's *Leçon de choses:* Myth and Ritual Displaced." *International Fiction Review* 5 (1978): 134-42.

――――."Du *Tricheur* à *Triptyque,* et inversement." *Etudes Littéraires* 9, no. 1 (April 1976): 137-60.

Raillard, G. *"Triptyque."* *Les Cahiers du Chemin* 18 (April 15, 1973): 96-106.

――――. "*Femmes:* Claude Simon dans les marges de Miró." *Cahiers du 20ᵉ siècle* 4 (1975): 123-37. See also *Claude Simon* Colloque de Cerisy, ed. by Jean Ricardou. Paris: Union Générale d'Editions. 1975, 73-87.

Raillon, Jean-Claude. "Propositions d'une théorie de la fiction." *Etudes Littéraires* 9, no. 7 (April 1976): 81-123.

Ricardou, Jean. "Un ordre dans le débâcle." *Critique* 16 (December 1960): 1011-24. Reprinted in *Les Critiques de notre temps et le Nouveau Roman.* Ed. by Réal Ouellet. Paris: Garnier, 1972, pp. 85-88.

――――. *Problèmes du Nouveau Roman.* Paris: Seuil, 1967.

――――. *Pour une Théorie du Nouveau Roman.* Paris: Seuil, 1971, pp. 118-58; 200-210.

————. *Le Nouveau Roman*. Paris: Seuil, 1973.

————. ed. *Claude Simon*. Colloque de Cerisy. Paris: Union Générale d'Editions, 1975. The essays in this volume are not listed separately.

————. "Le dispositif osiriaue." *Etudes littéraires* 9, no. 7 (1976): 9-79.

Rossum-Guyon, Françoise van. "De Claude Simon à Proust: un exemple d'intertextualité." *Les Lettres Nouvelles* 4 (September 1972): 107-137.

————. "Ut pictura poesis: une lecture de *La Bataille de Pharsale*." *Degrés* 3 (July 1973): k/1-k/15.

Roubichou, Gérard. "Continu et discontinu ou l'hérétique alinéa." *Etudes Littéraires* 9, no. 7 (April 1976): 125-36.

————. *Lecture de L'Herbe de Claude Simon*. Lausanne: L'Age d'Homme, 1976.

Roudiez, L. S. *French Fiction Today: A New Direction*. New Brunswick: Rutgers University Press, 1972, pp. 152-82.

Rousseaux, André. "L'Impressionisme de Claude Simon," in *Littérature du XXᵉ siècle*, vol. 7 ed. by André Rousseau. Paris: Albin Michel, 1961, pp. 173-79.

Rousset, Jean. "Trois Romans de la mémoire: Butor, Pinget, Simon." In *Formalisme et Signification. Cahiers Internationaux du Symbolisme* 9-10 (1965-1966): 79-81. Reprinted in *Les Critiques de notre temps et le Nouveau Roman*. Ed. by Réal Ouellet. Paris: Garnier, 1972, pp. 27-35.

Séguier, Marcel. "Proposition en lieu et place d'un avant-propos à une réflexion collective." *Entretiens* 31 (1972): 9-13.

————. Le Langage à la casse." *Entretiens* 31 (1972): 81-95.

Seylaz, Jean-Luc. "Du *Vent* à *La Route des Flandres*: la Conquête d'une forme romanesque." *Revue des Lettres Modernes* 94-99 (1964): 225-40.

Simon, John K. "Perception and Metaphor in the 'New Novel': Notes on Robbe-Grillet, Claude Simon, and Butor." *TriQuarterly* 4 (1965): 153-82.

Sims, Robert. "The Myths of Revolution and the City in Claude Simon's *Le Palace*." *Studies in the Twentieth Century* 16 (Fall 1975): 53-87.

Solomon, Philip H. "Claude Simon's *La Route des Flandres*: A Horse of a Different Color?" *Australian Journal of French Studies* 98 (1972): 190-201.

————. "Flights of Time Lost: Bird Imagery in Claude Simon's *Le Palace.*" In *Twentieth Century Fiction. Essays for Germaine Brée.* Ed. George Stambolian. New Brunswick: Rutgers University Press, 1975, pp. 166-83.

Sturrock, John. *The French New Novel: Claude Simon, Michel Butor, Alain Robbe-Grillet.* London: Oxford University Press, 1969, pp. 43-103.

Sykes, Stuart W. " 'Mise en abyme' in the Novels of Claude Simon." *Forum for Modern Language Studies* 9 (1973): 333-45.

————. *Les romans de Claude Simon.* Paris: Minuit, 1979.

————. "Claude Simon: Visions of Life in Microcosm." *Modern Language Review* 71, no. 7 (January 1976): 42-50.

————. "Ternary Form in Three Novels by Claude Simon." *Symposium* 32, no. 1 (Spring 1978): 25-40.

Thorsöe-Jacobson, Sören. "Claude Simon." In *Den Moderne roman i Frankrig. Analyser og synteser.* Ed. Hans Boll Johansen. Copenhagen: Akademisk Forlag, 1970, pp. 99-123.

Vidal, Jean-Pierre. "*Le Palace,* palais des mirages intestins ou l'auberge espagnole." *Etudes Littéraires* 9, no. 7 (April 1976): 189-214.

Weinstein, Arnold L. *Vision and Response in Modern Fiction.* Ithaca and London: Cornell University Press, 1974, pp. 215-56.

Wilhelm, Kurt. "Claude Simon als 'nouveau romancier'." *Zeitschrift für französische Sprache und Literatur* 75 (1965): 309-52.

Zeltner, Gerda. *Die Eigenmächtige Sprache.* Freiburg: Olten, 1965, pp. 35-52.

————. "Claude Simon." *Neue Rundschau* 81 (1970): 800-805.

————. "Ein Strukturalistischer Roman. Weg und Methode Claude Simons." *Neue Rundschau* 83 (1972): 715-21.

————. *Im Augenblick der Gegenwart. Moderne Formen des Französischen Romans.* Frankfurt / Main: Fischer, 1974, pp. 115-49.

Zwangenburg, W. "Phrase et énoncé dans '*La Route des Frandres*' de Claude Simon." In *Du Linguistique au textuel.* Ed. Charles Grivel and Aron Kibédi Varga. Amsterdam: Van Gorcum, 1974, pp. 61-69.

author and reader alike, for those who believe in a world that is at least potentially knowable, in which certain human values at least remain constant. Nothing in *Triptych* is constant, nothing finally knowable. One of the characters does complete a puzzle, but, as the film ends, he immediately scatters its pieces. "Their meandering edges have been deliberately cut in such a way that none of them, viewed individually, shows the entire image of a person, an animal, or even a face" (p. 171). The several sets of lovers, the several voyeurs, even the several landscapes are pieces of a puzzle that the rational reader can very nearly construct to his own satisfaction: the servants who make love in a barn as two boys spy on them belong to the country village, the drunken bridegroom and the barmaid in the alley to the industrial town, the middle-aged woman protecting her son in her luxurious bedroom to the seaside resort. The triptych seems complete, the metaphor fulfilled. But we may have had to force some of the pieces, or perhaps there are too many of them, for this seems not one puzzle but several, with compulsively interlocking parts and gaping voids. There is evidence to indicate that the woman's son may be the bridegroom and/or the sheep-faced actor in one of the films, perhaps the one about the drunken bridegroom who abandons his bride on their wedding night to seek out an old lover in town. The woman herself may be a character in the film (a film about making a film?) shown in the cinema alongside the alley (or in the barn), as well as in the filmstrips put together without sound by the boys. The boys, too, seem characters in some other film, and the servants seem figures in an engraving which decorates the wall of a luxurious bedroom, perhaps as background for one of these films. Even the different landscapes blur into one, "at once urban, industrial, and rural" (p. 21). Lured into assembling the narrative puzzle as a rational exercise, the reader is betrayed; the exercise alone remains. We are left like "the spectator" contemplating "the pathetic face of the clown" who performs for us [in a film? in the barn?—p. 13], the same clown seen on one or more of the posters, his face "frozen" beneath his makeup, contributing to "this impression of dehumanization" (pp. 119-20).

The way of life recorded in *Triptych* is like a movie set. "The entire décor leaves one with an impression of emptiness, impersonality, and desolation, as though the protagonists were merely passing through, staying for only a short time in a temporary and artificial ambiance that has nothing to do with them, set up the day before by stagehands standing ready to take it down and isolated from the rest of the world by floodlights, like a minuscule and ephemeral little island of light in the vast emptiness of the cosmos, or, more simply, that of a vast movie studio, equally black and equally empty" (pp. 130-31).

Viewed in this bleak light, such a reader-oriented approach to *Triptych* seems to negate the humanistic impulses, which link Simon to the Modernists (including, ironically, those of the reader), and to posit instead a perfect post-Modern critical solution: all theorizing and no emotion, but effected with great ingenuity and skill. There is pain in these events, according even to this approach, but no one to experience the pain; it is an abstract emotion apparently, a vestigial reminder of the suffering which informs all of Simon's previous novels and which singles out their protagonists. Even the reader's involvement is elicited, in this view, so that it might be betrayed. Surely Simon has repudiated here his own fictional past: there is no political import in *Triptych*, only the suspicion of a betrayal (but no single culprit) and no real love—merely some lovers to be described as frozen, geometric forms, as in a Robbe-Grillet tableau, fit alone for a pornographic film in a sleazy theatre. It is difficult to recall, when viewed from this critical perspective, that the distant recorder of the events of *Triptych* was once the creator of Georges and Blum and those other suffering (and involving) consciousnesses of the major novels. And it has not been necessary for the post-Modernist readers to invent this Simon; the evidence is undeniable: he seems detemined to shape his latest work precisely to fit this latest of critical forms.

But there is more: Simon rejects our involvement and then leads us on once again. There are palimpsests upon palimpsests in this ostensibly autonomous text, from "the layer upon layer of superimposed posters" (p. 6) which announce and then become the several performances that constitute so much of the narrative, to the filmstrip which the boy at his desk holds up to the light of the window, superimposed upon the world outside. The woman in the bedroom—the actress portraying the middle-aged woman—is Corinne de Reixach; the official who promises to aid her son is Lambert, Georges's old friend from *Histoire*: "But what wouldn't I be willing to do for the ravishingly beautiful cousin of my best friend from school" (p. 36); the father of her rebellious son is unknown: "I imagine, must have, father, somewhere, frightfully rich too" (p. 41). Could it be Georges? (They were lovers once, we know, in the country hotel in *The Flanders Road*, as Georges endeavors to comprehend the lives and deaths of de Reixach and Blum.) Why does Simon induce us to raise the issue? Is this autonomous text, after all, part of his slowly evolving, continuously involving personal universe?

The boy sitting at his desk and pondering his geometry lesson recalls the artist Simon at work at his desk. The figures that he draws, a study of certain and potential relationships, might conceivably serve as a metaphor of the narrative relationships seen in *Triptych*. The postcard lying on the kitchen table, with its view of palm trees along the arc of a tropical bay, echoes those postcards denoting foreign scenes and a missing father in *Histoire*. (There are older women in this household, but no men are evident.) This will become the setting of the scene played by Corinne in the seaside resort. These seem to be the scenes on the filmstrip held up by the boy to the light; the scene outside his window is of a rabbit being skinned; when we first see Corinne, she is unusually vulnerable, lying before Lambert, her "body sprawled out with its legs apart, too pink in certain places, . . . naked, stripped bare, . . . like the body of a skinned animal" (p. 36).

There are further connections. The boy's youthful voyeurism—spying on some lovers in a barn (the girl's "pink tongue" linked directly to the "pink body" of the dead rabbit, p. 63)—recalls that of the protagonist of *Conducting Bodies*, and there may be a hint here too of the homosexuality with his childhood companion seen in the stream of that older consciousness. The implicit act of betrayal is the death of a child (his younger sister?) abandoned by her nursemaid (occupied now in the barn) and by all those others delegated to care for her. The boy himself is not a betrayer but is somehow involved in the act (first associations of sexuality and guilt), and thus he will likely assume responsibility for the betrayal: this is, after all, the paradigm established in each of the novels from *The Palace* to *Histoire*. Does this mean that the boy, one of the few identifiable centers of consciousness in *Triptych*, is somehow related to Georges and those unnamed narrators who are so much like Georges—perhaps even, in certain respects, a younger Georges? The fact that we can ask such a question is a sign, will-he, nill-he, that Simon has not totally abandoned his old technique, his own history, his humanist needs and concerns.

There can be little doubt that a new Simon is operating in these later novels and that the new post-Modern, reader-oriented critical approach provides useful insights into these works. We are less moved now by the rhythms of the prose, less profoundly affected by the accretions of past history as they influence the characters, more aware of the act of writing as a significant theme in itself. Like Robbe-Grillet and Butor and those others who have made this difficult transition into a new literary age, Simon continues to play on and perhaps to expand Modernist advances in narrative technique (witness the beautifully sustained stream of consciousness in *Conducting Bodies* and what might be called the implied consciousness of the boy in *Triptych*). The expression of emotion in these later novels is increasingly indirect; but emotion remains. Simon does not abandon the humanistic concerns of his Modernist forebears. There is nothing in these books to equal the emotional depths of our discovery of Georges in *The Flanders Road*, left alone by Corinne in his hotel room, as he continues his monologue to the long-dead Blum. But Simon retains the ability to involve us in the lives of his people, however fragmented they may have become, and to remind us through them of the accretion of our own history, of the discontinuity of our lives. No text, Simon shows us in the